RESISTANCE AND COMPROMISE

Cambridge Studies in the History and Theory of Politics

RESISTANCE
AND
COMPROMISE

The Political Thought of the
Elizabethan Catholics

PETER HOLMES

CAMBRIDGE UNIVERSITY PRESS

CAMBRIDGE

LONDON   NEW YORK   NEW ROCHELLE

MELBOURNE   SYDNEY

Published by the Press Syndicate of the University of Cambridge
The Pitt Building, Trumpington Street, Cambridge CB2 1RP
32 East 57th Street, New York, NY 10022, USA
296 Beaconsfield Parade, Middle Park, Melbourne 3206, Australia

First published 1982

Printed in Great Britain at
Western Printing Services Ltd, Bristol

Library of Congress catalogue card number: 81–17990

British Library Cataloguing in Publication Data
Holmes, P. J.
Resistance and compromise: the
political thought of the Elizabethan
Catholics. – (Cambridge studies in the
history and theory of politics)
1. Catholics – England – History
2. Politics and literature – England –
History   3. Great Britain – Politics and
government – 1558–1603   4. Great Britain
– Tudors, 1485–1603
320.9′42′055   JN134

ISBN 0 521 24343 2

Contents

PART FOUR: NON-RESISTANCE AGAIN

Preface

This book has grown out of research I undertook a number of years ago at Cambridge. I tried to bear in mind, as I wrote, the interpretation of Elizabethan Catholicism which has become current in recent years, especially as a result of the studies of Professor Bossy, whose work remains the outstanding contribution in the field. I have sought at various points in the story to see what light my research could throw on our wider knowledge of Elizabethan Catholicism, and hence perhaps on the history of the reign as a whole.

A number of excellent studies covering part of the same ground have already appeared (these are discussed below in the introduction). My only excuse for adding to this weight of commentary is that I have – as I hope I show – something new to say on a number of points. Parts One, Three and Four of the book concern the central theme of this study, the question of Catholic allegiance to the Queen: theories of resistance and non-resistance. I treat the subject in a chronological fashion, beginning with the writings of Catholics in the first half of the reign, who were generally in favour of non-resistance, dealing in Part Three with the ideas of resistance put forward in the critical decade after 1584, and concluding in Part Four with the works of the Appellants and their opponents at the end of the reign. In Part Two I discuss the reaction of Catholics to laws which proscribed the practice of their religion and enforced attendance at Protestant services. I felt compelled at one point (Chapter 16) to attempt a few comments on the political ideas of the Catholic laity, and this must of necessity be the least reliable part of this study since the evidence is so sparse.

It is a pleasure to be able to acknowledge here the help I

received while working on this book. My principal debt is to my former Research Supervisor, Professor G. R. Elton, and what there is of value in this study is largely due to his instruction and encouragement. At every stage, from research, through doctoral thesis, to publication, his advice has been my unfailing guide. Professor John Bossy and Mr Christopher Morris made valuable comments on earlier drafts of the book, suggesting new avenues to explore. The staff of many libraries and archives made my research possible: the University Library, Cambridge (especially), the Bodleian Library at Oxford, the British Library, the Public Record Office, and the John Rylands Library, Manchester. I was warmly and often hospitably received by the custodians of various private collections: the Inner Temple Library, Lambeth Library, Oscott College Library, the Muniments Room of Westminster Abbey, Miss Elizabeth Poyser of Westminster Cathedral Archives, Fr Francis Edwards S.J. of the Archives of the English Province of the Society of Jesus at Mount Street, Fr Frederick Turner S.J. of Stonyhurst, and Dom Placid Spearitt O.S.B. of Ampleforth. Requests for microfilm and enquiries were answered most helpfully by the staff of the Vatican Archives, by Madame Y. Duhamel of the Bibliothèque Municipale of Douai, and by the Rev. C. P. F. Chavasse, Archivist of the Venerable English College at Rome. Finally my thanks are also due to the staff of the Cambridge University Press for the care with which they have prepared the book for publication. Expenses in completing research for this study were defrayed in part by a grant from the Twenty-Seven Foundation Award of the Institute of Historical Research.

All quotations have been modernised in spelling and punctuation. In the endnotes reference is made in rather abbreviated form to early printed books, but a key to these works is provided in the bibliography, where a fuller description is made.

Introduction

The Catholics of Elizabethan England faced problems similar to those which confronted men in various other parts of Europe at the time: these problems stemmed from the fact that they differed from their sovereign in religion. By the second half of the century the Holy Roman Emperor ruled over a large number of Lutherans; in France the Huguenots formed a sizable minority under the Most Christian King; in the Netherlands a Catholic king faced a growing body of Calvinists. To a greater or lesser extent this pattern was repeated all over Western Christendom. Thus the Elizabethan Catholics were not unique; indeed, their difficulties and the answers they found to them are in some ways typical of European history in the era of Reformation and Counter-Reformation. In one important respect they were unusual, however: the experience of being in a minority as a religious group was generally that of Protestants. The only other Catholic minorities which spring easily to mind are the Scots, who were naturally rather closely associated with the English in any case; and rather later the Dutch Papists in the United Provinces. This made it more difficult for Catholics in England – lacking the support and example of men of the same church in the same position – to adapt to their position under Elizabeth. Differing from their prince in religion brought for English Catholics, as it did for other minority groups at the time, many difficulties. These were partly of their own making, resulting from their desire to pursue their religious observances and to separate themselves from those of the Church of England. The response of the Queen's government to this non-conformity then itself created further problems, as gradually during the course of the reign Catholics faced persecution, which, while it did not match the cruelty of that suffered by the Marian Protestants, was nevertheless real enough. The purpose of this book is to analyse the difficulties of the Elizabethan Catholics and the solutions they found to them.

The field of options open to a persecuted religious minority in sixteenth-century Europe may be narrowed to two fundamental issues. First, what forms of religious observance could be maintained under persecution and how far could the dissenter go in accommodating himself to the ecclesiastical and doctrinal order established by his ruler? In short, what form should his religious opposition or resistance take to a church which he considered heretical or idolatrous? The second problem was more obviously political: was the political regime of the sovereign to be recognised and were his commands to be obeyed; or might disobedience, even rebellion, be lawful? It is in terms of these two central themes that I have described the opinions and ideas of the Elizabethan Catholics.

The first of these problems – the question of religious resistance – is clearly central to an understanding of the sixteenth-century minority groups, although it has not received the attention from historians which it deserves. *Prima facie*, there seems to be little difficulty: the very definition of a group with a separate religious identity depends upon a degree of religious resistance to the established church. Indeed, the great text of the period was Acts 5. 29: 'We ought to obey God rather than men.' If the prince commanded a man to disobey the divine law, his commands were not to be obeyed. On this basis, a separation of Huguenots from Catholic France and of Catholics from Anglican England was established. But much practical complexity underlies this seeming theoretical simplicity. Under persecution, what forms of obedience to God were absolutely necessary and which might be set aside in order to avoid punishment? How could the ecclesiastical ideals of a religion practised under royal approval be achieved by a scattered community subject to the pressures of a hostile society? Which was preferable: exile or martyrdom; stealth or discovery; a measured degree of conformity or extirpation? Martin Luther counselled his followers to obey their rulers without rebellion in all things except those which affected their religious observances. But the reaction of another reformer was markedly different. Otto Brunfels enunciated the doctrine first in 1527, in response to the Peasants' War (which itself helped Luther to develop his own political ideas) that to avoid persecution even obedience to the religious commands of an idolatrous prince might be lawful. If rebellion was not licit, only death at the hands of a Papist ruler faced a believer who practised his religion openly. The vehemence with which the leading reformers, notably John Calvin, denounced this doctrine suggests that it was widely held and practised in various parts of Europe in the sixteenth century by those who faced Catholic persecution. Especially in places like Italy and pre-Huguenot France, where heresy was thinly spread and subject to severe penalties, the practice of 'Nicodemism', or secret adherence internally to reformed doctrine, while openly following Catholicism, was perhaps almost the norm.[1] As will be seen in the course of this present study, the Catholics of Elizabethan England faced a similar dilemma.

More attention has been given by the historians of political opinions to the second of our major themes: the question of political obedience. To simplify, the Catholics of Elizabethan England, like the other religious minorities, could choose between two ideologies. On the one hand, the most popular doctrine of the period taught that the political (or non-religious) commands of a king should be obeyed whatever his theological views or however harsh his government. Such a ruler was not, of course, praised – indeed, he might, by Luther for example, be severely rebuked – but his punishment should be left to God, and his subjects could comfort themselves with the knowledge that their suffering would be rewarded by the same agency. The alternative ideology rejected this long-suffering quietism, and held that there might be lawful resistance to a ruler who persecuted the true religion or who misused his power. There was, of course, a middle ground between these starkly opposed political theories, although it is not to be found expressed with great enthusiasm by members of religious minority groups. These competing ideologies developed and hardened, partly as a result of the tensions created by the religious strife of the period, emerging into the seventeenth century as full-blown theories of divine-right absolute kingship or of popular sovereignty and the right of resistance.

What is remarkable is the ease with which religious leaders transferred from one of these political theories to another. In

1547, for example, the Edwardian *Book of homilies* was published, containing a brief essay in non-resistance in the form of 'An exhortation concerning good order, and obedience to rulers and magistrates'. This work expressed the orthodox view (at the time) of the Church of England, that rebellion and disobedience to royal authority were sinful:

it is an intolerable ignorance, madness and wickedness, for subjects to make any murmuring, rebellion, or resistance, or withstanding, commotion, or insurrection, against their most dear and most dread sovereign lord and king, ordained and appointed of God's goodness for their commodity, peace and quietness.[2]

But within a decade the Bishop of Winchester (among other divines) had completely abandoned this view of politics. In his *Short treatise of politic power* (1556), Bishop Ponet maintained that royal authority was derived from the people, who were able to choose their government and to change it if necessary. The power of a king was limited: he was bound both by the laws of God and by the positive laws of the commonwealth. Obedience was a virtue only in moderation, Ponet maintained, 'for too much maketh the governors to forget their vocation and to usurp upon their subjects'. If a king ruled badly, he became a tyrant and could legitimately be killed by his subjects.[3] Clearly this rapid conversion from non-resistance to a defence of tyrannicide owed everything to political circumstances, the change from Edward VI to Mary Tudor. The same ideological agility is to be found in the history of German Lutheranism, of both Huguenotism and Catholicism in France, and of Catholicism in Elizabethan England itself.

The political and religious debates of the Reformation era were encouraged by the growth of printing in Europe, and the consequent and attendant developments of both lay and (sometimes overlooked) clerical education in the period. The Elizabethan Catholics excelled in both fields. Led by William Allen and Robert Persons, the Papists in exile founded colleges, largely to train priests, in the Low Countries, France, Spain and at Rome. Some attempt has been made in the following pages to establish what the seminarists were taught in these establishments. But the main source for a study of the political opinions of the Catholics of Elizabethan England is in their printed works, although manuscript books still circulated as a relic of more primitive and, under persecution, perhaps safer forms of communication. The standard catalogue of post-Reformation Catholic printed books (the invaluable guide of Messrs Allison and Rogers) lists over 260 English books published in the reign of Elizabeth, and very many of these can be made to yield evidence of political attitudes.[4] In addition, a number of English Catholic authors continued to develop their ideas in Latin and in other languages. Several of these books are well-studied and available in modern editions, although others were rare when they were first published and now survive in only one or two copies, while their authorship and the circumstances of their composition remain obscure and doubtful.[5] Reading these pamphlets is often, to twentieth-century taste, tedious work, but several show considerable stylistic ability, powers of scholarship and strength of argument. Catholicism represented a threat to Elizabeth greater than the figures in the Recusant Rolls suggest it should, partly because it had at its disposal the intellectual dynamism of the Counter-Reformation which attracted and stimulated the minds of men like Robert Persons, William Allen, Robert Southwell and Thomas Stapleton, whose talents shine bright even in the Elizabethan age.

The broad range of political ideas expressed by the Elizabethan Catholics and the other religious minorities of the period has been dealt with in several general surveys of sixteenth-century political thought. The works of J. N. Figgis and C. H. McIlwain will continue to be read, both for their scholarship and their stylistic vitality. The studies of Christopher Morris and J. W. Allen provide a stable, workmanlike foundation of knowledge for all students to build on, and more recently Professor Skinner's study of *The foundations of modern political thought* (while it does not directly deal with the writings of the Catholics under Elizabeth) has added considerably to our understanding of the complexity of the Protestant response to the political problems of the day.[6] In my own field there have been two detailed studies, by Fr Clancy and Dr Pritchard, of the political ideas of the 'Allen–Persons party' and of the Catholic loyalists under Elizabeth.[7] In treating the reign as a whole and presenting my analysis largely in chronological form I hope to have added somewhat to their findings. The evidence of the printed books and the opinions they express leads me to believe that there were no distinct parties or groups among the Elizabethan Catholics, with their own separate responses to the political problems of the day. It is undeniable that, at the end of the reign, two groups – the Appellants and the supporters of the Archpriest – developed, but, as I will argue, I cannot accept that there were profound ideological differences between these groups. Nor does the evidence of the printed books – on which a historian of political opinions in the sixteenth century of necessity must rely in large part – support the view that there was ever in the reign of Elizabeth a 'loyalist' group who presented a sustained critique of the ideas of a party led by Allen and Persons. What emerged rather surprisingly from my research was a clearly defined chronological rhythm to the development of the political ideas of the Elizabethan Catholics, taken as a whole and not divided into groups or parties.

The political, social and religious history of Catholics in Elizabethan England has been the subject of a number of excellent studies. Most attention has been focused on government policy towards Catholics, on the international and diplomatic ramifications of Catholic resistance to Elizabeth, and on the hagiography of the mission itself. The work of J. H. Pollen, A. O. Meyer, and more recently of Fr Loomie and Professor Bossy has added considerably both to our knowledge of the Catholics themselves and by extension of the Elizabethan period as a whole.[8] The internal history of Elizabethan Catholicism itself, especially at home in England and especially with reference to the laity, has been rather neglected. Professor Trimble's study of the 'Catholic laity' under Elizabeth was largely a discussion (and a very good one) of government policy. Recent local studies and the work on a broader time scale of Professor Bossy and J. C. H. Aveling point the way for further research.[9] At various points in this book I have attempted to show how my own studies seem to conflict with the established view of Elizabethan Catholicism, especially that contained in Bossy's seminal essay on the 'Character of Elizabethan Catholicism'. To summarise briefly here, I consider that there is considerably more continuity between the early years of Elizabeth's reign and the more heroic days of the seminarists than Bossy allows. Secondly, I disagree with the view that Elizabethan Catholicism is best understood in terms of division, especially division between laity and clergy. There is little evidence in the printed books of the period for any disagreement between priests and laymen over political ideas.

What is not in doubt, however, as a result of the work of Professor Bossy and other scholars in this field, is the importance of a study of the Catholic minority to our understanding of the Tudor period. To adapt a phrase of Professor Elton there was no 'high road' to Catholic extinction, and the Elizabethans regarded Popery as immeasurably more dangerous than Puritanism. Indeed, the threat of Catholicism, with its international ramifications, its connection with the question of the succession, and its insidious danger to internal security, may be seen as the central and most important theme in the history of Elizabeth's reign. In the following pages, I hope to cast some light on one aspect of this theme and hence on our understanding of the period as a whole.

→ a bit of an overstatement!

Part One

POLITICAL NON-RESISTANCE

I

Half-hearted non-resistance: the Louvainists 1558–68

THE FIRST YEARS OF THE REIGN

Evidence of Catholic activity and for Catholic opinions in the early years of the reign of Queen Elizabeth is rather scarce. By comparison, the sources for a study of Catholicism later in the century are ample both on the government side and in the papers of Catholics themselves. This shortage of documentary material has, understandably, left the first decade of the reign suffering from historiographical neglect, and this neglect has tended to breed contempt. Recent studies of Elizabethan Catholicism have seen these as years of 'drift' and 'decline', which witnessed the death of the old Church. It was not until the 1570s, according to this view, that an English Catholic resistance to the Elizabethan settlement developed, and it was a rebirth not a revival.[1] The scarcity of political writings in the period might be held to confirm this view. Evidence for the political ideas of the Elizabethan Catholics in this first decade is scattered and contradictory in what it reveals. On the whole, however, I feel that it is best to see the period in a more sympathetic light. Two substantial achievements of Catholics in the face of Elizabeth's accession and the consolidation of her regime cannot be ignored. First, the Catholic hierarchy and a proportion of the clergy refused to conform to the new settlement of 1559; and second, a number of these non-conformists organised themselves in the Netherlands and began to publish a large number of works of religious controversy. From this community of exiles there emerged gradually the features which best characterise the Catholic resistance to Elizabeth: plots to dethrone the Queen and seminaries to train priests who would attend to the religious needs of the laity at home. Similarly, though scattered and brief, the published political statements of the earliest

Elizabethan Catholics give a foretaste of the principal themes
which were to dominate the political literature of the whole reign.
If the Louvainists failed to resolve adequately the ideological
dilemma facing them, their more illustrious descendants had,
taken altogether, hardly more success, though their writings were
more voluminous and systematic.

Through the confusion and the paucity of sources a pattern
emerges. The dominant theme in the political statements of the
early Catholics is that of political non-resistance. They expressed,
on the whole, their loyalty to the Queen, despite their religious
opposition to her, and refused to countenance opposition to her
political regime. In this the Louvainists foreshadowed again the
history of Catholicism in the whole of Elizabeth's reign, since this
was also the most popular ideological stance taken by Catholic
writers throughout the period.

If the first decade of the reign is lacking in evidence of the
political opinions of Catholics, this is doubly true of the first few
years, before the Louvainists began to publish their religious
polemics. This very interesting period, when the bishops were
deciding to resign and to oppose the religious settlement in parliament, and as the first Catholics moved abroad to the Low
Countries, is particularly badly documented. The record of a few
speeches made mainly in parliament by Catholic prelates has,
however, survived, and in these we read a few fairly conventional
protestations of loyalty to the Queen, and expressions of a belief
in the illegality of revolt and of political opposition to her.

The senior surviving representative of the Catholic hierarchy,
Archbishop Heath of York, delivered a speech in the Lords against
the Supremacy Bill in which he declared his complete willingness
to acknowledge the Queen's temporal supremacy. She was 'our
sovereign lord and lady, our king and queen, our emperor and
empress', he said, 'by right and inheritance' and 'by the appointment of God'. Elizabeth owed no foreign prince tribute, and she
was as humble, virtuous and godly as any ruler of England ever
had been. The reigning Pope, on the other hand, Heath maintained, had been 'a very austere, stern father unto us, ever since
his first entrance into Peter's chair'.[2] The Bishop of Chester,
speaking on the same occasion, also affirmed his loyalty to the
Queen 'not only for wrath and displeasure's sake, but for con-

science sake, and that by the scriptures of God'.[3] The Abbot of Westminster urged the Queen, when speaking against the Bill of Uniformity in Parliament, to reject Protestantism, on the grounds that Catholicism taught obedience to political authority more firmly than heresy did; this was to be a very common theme in Catholic political literature later in the reign.[4] In the same vein, Lord Montague and Robert Atkinson, two Catholic opponents of the parliamentary bill of 1563 which extended the penalties of the Act of Supremacy, emphasised the quietness and loyalty to the Queen of her Catholic subjects: 'they dispute not, they preach not, they disobey not the Queen, they cause no trouble, nor tumults among the people'.[5] Atkinson praised Elizabeth, saying that she had reigned 'in a quieter peace, with more love and less exaction' than any other ruler since the Norman Conquest.[6] An anonymous Catholic manuscript against the royal supremacy, from the same period, also expressed a belief in the illegality of political resistance to the Queen: 'we are...sharply commanded by the Apostles to be obedient to our king and rulers', the author maintained. This doctrine applied to rulers both good and bad, the paper said, citing the examples of St Peter, who had obeyed Nero, and of St Ambrose, who had recognised the temporal authority of Theodosius.[7] John Murren, who wrote in 1561 instructing Catholics to abstain from Anglican communion, told 'both priests and the laity' to obey the Queen in all other respects, 'as far as God's law will permit'. These were the conventional slogans of sixteenth-century loyalism and non-resistance, of the belief, so strongly expressed in most political literature of the day, that rebellion and disloyalty were sinful.[8]

LOUVAINIST LOYALTY

These early political pronouncements of Catholics, especially when made in the Houses of Parliament, can hardly have been totally free expressions of opinion; the Marian ecclesiastics had every reason from their recent experience to fear for their lives and were clearly not in a position which would encourage them to antagonise the Queen. But the same cannot be said of the Louvainist writers who after 1564 provide us with the next source for the political ideas of the Elizabethan Catholics. Having uprooted themselves from Oxford and Cambridge, these Catholic intellectuals had little to gain personally from sycophancy and a hypocritical expression of loyalty to the Queen, although it may, of course, be that they wished to avoid causing difficulties for their fellows who had not fled and who remained as hostages for the political good behaviour of the exiles. For whatever reason, when these writers discussed political issues, they tended to agree with the Marian prelates and to express their loyalty to the Queen and their support for a policy of non-resistance. Indeed, on the whole the Louvainists preferred not to be drawn into the discussion of political questions and stuck to safer, more theological ground. This reluctance to deal with politics is itself perhaps indicative of a quietist, non-resistant attitude.

The aim of the Louvainist writers was to discuss 'points of doctrine', as John Fowler, their principal publisher, said; not to interfere in 'the affairs and politic government of the realm'.[9] Richard Shacklock contrasted the literary activities of the Marian exiles with those of his fellow Louvainists, 'all whose diligence and study intendeth nothing less than to write one word willingly which might displease Your Majesty, which may sow any seeds of sedition, which may disquiet the peace of our native country (as in your grace's dear sister's days divers seditious sectaries did) but only to further and to prefer as much as is possible this princely desire of knowing the truth which we hear with great joy to be reported of Your Majesty'.[10] When political matters were touched upon by the Louvainists, it was almost always to express loyalty to the Queen, to denounce Protestants as rebels,[11] and to affirm a belief in political non-resistance. 'Points of doctrine', such as Papal power in temporals, which might be considered disloyal or might encourage rebelliousness in Catholic readers, were by and large avoided, even though the question of Papal supremacy, a favourite controversial issue, rather invited such a discussion.

Four books printed by the Catholic exiles were dedicated to the Queen herself, and Thomas Stapleton even gave her the title 'Defender of the Faith' in the dedication of his translation of Bede, apologising that the 'base subject attempteth to talk with a right mighty princess and his learned sovereign'.[12] In their dedicatory letters to the Queen these authors spoke of their hope for her conversion to Catholicism, and John Martial in his *Treatise of the Cross* commended her taste for crosses.[13] The Antwerp printer, Jan Laet, had a plate made of the royal arms with 'God save the Queen' inscribed underneath, and this was used as the frontispiece of three books.[14] Abbot Feckenham promised to obey Elizabeth 'with no less loyalty and faithfulness' than he had shown to Queen Mary, 'unto whom I was a sworn chaplain and most bounden'.[15]

Catholics were not disloyal to the Queen, Lewis Evans told his reader: 'for I assure thee, that in this their adversity, they do upon their knees pray unto God for the preservation of our most gracious prince and queen'. Protestants, on the other hand, he said, were by nature rebellious, as the recent Vestiarian Controversy had shown.[16] Thomas Dorman pledged to the Queen the loyalty of Catholics, 'who protest never to desire to live hour longer than we shall be contented to live like true subjects under the humble obedience of our gracious sovereign whom we acknowledge to be the image of God in earth in all civil and politic government'.[17] Stapleton rejected the accusation that Catholics were disloyal, and, using many examples, showed the rebelliousness of Protestants. He admitted that Feckenham and others had refused to take the Oath of Supremacy for conscientious reasons and quoted Acts 5.29 ('We ought to obey God rather than men') as their justification, but said that in political matters Catholics were the Queen's 'most loyal and obedient subjects':

the Catholics wish to the Queen's Majesty as quiet, as prosperous, as long, and as honourable an empire to the honour of God as ever had prince in the world and are as well affected to her highness as ever were good subjects to their noble princes.[18]

Catholics were all willing 'to employ, if the case so require, wit, body and life also' for the preservation of the Queen and of England, even though they were badly treated by her. Recent history proved this:

It may seem a good and a convenient proof of their quietness and obedience that all this eight years and more there hath not been in the realm, no not one, that I can hear of, that hath been convicted of disloyalty, for word or deed, concerning the prince's civil regiment, which they all wish were as large and ample and as honourable as ever was our noble countryman's, the great Constantine's.[19]

John Martial likewise pointed to the loyalty of the Catholics under Elizabeth, contrasting it (as most of the Louvainists did) with the rebelliousness of Protestants under Mary and under Elizabeth herself:

There is no blast blown against the monstrous regiment of women; there is no libel set forth for order of succession; there is no word uttered against due obedience to the sovereign.[20]

Thomas Harding, writing in 1568, made quite a lengthy defence of the doctrine of political non-resistance. He was replying to the Protestant John Jewel who (he said) had used the texts Acts 5. 29, and Psalm 118. 9 ('it is better to trust in the Lord than to put confidence in princes') to justify the rebellion of Protestants in Scotland against Queen Mary. Harding denied that these verses allowed rebellion. In matters of conscience it was quite correct to refuse to obey the Queen's laws, in the same way that St Peter (who spoke in Acts) 'suffered scourging, contumelies and imprisonment rather than he would obey the magistrate commanding him not to preach, nor teach in the name of Jesus'. But political resistance, rebellion, was not lawful:

If the prince command heresy or idolatry, the way to obey both God and the prince is to keep thee from yielding to heresy or committing of idolatry, and for God's sake to sustain the punishment whatsoever the prince putteth upon the breakers of his commandment.

Harding contrasted the doctrine of non-resistance, which he espoused, with that of resistance and rebellion which Jewel (he claimed) held: 'for it is two things, and much different, to [dis]obey the prince in an unlawful request, and to take arms against the prince.' He stated his belief in non-resistance quite unequivocally:

But we openly protest before God and the world that we condemn and defy all such attempts. I mean that any subject or subjects whatsoever of their own private authority should take arms against their prince for matters of religion. This we do teach to be plain disobedience both to God and to the prince.

The policy of political resistance, Harding said, would cause ruin. He imagined a country in which half the inhabitants were Protestants and half were Catholics; it would cause chaos in such circumstances for Catholics to think they could rebel against a

Protestant prince and for the Protestants to rebel against a Catholic ruler.[21]

THE LOUVAINISTS AND PAPAL POLITICAL POWER

The reasons for the expression by the Louvainist authors of loyalty to the Queen and their insistence on non-resistance will be described later;[22] briefly, it seems that English Catholics were influenced by the general inclination of European Catholicism towards it, and by what they saw as the essentially conservative nature of Catholicism. They liked, as one or two of the examples above have already shown, to contrast their doctrine with the seditious writings of the Protestants, Knox, Goodman and Ponet, who had advocated resistance during the reign of Queen Mary I. One may doubt whether non-resistance was really best suited to their position in Elizabethan England at the time, but it was the political doctrine which appeared most attractive to English Catholic writers throughout this period, and in this respect, as in others, the Louvainists were setting the tone for the rest of the reign. But the early Elizabethan Catholics were aware of the alternative to non-resistance, even if they felt unable to embrace it fully. It is possible that the Marian bishops had in 1558 discussed whether to excommunicate Elizabeth;[23] and certainly the Louvainists put plans of that sort before Papal and Conciliar officials in the early 1560s.[24] None of this is apparent in the published utterances of the early Elizabethan Catholics, but there are in their books occasional hints of a desire for political action against the Queen and of a belief in the rectitude of such resistance.

Two Louvainist authors, Thomas Harding and John Rastell, allowed themselves to discuss the doctrine of Papal political power, the cornerstone of Catholic resistance theory as it developed later in the reign. Both were rather apologetic about dealing with this subject and discussed it quite briefly and as a theoretical point. Their exposition of the doctrine shows, nevertheless, a lurking belief in the right of resistance. Harding was driven to defend this aspect of Catholic theology in response to the Anglican, John Jewel, who in his *Apology, or answer, in defence of the Church of England*, had accused the Pope of interference in politics and had described how medieval Popes had excommunicated and deposed kings.[25] Harding showed himself sensitive to the controversial force, if not the theological value, of such an argument: in one of his books he declared, 'I do not here justify all the deeds of the Popes'.[26] But he felt bound to reply to Jewel partly because the issue was associated with the question of Papal primacy which it was important to maintain against the Anglican doctrine of royal supremacy. He said that priests and bishops were superior to kings, and applied the words of Jeremiah i. 10 to the clergy: 'Behold I have set thee over nations and kingdoms, to the intent thou mayest pull up and scatter, and build, and plant.' This was the text used later by Pius V in *Regnans in excelsis*, the bull of 1570 which excommunicated Elizabeth.[27] Priests had their power from God, Harding said, while kings took their authority from the people, and hence priests were superior, which the fact that kings were anointed and blessed by bishops at their coronation demonstrated.[28] This was above all the case with the Pope, who had been given special authority by Christ, as His Vicar or representative on earth. Christ was the king of kings and 'all the right of all kings' came from Him; the Pope, as Christ's Vicar, had the same power over rulers as Christ Himself. This power was used only occasionally, and Popes usually preferred to admonish kings rather than punish them. But in some cases they were forced to act: thus, for example, the Pope had deprived the rulers of Byzantium of their imperial title; Pope Zacharias had deposed King Childeric of the Franks, and Philip the Fair had been chastised by Pope Boniface VIII. It might be true, Harding acknowledged, that some Popes had been rather over-zealous in their punishment of kings, but generally their political activity had been directed by God and could be shown to have been of divine origin by the providential success which ensued for the beneficiaries of it. For example, Florence flourished as a duchy more than as a republic (the transition had been effected by the Pope), and Pippin, placed on Childeric's throne by the Pope, began a long line of successful kings.[29]

Harding's theory of Papal power in temporals, therefore, was based on the belief that ultimately all political authority belonged to the Pope as Christ's Vicar. John Rastell's doctrine was the same, although he gave far less space to discussing the matter.

Like Harding, he defended the terminology of Boniface VIII's bull *Unam sanctam*, where spiritual authority was compared to the sun and temporal authority to the moon, and he concluded from it that all priests were 'higher and honourabler' than the greatest emperor in the world.[30] Like Harding, he used St Bernard's metaphor of the two swords: the spiritual sword in the hands of the Pope, the temporal sword in the hands of the king, but at the Pope's disposal.[31] The Pope, he concluded, could excommunicate an emperor as easily as he could 'the basest man in a whole city'.[32]

The other Louvainists avoided discussing the contentious matter of Papal power in temporals and even Harding and Rastell treated it in a theoretical way, without applying it to the case of Elizabeth of England (who had not yet been excommunicated, of course) and without allowing the doctrine to prevent them expressing their loyalty to the Queen and belief in non-resistance. In view of the great importance which the theory of Papal political power assumed in Catholic (and anti-Catholic) polemic later in the reign and during the course of the next century, it is rather surprising, and indicative of a non-resistant frame of mind, that Catholic literature of the first decade of Elizabeth's reign contained so little discussion of it.

OTHER DISSENTIENT VOICES: WHITE AND MARTIAL

Before leaving the ideas of the first decade of Elizabeth's reign it is necessary also to mention two men who briefly cast rather a different shadow over the loyalism and non-resistance of Catholics to Elizabeth. The first and more important was Bishop White of Winchester, who appeared in the opening weeks of the reign, like the bad fairy at the christening, and delivered a few rather vague threats, expressing perhaps a deep-felt gut reaction to the accession of the Protestant Queen, rather than hoping to begin a tradition of Catholic resistance theory. The occasion which allowed White to express himself thus was the funeral of Mary Tudor on 13 December 1558, and his was the first lengthy political statement made by a Catholic in Elizabeth's reign. White's sermon is a fine piece of sixteenth-century pulpit oratory, on the rather uncompromising text, Ecclesiastes 4. 2–3: 'Where-

fore I praised the dead which are already dead more than the
living which are yet alive. Yea, better is he than both they, which
hath not yet been, who hath not seen the evil work that is done
under the sun.'[33] The bishop, who as a result was imprisoned,
began by condemning as sinners those who attended church while
disliking the form of service used there – which applied to the
Queen and her Protestant courtiers at Mary's funeral. It was
better not to have been born at all, the bishop said, than to have
been born 'a rebeller, a murderer, a heretic, a blasphemer'.[34] He
contrasted those people who died within the unity of the Church
with those who died 'in the sedition of Core'; those who died in
the gospel with those who died 'under the Alcoran'. The latter, it
was sufficient to say, after death, 'be in pain, in dolour, in ire, in
fire, in darkness, and horror: the indignation, the scourge, the
vengeance of God, with confusion and damnation everlasting, is
poured on them. Neither have they qualification of pain, nor
intermission of time, nor hope of end'.[35] This severe denunciation
of heresy, while no doubt not actually constituting a call to
Catholic arms nor any political criticism of Elizabeth's new
government, was clearly embarrassing to a Protestant Queen,
especially when uttered on such an occasion.

    White came even closer to a direct political attack on the
Queen and her government in the next section of the speech,
where he exhorted men to defend the Church against heresy.
Priests were to keep 'watch and ward' and give warning if they
saw the enemy approaching or if they saw wolves coming towards
their flocks, 'as at present, I warn you, the wolves be coming out
of Geneva, and other places of Germany, and hath sent their
books before, full of pestilent doctrines, blasphemy, and heresy,
to infect the people'. If bishops or ministers neglected their duty to
protect their flocks 'for fear or flattery with the world', they
would be mightily scourged and the blood of the people required
at their hands. The same was true, he said, of laymen: of princes,
dukes and magistrates. These men were given authority by the
prince, 'as Trajan the Emperor did deliver the sword of justice to
his chief officer, with this charge, Hoc gladio pro me utere, si
justa impero, contra me, si injusta: expressly commanding his
own authority and sword of justice to be used against himself,
when the equity of the law should so require.' This was the nearest

to the expression of ideas of resistance that White came; the example he used was a favourite with opponents of royal authority, who employed it to justify the right of resistance vested in inferior magistrates.[36] But it is not clear exactly what the bishop meant by this phrase. He finished his speech in the same threatening, but vague, fashion. Lay magistrates, he said, should not neglect their duties to rule rightly, judge justly and give faithful counsel, and he warned them that if they did fail in these respects their punishment would be sharper and fiercer than the punishment poor, simple men received. Magistrates should speak out against injuries, extortion, sedition and rebellion and not allow the Christian religion to decay and the public weal to be subverted; it was better to live as a dog, barking against heresy, than be a dead, dreaming lion who allowed heresy to infect the commonwealth.[37]

The other early Elizabethan Catholic actually to express criticism of the Queen's political regime was John Martial, who made some similarly obscure complaints about Protestant policy in *A treatise of the cross*, published in 1564, a book in which, it should be said, Martial also expressed his loyalty to the Queen. Having first attacked the rebelliousness of Protestants, Martial went on to describe how they observed 'no ordinary debating of matters by law', disregarded old laws, and did everything 'fiercely, rashly and seditiously, with much corruption and partiality'. Partiality was shown towards Protestants in England, while Catholics were punished:

Some of late [have been] put to open penance, prison and further trouble for speaking of a sprite walking under a nut tree in W park. And he that broke down the pale, hunted without his lady's warrant, embossed the white doe, and made the cockerel crack, never touched? but by his holy brother adjudged innocent?

This passage presumably refers to some court or political scandal of the early 1560s. Martial continued to complain about the political state of England:

Be not lords' heastes, na scribes' fantasies, parasites' pleasures, Machiavellians' policies holden and followed for laws? Are not many matters huddled up in corners? examined in chambers? and determined without ordinary process of the law? Have not some been borne withal because they were Protestants? some overborne because they were Papists?

After these brief and rather cryptic passages, Martial returned to theology.[38]

The defence of Papal political power made by Harding and by Rastell, White's fulminations and Martial's strange accusations do not outweigh the far more frequently expressed non-resistance of the Catholic leaders at the beginning of Elizabeth's reign, but they do show the strain which such doctrine imposed upon the Catholics of England, and they do hint at a certain degree of support for the alternative ideology of resistance.

2

Resistance and the return to
non-resistance 1569–79

THE RESISTANCE THEORY OF JOHN LESLIE

The Louvainists published in all about forty works of religious controversy; after four years, by 1568, they seemed to have exhausted their repertoire, and possibly their funds.[1] In 1569 there came a change in their publishing policy, and the detailed theological wrangling with Jewel and the other Anglican champions drew to its inconclusive close. During the next five years (1569–73) a handful of pamphlets of a purely political sort were for the first time printed by the Catholic exiles in the Netherlands. In these works, political opposition to the government of Elizabethan England was openly and clearly expressed. The tracts of this period were the work in the main of two men, John Leslie and Nicholas Sander, and they provide us with the first taste of Catholic ideas of political resistance. What is surprising is that this was merely a taste: the ideas of Leslie and Sander were not developed further in other books. After 1573 Catholics deliberately drew back from resistance theory and for another decade expressed loyalty to the Queen and a belief in passive obedience.

The abandonment of political non-resistance by the Louvainists and the publication from their presses of works of resistance is easy to understand. The international political climate changed considerably in the late 1560s. Tension between Spain and England increased and religious conflict became more bitter over much of Western Europe – in the Netherlands, France, and Scotland especially. In England itself the Rising of the Northern Earls in 1569 cast a shadow over the shaping of the new regime; court intrigues involving Mary Queen of Scots and the greatest noble in the country were revealed; and the Pope, on the advice of some of the English Catholic exiles, reacted to the Rising by issuing his bull *Regnans in excelsis* in 1570 by which the Queen was declared excommunicate and deprived of all political authority. In such circumstances it is not surprising that the Louvainists should have ceased writing works which expressed loyalty to the Queen and that, in their place, these works of resistance should have been published.

John Leslie, Bishop of Ross and agent of Mary Queen of Scots, published three books in five separate editions in the years 1569–73, all generally supporting the cause of his mistress and expressing opposition to the government of Elizabethan England. In this he enjoyed the collaboration of English Catholics, especially of the Louvainist publisher, John Fowler, who helped with the printing of his books.[2] Leslie's first concern was to defend Mary Stuart's claim to the English succession.[3] Here he relied on the researches undertaken a few years before by Catholic lawyers, especially Edmund Plowden and Sir Anthony Browne, in reply to the agitation of Protestants in favour of Lady Catherine Grey.[4] The prevalent non-resistance of the mid-1560s had prevented the publication of Browne's work, but by 1569 Leslie felt able to have this tract printed. The succession question was one of the most important political issues of the time and for Catholics one which held out most hope of a successful solution to their problems. To publish a book defending Mary's title (as Leslie did in 1569) was not necessarily to support resistance to Elizabeth, but it implied a far greater degree of political awareness than the Louvainists had shown and a willingness to discuss a contentious issue which Elizabeth had made it clear she wished to remain undiscussed. Leslie vindicated Mary's rights against those who had alleged that Henry VIII's will and her own foreign birth debarred her from the English throne. To make things clearer still he appended to his succession tract an attack on the theory that women could not bear rule over men. He dealt with biblical texts which seemed to support male chauvinism, appealed to the authority of Plato and Aristotle, and described how in various parts of the world and at various times women had ruled successfully.[5]

No doubt this thesis would have been as acceptable to Elizabeth as to Mary, but Leslie's tone was not consistently eirenic. In the preface to the 1571 edition of his defence of Mary's title he thundered warnings to the nobility of England:

If manifest injustice should so far prevail (which God of His infinite mercy forbid) as that her just and rightful title be suffered any way to be touched or defaced by colour or pretence of any law or authority, then undoubtedly, as the same unjust law must be accounted by all wise and good men, non lex, sed foex and as the learned civilian Baldus termeth it, non lex, sed lis, even so will the horrible and irrecoverable confusion, desolation and utter subversion of the whole realm necessarily and certainly ensue thereupon by continual terrible wars, and many bloody battles, with fire and sword to be most cruelly pursued, the end whereof Almighty God only knoweth, and few or none now alive are ever like to see.[6]

The same stern tone is to be found in *A treatise of treasons against Queen Elizabeth and the crown of England* (1572), a pamphlet devoted entirely to the criticism of English politics.[7] The authorship of this tract is not certain: the bibliographers, Messrs Allison and Rogers, and A. C. Southern, attribute it to Leslie; but D. M. Lockie does not, and John Bossy ascribes it to the nobles who left England after the failure of the Northern Rising of 1569.[8] Internal evidence perhaps suggests that Leslie was the author: favourable references to the bishop himself; the concern with the succession; the interest in Scottish affairs and the attack on the Earl of Moray (a principal theme of Leslie's in other of his pamphlets); and the defence of Mary Stuart.[9] Whether or not the author was Leslie, it was certainly published by John Fowler and was presumably, therefore, approved by the leading exiles in the Netherlands.[10]

The book was made up of a series of bitter attacks on the conduct of English policy, in which the Villainies of Cecil and Bacon were especially denounced. Elizabeth herself was described as the innocent victim of the knavery and treason of her evil councillors.[11] At the start of the reign they had persuaded the Queen to change the country's religion and to adopt 'a religion of negatives, a religion of lies, a religion of liberty, a religion that leadeth to looseness and to all lewd life'.[12] They had then sought to tamper with the succession, persuading Elizabeth not to marry, and seeking to prevent Mary Queen of Scots from enjoying her rights. To exclude the legitimate heir was to attack the foundations of monarchical rule:

no man should look for an end thereof, when it were come to that, nor expect any less, but that when these two first families shall be weeded out for that third, that also shall be weeded out for another, and so that fourth for a fifth, till none be left of the blood royal, but the realm come to be governed, either by a foreigner, or by a popular state.[13]

The policy of Cecil and Bacon had led the country into a miserable state: allies abroad had been lost; pirates and rebels in France, Flanders and Scotland had been encouraged; taxes were high; the old nobility had been replaced by upstarts; 'floods of foreigners' covered the land; England was divided into political and religious factions. Even the Papal excommunication of Elizabeth was the fault of the two evil ministers, for by refusing admittance to the Papal legates and by persecuting Catholics, the Pope ('being the supreme judge of all obedience among Christian men') had – after years of forbearance – been forced to 'set her Christian subjects free from obeying her for conscience sake'.[14] The pamphlet ended with some advice for Elizabeth: she should return to the obedience of the Apostolic See and to her old alliances, restore Mary as Queen of Scotland, marry and have children, revive the power of the old nobility, rule in religion and justice, and repair the economy of her country. If she followed this course she would have a long and prosperous reign; if she did not, 'she hath already seen the best and the quietest of her time'.[15]

THE RESISTANCE THEORY OF NICHOLAS SANDER

A treatise of treasons, although severely critical of the Elizabethan regime, did not contain a theoretical justification for resistance. This was provided in the first period of Catholic opposition to Elizabeth by a work written by Nicholas Sander, entitled *De visibili monarchia*, and published in 1571 by John Fowler.[16] Sander's book falls into three parts. It is principally a defence of Papal ecclesiastical supremacy, presented first in a theological way, and then at length in Book Seven as a historical exposition of the Pope's primacy. This was fairly run-of-the-mill Catholic scholarship and differed little in ideological terms from the works of the other Louvainists. Secondly, at the end of Book Seven, Sander gave a brief history of Catholic opposition to Queen Elizabeth and crossed the line from political non-resistance to resistance. It was passages from this short section of his very long book that the government found most objectionable and included in the 'bloody questions' put together in 1581 as a shibboleth to test the loyalty of priests.[17] Sander described the sufferings of Catholics under Elizabeth, the fortitude of the exiles, and the ill-treatment of Mary Queen of Scots. He proceeded to relate how Nicholas Morton had been sent by the Pope to tell Catholic noblemen that Elizabeth was a heretic and for that reason deprived of all dominion and power, to be treated as an ethnic and publican, and her laws not to be obeyed. Sander praised the Rising of the Northern Earls, describing it as a miracle and calling those who were executed after the rebellion martyrs. The Rising had failed because all Catholics had not been aware at the time that Elizabeth had been declared a heretic by public authority or because God wished to punish the defection of England from the Church further. Sander went on to describe the publication of the Bull of Excommunication and the 'martyrdom' of John Felton, who attached the bull to the door of the Bishop of London's palace.[18]

Although these passages from Sander's book were those most offensive to the government, there was a third, and in some ways more dangerous, part to the *De visibili monarchia*, for in its opening chapters Sander set out a theoretical justification for the Bull of Excommunication, a defence of Papal political power.[19] Three years before the *De visibili monarchia* appeared, at the very end of the period of Louvainist non-resistance, Sander had published a work entitled the *Rock of the Church*, in which he had also touched on politics, and it is interesting to compare the doctrine of the two books. In the *Rock of the Church* Sander adopted a most condescending attitude towards political power: kings were instituted, he said, as a punishment from God, 'somewhere to stay violent injuries and robberies and other where permitted of God for our just punishment'.[20] Priests, on the other hand, were exalted far above kings in the *Rock of the Church*: even a wicked priest, Sander maintained, did less harm to the people than a good king. But although the ground-plan for a theory of sacerdotal political power was contained in this book, in 1568 Sander was not prepared to proceed to its erection. Indeed, he specifically denied that priests exercised dominion – the power of life and death – over men. Priests were servants and ministers, the Pope above all. The Pope had none of the sovereignty of a secular prince, he could compel no one to accept the faith, and he had no right to punish heretics himself: he was truly the servant of the servants of God.[21] It is remarkable to see how rapidly Sander's opinion had changed in the three years between 1568 and the publication of the *De visibili monarchia*, for by then this idea of a peaceful pope exercising no political power and suffering with the people whatever tyranny God should inflict upon him had given way to a theory which placed all political power entirely under the Pope's control.

In the *De visibili monarchia* Sander approached the question of Papal political power from several angles, presenting a number of arguments for it. He spoke of the commission to 'bind and loose' given to St Peter and handed on by him to the Popes and of the Church's need to defend its members from attack, and he used biblical and historical examples to show how Popes and priests in the past had chastised rulers. But in a large part of his discussion of the subject, he adopted an interesting and original approach, not to be found elsewhere in Elizabethan Catholic literature. To show that the Pope had power over kings, Sander looked at the question from the point of view of the king. First, he defined political authority in terms of its origins. There were three stages of development in the history of kingship, Sander maintained. The first form of authority was patriarchal, that of the father over the son, the elder over the younger brother, and it derived from the law of nature. This primitive sort of dominion had given way in time to the authority of king over subject, which had its origin in the consent of the subject, in human law. Finally, with the coming of Christ, a third and more perfect kingship had been established with the setting up of the Christian commonwealth. Christian kings alone ruled with divine support; indeed, they were in some ways like priests – mixed persons, whose duties were both secular and spiritual. But there was another side to the coin: since the Christian prince ruled over a community whose ultimate goal was eternal felicity rather than material safety, he was subject to the advice and the control of the priesthood. The king himself agreed to this twice: first, at his baptism when he joined the Church, and then at his coronation, when he submitted to the unction of a priest and swore to protect religion. The baptism and coronation were contracts between prince and Church; if the prince failed in his religious duty, his position at the head of the Christian commonwealth was endangered. Sander did not really think in terms of two kingdoms – a Church and a State, one subordinate to the other; he saw the Christian commonwealth as in essence a single entity, a single Church. In this way, he justified the Papal right to depose a king who ruled irreligiously, and made it appear in some ways the result of an agreement freely entered into by the ruler himself. All this applied to Elizabeth, although Sander did not in this section of his book make it explicit: she was baptised and crowned as a Christian and hence was subject to the control of the head of the Church.

RICHARD BRISTOW AND THE RETREAT FROM RESISTANCE

The *De visibili monarchia* and *A treatise of treasons* complement one another, the theoretical discussion of the right of resistance in a theological work written in Latin, and the detailed critique of the personalities and policies of the Elizabethan regime in a short English pamphlet, which was further circulated as a news-sheet. Leslie's tract on the succession then provided a Catholic solution to English problems, but further exasperated the government by stirring up a matter which they wished to be forgotten. But the first period of Elizabethan Catholic resistance was confined to this handful of books, and was extremely short-lived. The crisis of 1569–70 passed: the Northern Earls failed, Philip II and Alva cried off, the bull was published, but Elizabeth still prospered. After 1573, Elizabethan Catholic authors avoided political controversy for a decade and returned to non-resistance; Leslie's and Sander's brief propaganda campaign had come to nothing.

There seems to have been a conscious decision by the Catholic leaders after 1573 to draw back from resistance and to revert in their books to their usual, rather insincere, loyalism. The reason for this change must lie with William Allen's plan to train missionaries to return – as he himself had in the 1560s – to England to confirm the remnants of the Church in their faith. Allen appears to have decided to adopt this strategy soon after the failure of the Northern Rising and of *Regnans in excelsis* to achieve the deposition of the Queen and the restoration of Catholicism. The defeat of this attempt to overthrow Elizabethan Protestantism by political action led Allen to send his missionaries into England, in anticipation of a reasonably long period of Catholic proscription, but with the hope of an eventual restoration under a Stuart heir. The missionaries would reorganise Catholics, confirm their faith, and replace the dwindling band of Marian priests. But it would be dangerous to encourage them to engage in political activity, or to exasperate the government with ill-timed printed attacks on the Queen and her ministers. The missionaries would be hostages whose preservation depended to some extent on the abstention by the exiles from extremist political thought. Sander and Leslie had to be silenced.

In one of his books, Allen describes how Nicholas Sander was persuaded by his fellow exiles to avoid further essays in resistance theory after the publication of the *De visibili monarchia*. Sander, apparently, had written a book entitled *Pro defensione excommunicationis Pii V^i latae in Elizabetha Angliae* in about 1570, which was a more detailed discussion of *Regnans in excelsis* and its theologico-political background than that contained in the *De visibili monarchia*, but publication of it was stopped to avoid causing trouble in England.[22] Sander did write another book, similar in some ways to the *De visibili monarchia*, in the 1570s, which contained a brief defence of Papal political power, but this was not published until after his death.[23] The other writer of this brief period of resistance, John Leslie, made his peace with Elizabeth in the elaborate Latin of his *Oratio*, published in 1574, in which he pledged his loyalty to the Queen and praised her virtues.[24] His flattery of her was so extreme that in 1580 Richard Shelley denounced the book in Rome, quoting the more extravagant passages in which Elizabeth's good government, her hospitality towards Mary Queen of Scots, and care generally for exiles were mentioned.[25] Leslie continued to defend the claims of his mistress, Mary Stuart, to the English succession, publishing a Latin book on this subject in 1580, but he carefully avoided any reference to recent political events – even in Scotland – in this version, which was in any case probably intended for a European rather than an English audience.[26]

The new ideological position adopted by Allen and the English

Catholic exiles was expressed briefly in a book published first in 1574, Richard Bristow's *A brief treatise of divers plain and sure ways*, often known as 'Bristow's Motives'. In this work Bristow gave forty-eight motives for being a Catholic rather than a Protestant, following a plan for a book made some years before by William Allen. It is, therefore, largely a work of controversial theology, aimed, as Bristow says in his introduction, at a rather wider public than some of the more pedantic publications of the Louvainists. Three of his 'motives' discuss, briefly, political matters; that is, in three out of three hundred and fifty pages. It would not be correct, therefore, to describe Bristow's book as a work of politics. But the political ideas expressed by Bristow were considered offensive by the government in England, and in 1581 passages from his book as well as from Sander's *De visibili monarchia* were included in the 'bloody questions' which were asked of the imprisoned priests and then published as evidence of Catholic disloyalty and the treason of the priests.[27] In a sense it is true that the political passages in Bristow's book might be interpreted as the last example of the political ideas of resistance expressed in the years 1569–73 by Sander and Leslie; this, at least, was how the government chose to see them. In one place Bristow spoke of the holy martyrs in England who suffered 'by loss of their livings, by prison, by poison, by whipping, by famishing, by banishment', and named as martyrs who had 'openly suffered' Sir Thomas More, Bishop Fisher and the Carthusian monks who were executed by Henry VIII, and 'the good Earl of Northumberland, Dr Storey, Felton, the Nortons, Mr Woodhouse, Mr Plumtree and so many hundreds of the Northernmen'.[28] Thus, following Sander, he described those executed for their part in the Rising of the Northern Earls as religious martyrs.

In another of his 'motives' Bristow spoke of miracles and said that excommunication was a miraculous power: 'whereby it is manifest that they do miserably forget themselves who fear not the excommunications of Pius Quintus', because Christ himself acted through them.[29] By putting 'excommunications' in the plural, of course, Bristow made this reference unspecific and oblique. He was slightly more direct, however, in another part of the book where he defended Papal political power. The compilers of the 'bloody questions' selected a sentence from this 'motive' in which

Bristow said that rulers who were 'very wicked and notorious apostates or heretics', and who held out 'no other hope of amendment...but the filthy more and more daily defiling himself and others', could be deposed by the 'pastor' (or Pope, presumably) and their subjects discharged of the duty to obey them. This, indeed, seems to be a clear defence of the Papal power to depose princes which had so recently been exercised in Pius V's bull. But if one reads the whole passage from which the government extracted this sentence Bristow's doctrine appears to be far less extreme and far more interesting.

Bristow discussed the Papal power of deposition in a section of his book devoted to showing that Catholics were more obedient subjects than Protestants, a thesis to which, as we shall see, much Catholic ink had already been dedicated and which was to continue a central theme in Catholic political thought for many years to come. Bristow admitted quite candidly that he presented this argument as a motive for 'governors', or rulers, to be converted to Catholicism. Catholics were, he said, good and obedient subjects and were taught by the Catholic Church to believe that they were obliged in conscience to obey their rulers. He then brought in the brief passage describing Papal temporal power which the composers of the 'bloody questions' seized upon as evidence of his rebellious doctrine. He next said, however, that the Catholic subjects of a prince who had been deposed by the Pope prayed to God and appealed to the prince himself for his reconciliation to the Church, 'neither in the mean time denying him such love and worship as we may'. Protestants, on the other hand, habitually attacked both ecclesiastical and political superiors, and rose in bloody rebellion against their rulers. Catholics, even after Papal sentence, 'though discharged of their fealty', continued to obey their rulers, 'for common humanity, for their accustomed use, for their continual and (as it were) natural institution'.[30]

'Bristow's Motives' saw, therefore, the first attempt by an Elizabethan Catholic writer to reconcile the bull deposing Elizabeth with Catholic loyalty to the Queen, a balancing act which later became a common part of the Elizabethan Catholic ideological repertoire. Bristow, writing probably with William Allen's approval, anticipated by six years the Papal 'rescript' of

Because of the way the Elizabethan ruined the subject. [handwritten annotation]

the bull delivered by Gregory XIII which plays such a large part in the standard histories of Elizabethan Catholicism. Only four years after *Regnans in excelsis* the English Catholic leaders, without official Papal faculty, were publicly urging Catholics to ignore the bull. This ideological tight-rope had to be trodden when the first missionary priests returned, in 1574; it would not wait for Gregory XIII and the mission of Persons and Campion.

Even 'Bristow's Motives', however, was too strong for the Elizabethan Catholic leaders in their new mood of non-resistance, and when in 1576 it was republished the political passages we have just discussed were removed entirely.[31] Between 1574 and 1579 twenty-two other English Catholic books were published: all were studiously non-political. Two of them were catechisms, one was a pamphlet giving instructions on how to confess; two were works of consolation to the afflicted Catholics in England, encouraging them to stay firm in the faith; one book sought to persuade Catholics to be recusants; three were works of controversial theology; and thirteen were prayer-books or manuals of meditation.[32] Only very occasionally did these works (mainly the catechisms and works of religious instruction) touch, even vaguely, on political matters, and where they did so they were uniformly in favour of obedience to superiors, both religious and political. Thus, in *A brief form of confession*, young Catholics were urged, with reference to the fourth commandment, to honour not only their mothers and fathers but also 'prelates, bishops, pastors, preachers, doctors, schoolmasters', 'all temporal governors' and 'elders and all aged persons'. This meant that children should 'think well of them, reverence them, obey them, help and succour them in their needs, wish them well, and procure the same, and ...pray to God specially for them'. It was forbidden 'to curse or speak ill' of them, 'not to help them, not to obey them, to give them ill answers, to mock and scoff at them, to murmur, grudge and think ill of them, to dishonour, contemne and despise them'.[33]

The first missionaries came to England not accompanied by seditious pasquils or even by the staple of the Louvainists, works of positive or controversial theology, but by books entitled *Godly contemplations for the unlearned*, *The Godly garden of Gethsemane, furnished with wholesome fruits of meditation and prayer*, or *Certain devout and Godly petitions, commonly called Jesus psalter*.[34] Such books would start no revolution, or at least only the spiritual revolution Allen hoped for. This was not so much non-resistance as non-politics; a withdrawal from the political field, an abnegation of clerical responsibility to give its flock ideological guidance, but, Allen hoped, the safest way out of a very grave dilemma. In 1580, however, this changed quite abruptly, and for a brief period the Elizabethan Catholics published books in which once again political issues were freely discussed.

3

Enthusiastic non-resistance 1580–83

THE NEW IDEAS OF ROBERT PERSONS AND
WILLIAM ALLEN

The mission of Robert Persons and Edmund Campion to England in 1580 cannot now be regarded as a 'Jesuit invasion',[1] but although these were only two among hundreds of Elizabethan missionaries, it is hard not to be intrigued and attracted by their expedition, nor to regard 1580 as being of some particular importance in the history of Elizabethan Catholicism. This mission was after all intended to be rather special: the first Jesuits to work at length in England, equipped with highly important faculties by the Pope, and to be accompanied back to England by one of the last surviving Marian bishops, Thomas Goldwell – a symbol of continuity which Goldwell's ill-health prevented from being fully exploited. Campion and Persons at the head of the expedition, two brilliant young converts – the son of a merchant and of a blacksmith, yet specifically commanded by their superiors to address themselves as missionaries to the nobility of England.[2] The whole story is rather too large for life: the blessing from Borromeo in Milan, meeting Beza in Geneva, the disguises to effect a passage across the Channel, the escapes in England. It ended, of course, in failure and tragedy: Persons fled, and Campion, before his heroic martyrdom, seems to have broken down under torture and revealed the places he had visited. With them Campion and Persons brought a new political message, or at least a brightly polished and tastefully modernised version of the political message of the Louvainists: once again it was slightly larger than life.

To accompany and follow the mission of Campion, Persons and their fellows, a new publishing programme was launched by the leaders of the English Catholics, and it is in the books which formed part of this campaign that their bright new ideas were expressed. Between 1580 and 1583 as many English Catholic books were printed as in the previous ten years together,[3] and once again controversial theology and apologetics formed the bulk of this programme. Many of these books were published by Persons himself, at first in England and then at Rouen; most of the others were seen through the press by William Allen in Rheims, where the seminary (formerly of Douai) was now established. Through this medium the Catholic leaders affirmed their loyalty to the Queen and their acceptance of the doctrine of non-resistance with great vigour.

Persons and Campion proclaimed their belief in political non-resistance as soon as they landed in England. On or about 18 July 1580, they met at Hoxton, a village near Islington outside the city of London, and the following day each composed a short tract in which he stated their reasons for coming to England and said what they intended to do there.[4] Like Campion in his 'Letter to the Lords of the Privy Council' or 'Brag', Persons in his 'Confessio Fidei' was concerned to repudiate the charge that they came as political agents to stir up rebellion against the Queen.[5] They came, Persons said, like missionaries in India or Turkey to teach the rudiments of the Catholic faith:

And that obedience which they [Christians] owe to their sovereign we inculcate not less but truly much more than does any of the Protestants. For we preach that princes should be obeyed not merely for fear of punishment or for the sake of avoiding scandal but for conscience's sake as well; and that he may be condemned who does not obey his prince even in the utmost secrecy of his closet [in cubiculo suo secretissimo] where no fear of punishment or scandal exists.

Catholics in England would be taught by the missionary priests, Persons said, to lead lives of moral uprightness, obeying the commandments of God, avoiding 'stealing, licentiousness, bribery and other sins of that kind', returning what they might have got unjustly and doing works of charity. Persons declared to the 'magistrates' of London:

In fine we incline your people to patience in all things and counsel them to endure any punishment which your worships may yourselves inflict, without resentment, taking comfort only in the testimony of a good conscience. And so far are we from encouraging resistance in any way to any person's authority, that we exhort them much to pray God for us all in Christ our Lord, who, though for our sakes He suffered far more, was willing to endure it all with such patience that He would not open His mouth.[6]

Persons' *Confessio Fidei* shows a new willingness to discuss political matters, and to use them as part of Catholic propaganda. This same lack of embarrassment with the difficult issues of political allegiance is seen in many of the other books of the period 1580–3. Allen and Persons (the principal authors of those years) confidently, almost defiantly, stressed their loyalty to the Queen, and their belief in non-resistance and passive acceptance of persecution. In a book of 1582, Allen described Elizabeth as 'liege and sovereign' of all Catholics and said they would do 'all duties of subjection to her that the laws of God, nature or the realm and all nations require', except recognise her supremacy in the Church. He complained of the way the propaganda of the government, by means of the 'bloody questions' proposed to Catholic priests in prison, had revived the 'old sore of the excommunication'. He said that *Regnans in excelsis* 'hath lain dead, and so might for us Catholics have been dead with Pius Quintus the author and publisher thereof for ever'. It was bad policy to rake up the question of the excommunication again, and Allen said he marvelled that the government should reveal to the people the opinions of Sander and Bristow about the bull (as they had done by publishing the 'bloody questions') since the people might easily be influenced by the writing of such famous and learned men.[7]

In his *Apology* of 1581 Allen praised the government of Elizabeth. Apart from the change of religion, which had 'contaminated' it, he would, he said, have described it as 'glorious, renowned to the world', and 'secure and happy' at home. It was not for dislike of her political regime that Catholics had left England, he assured the Queen.[8] Catholics in England did not 'repugn' or 'resist' any of the realm's temporal laws, but simply refused to obey the 'pretended laws of religion' because they believed in conscience and could prove that they were 'against the laws of God and not consonant to any just and truly called laws of our country'.[9] Catholics were not rebellious, Allen said, but heretics were:

Is our doctrine seditious? be Catholics by nature or profession un-quiet persons? are they desirous of disorder, change and novelty, or weary of peace, order and antiquity? are they libertines, despisers of authority, seekers of spoil, sack and garboil? are they given to sacri-lege, to irreligiosity, Epicurism, Sadducism, or atheism?

He asked his readers to compare Protestants and Catholics. Catholics in every country were known for their 'constancy, gravity, patience, peaceable, civil and sweet behaviour', while Protestants were rebellious everywhere. Rebellion as a result of repression was understandable, he claimed; even God's people had rebelled against Moses and Aaron, and even Catholics (despite the doctrine of their leaders) had in the days of the Primitive Church rebelled against their persecutors; nevertheless, during the whole of Elizabeth's reign there had only been one Catholic rebellion in England, and one in Ireland.[10] English Catholics, Allen said, were 'most obediently, dutifully and naturally affectioned to Her Majesty', to her councillors and to 'our dearest country', as far as they possibly could be, that is, bearing in mind their subjection to God's and the Church's law.[11] He admonished Catholics in England to 'be humble, wise, meek, peaceable, patient and constant in all your cogitations, words, answers, doings and sufferings', and hence procure the intercession of Jesus, who would remove the persecution by opening the eyes of the Queen and her councillors to the truth of the Catholic religion.[12]

In a book printed secretly in England in 1580, Robert Persons described the Queen as 'the substitute and Angel of God' and 'Vicegerent' in God's place.[13] Catholics had supported the Queen at her accession and were ready to defend her 'in all safety, peace and quietness unto the end', 'with the uttermost drop of their blood', 'to spend their goods, lands, livings and life...in the service of Your Majesty' and England.[14] They only refused to obey her religious laws. Catholics (unlike Protestants) were taught

true obedience to their princes, for conscience sake, even as unto God Himself, whose room they do possess, and to whom they are bound, under the pain of mortal sin and eternal damnation patiently to obey, how hardly soever they deal with them in their government otherwise.[15]

Persons promised the publication of a book in which he would exhort all Catholics to 'bear out with Christian courage, what tempests soever shall storm upon them' and to do so in a patient and quiet way, 'assuring them that this is the best and only way to please God and to save their own souls, to advance also the Catholic faith, and to mollify and confound their enemies and detractors'.[16] In another book printed secretly in England in 1581 Persons denied that Catholics were enemies to the state of England and rejected the general proposition that those citizens who disliked a state's religion were necessarily enemies to that state. He took the example of the Apostles to disprove this, and described how they and the early Christian Fathers had 'taught all dutiful obedience in temporal matters' to their rulers, even though they were 'infidels and otherwise wicked men', and had told Christians to obey them 'as substitutes of God'.[17] In his *Epistle of the persecution* of 1582, Persons said that Catholics were 'most ready both with life and goods' and 'with all dutiful and faithful good will' to serve the Queen and her councillors.[18] He exhorted Catholics to passive obedience:

For I deem it not the part of Catholics to recompense injury with injury, or to requite injustice with acerbity of speech. For that we have a merciful and mighty lord to whose only arbitrement all injuries are to be referred: he hath care of us (as the Scripture saith) to him let us leave revenge.

God would deliver them from their torments, and they should leave the policy of rebellion to heretics.[19] In the same spirit another Catholic author, Thomas Alfield, concluded his account of the death of Edmund Campion with a poem which included this patriotic stanza:

> God save Elizabeth our Queen,
> God send her happy reign,
> And after early honours here,
> The heavenly joys to gain.[20]

THE POLITICAL IDEAS OF THE RHEIMS NEW TESTAMENT

It was at this time that in the seminary of Rheims the finishing touches were being put by Gregory Martin (with the assistance of Allen, Bristow and others) to the Rheims New Testament, published in 1582.[21] At the end of each chapter of this translation of the Bible, annotations on important passages in the text were to be found. They were principally used as a vehicle for religious instruction, but they also contained moral and political precepts. This influential work reflects in its annotations the non-resistance which was expressed in the 1580s in the pamphlets of Allen and Persons. It is interesting to speculate on how different the political propaganda of the Testament would have been if publication had been delayed for half a dozen years or so, when the ideology prevalent among the Catholic leaders was very different. But in 1582 the Bible was non-resistant.

The Rheims Testament stressed the need for religious opposition to the Elizabethan settlement, for the segregation of Catholics from heretics, and for refusal to bend before the persecution. It took every opportunity to impress on Catholics that they should obey priests and religious authority,[22] but it also reinforced the need for political obedience, even to persecutors and infidels. This is shown in the annotations to the most famous political texts in the New Testament, Romans 13. 1–6 and I Peter 2. 13. The gloss on the first of these texts begins by saying that the Apostles had taught 'liberty by Christ from the yoke of the law and servitude of sin' and had impressed on the faithful that they should obey God more than men and be obedient to their 'prelates'. As a result many new converts had thought that they were free from all bonds of temporal obedience and the Apostles had to reply to the accusation 'that they withdrew men from order and obedience to civil laws and officers'. Thus, St Paul 'here...cleareth himself and expressly chargeth every man to be subject to his temporal prince and superior', not in religious matters, 'but to them in such things only as concern the public peace and policy, and what other causes soever consist with God's holy will and ordinance'. No political resistance is lawful:

Whosoever resisteth or obeyeth not his lawful superior in those causes wherein he is subject unto him, withstandeth God's appointment, and sinneth deadly, and is worthy to be punished both in this world by his superior and by God in the next life.

Catholics followed this precept, the annotation went on, obeying both spiritual and secular superiors, while heretics refused obedience to the prince, except where it was to their advantage.[23]

The Rhemish annotation on the first epistle of St Peter also taught non-resistance. It began by saying, once again, that it was necessary for St Peter to impress obedience on the early converts to Christianity because there was a risk that they might neglect this duty through being so often told to obey their spiritual governors and because their rulers were infidels and tyrants, like Nero. The Apostles had, therefore, been at pains, the gloss said, to warn the faithful not to give heathens any opportunity to call them 'disobedient or seditious workers against the states of the world'. Christians, St Peter had said in this text, were 'bound in temporal things to obey the heathen. . . lawful kings, to be subject to them even for conscience, to keep their temporal laws, to pay them tribute, to pray for them and to do them all other natural duties'.[24]

The New Testament was eloquent also in its omissions. The keystone of Catholic resistance theory, as Sander showed in *De visibili monarchia*, was the theory of papal political power. This was likewise the theoretical basis for the bull *Regnans in excelsis*, the most authoritative and important papal pronouncement on English affairs made in the reign of Elizabeth. But not only does the first official Catholic translation of the New Testament, published only twelve years after the bull, not mention that important document, it also avoids any reference to the doctrine of papal political power which lay behind it. The obvious place for such a reference would have been in the annotation on the famous text Matthew 16. 18–19, where Peter was given the keys of the kingdom of heaven and told that whatsoever he should bind or loose on earth should be bound and loosed in heaven. There the gloss reads: 'All kinds of discipline and punishment of offenders, either spiritual (which directly is here meant) or corporal so far as it tendeth to the execution of the spiritual charge, is comprised under the word "bind" '.[25] This was extremely tame, and the authors of the Testament seem deliberately to have omitted more than this very cursory discussion of the subject.

NON-RESISTANCE AND REGNANS IN EXCELSIS

It was possible for the Rheims New Testament to ignore the bull *Regnans in excelsis*, and Allen and Persons could pour out their professions of loyalty to the Queen in print because of the faculties granted, on 14 April 1580 by Gregory XIII to Edmund Campion, Robert Persons and the other missionaries who were setting out for England. In their faculties the missionaries were told that the bull by which Elizabeth had been excommunicated in 1570 bound the Queen and heretics, but did not bind Catholics in present circumstances.[26] In the instructions given at the same time to Campion and Persons by their Jesuit superiors, they were likewise told not to meddle in affairs of state, not to include the discussion of political matters in their letters and not to indulge in talk against the Queen, except with trustworthy Catholics, and even then only for very good reasons. In the instructions given a year later to other Jesuits bound for England the final clause which allowed discussion of matters of state in certain circumstances was removed, making them unequivocally non-resistant (although when in 1588 Fathers Holt and Cresswell set out for Scotland and England a rather similar piece was put back in their instructions).[27] As we have seen, Bristow anticipated the doctrine of the papal faculty by six years,[28] and, apparently, Bishop Leslie had held the same doctrine soon after the bull had been published.[29] But, until the Pontiff had spoken himself, it was not easy for Catholics to express themselves openly on the subject. In 1576 Bristow's book was republished, but with the political sections expurgated, and during the later 1570s Catholic authors avoided political discussion. The faculties given to Campion and Persons enabled the Catholic leaders openly and fully to express their loyalty to the Queen.

It is quite true, as the English government's propagandists noticed at the time, that the faculties and instructions given to the missionaries were not unconditional: the Queen was to be obeyed for the time being; the discussion of politics was to be avoided, except for very good reason.[30] Indeed, a document connected with the faculty of 1580 throws papal and English Catholic motives into an even worse light. This document consists of a series of questions, mainly concerned with the Bull of Excommunication and presumably drawn up by an English Catholic, put in about 1578 to a learned theologian at the Papal Court, possibly (it has been suggested) the Jesuit, Antonio Possevino.[31] Many of the questions confirm that the English Catholic leaders wished to be rid of the obligation imposed by *Regnans in excelsis*.

They seek in various ways to impugn the bull's validity: it was not published in Rome or England in the proper way, they say, and since it had not helped Catholics in England – which was the intention of its author – it might, therefore, be withdrawn. But other questions do not suggest a great faith in non-resistance. They ask, for example, if it is lawful to assassinate the Queen, and say that the bull can be withdrawn since it is quite lawful to rebel against a heretic ruler without papal authorisation. Possevino's answers suggest even greater deviousness and an even deeper dislike for Elizabeth, but do recommend some modification or withdrawal of the bull. But in the printed books of 1580–3, the Catholic leaders betrayed no such reservations about their loyalty to the Queen. Neither should we infer from the papal faculty or from Possevino's document that there was some sinister plot to mask Catholic preparations for rebellion by protestations of loyalty.

Two important casuist documents closely connected with the leaders of Elizabethan Catholicism dating roughly from this period corroborate the evidence of the printed books and confirm that the political message the early seminarists brought to England was that of non-resistance and passive obedience. One such document, which dates from the early 1580s, discussed the question, 'Is it lawful for Catholics in England to obey the Queen in all political matters after the bull of Pius V in the same way as they did before?' The resolution of the case said at first that a decision depended rather on the 'judgment of Catholics in England who know all the facts of the matter well'. It went on to say, however, that it seemed that it was lawful, in order to avoid 'worse evils befalling them', for Catholics to obey the Queen in everything of a purely political sort, as long as it did not involve the persecution of Catholics. They were not, however, bound to do so. The resolution concluded by explaining that Catholics could obey the Queen after the bull, as before, since the bull had failed to achieve its purpose. After this 'resolution' – or explanation of the case – came the final 'solution' of the discussion, written by William Allen and Robert Persons. They said that it was lawful to obey the Queen, but that there was a further comment on this case which had to be given in secret. I think that this further comment must have been connected with the papal faculty of 1580. We can assume, therefore, that in the confessional Catholics were told that they could obey the Queen in present circumstances, but also may have been warned that this situation might change.[32]

The other casuist manual, of 1578–9, does not actually deal with this question of political obedience, but one case is of some relevance.[33] It discussed what answers a Catholic should make to certain questions asked him by a heretic judge. The resolution said first that the best policy was to answer all questions clearly and without shame, and hence invite martyrdom, but that, on the other hand, it was quite lawful to reply 'sophistically' to the questions, even under oath, as long as one did not actually deny the Faith.[34] Thus, if asked when and with whom he last heard mass, and whether he had reconciled anyone to the Church, a Catholic could explain that he was not bound to answer such questions. The answers to the political questions were more 'sophistical' still. To the question whether the Queen was a heretic or schismatic, the Catholic was advised to reply:

What about you? Who gave you the right to judge her? Although everyone must denounce heretics and bring them to book if heresy is going to harm the Church . . . I am not bound to accuse or denounce anyone to a judge who has no jurisdiction in matters of heresy. If you say she is a heretic, you have your laws, judge according to them! If anyone says I have called her a heretic, let him appear and accuse me![35]

If he was asked whether the Queen was still Queen despite the excommunication the Catholic should reply: 'If you want to enquire into particular matters you should prove that I have committed a crime. . .meanwhile let me live in peace'.[36] The final question was whether the Queen could be deposed 'for any fact by any authority hereafter'. Two answers were suggested:

I cannot answer this question unless you first decide whether she has committed a crime worthy of deposition, who is her judge and what are her crimes. Or: kings and queens cannot be deposed for any crime. Unless these things are certain the question is captious because it is not based on a sure foundation.[37]

One manuscript version of this text then adds in English what seems to be an extremely non-resistant alternative reply: 'well, we say for no fact, and by none authority'. These questions and answers show that in 1578–9 the Catholic leaders had foreseen

that Catholics (especially priests) would be questioned closely on
these political points and advised them to answer the questions put
to them obliquely and, generally, in a rather non-resistant way.
They did not, it is true, tell them to proclaim their loyalty to the
Queen in the same way as it was expressed in the printed books of
the period. But, on the other hand, these manuals of casuistry did
not seem to envisage the dissemination of subversive political ideas
(even if based upon sound Catholic theology) among the Catholic
laity in England.

The replies to these questions suggested in this casuist manual
are reflected in the answers actually made by missionary priests in
England to the 'bloody questions'. The bloody questions sought to
determine the political ideas of the examinee, especially with
reference to the bull of 1570: was the bull to be obeyed? was the
Queen still lawful queen? could the Pope authorise rebellion?
could the Pope absolve subjects of their allegiance? were certain
seditious passages in Sander's and Bristow's books true? which
side would a Catholic take if a papal invasion should be launched
against England? Of the thirteen priests tried at the same time as
Campion, two gave answers to these questions which were entirely
favourable to the Queen. Nearly all the other answers were
evasive, although four priests answered the fourth question
(whether the Pope had power to absolve subjects from their
allegiance) in the affirmative. For the majority of the answers, the
reply of Briant to the second question (is the Queen to be obeyed
notwithstanding the bull?) is representative: 'that question is too
high and dangerous for him to answer'. Campion's answer to all
the questions is similar: 'he meddleth neither to nor fro, and will
not further answer, but requireth that they may answer'. Curiously
enough both the Protestants and Catholics used these answers in
their propaganda; they were published both in a government
pamphlet and in a work by William Allen.[38] The government
saw the evasive answers as evidence of Catholic subtlety and
refusal to profess open and unequivocal obedience to the Queen;
Allen saw them as proof of Catholic loyalty and government
cruelty.

The bloody questions did present a dilemma, as the casuists
had foreseen in 1578–9. It was all very well for Allen and Persons
to cover the difficulties of their ideological position with rhetorical

professions of loyalty to the Queen. But if asked directly to choose between the Pope and the Queen they had to resort to sophistry or silence. The non-resistance of the early 1580s was still unreal, despite the faculty of 1580. Gradually, however, the pressure of events was pushing the Catholic leaders towards the only possible resolution of this dilemma, total political resistance to the Elizabethan regime. By 1584 the loyalism of Catholic authors had disappeared. But this still left the missionaries in the field on the spot: their only resort was sophistry, and so it remained until the end of the reign.

All of this should be placed in the larger picture of the growth of "new monarchies" & the notion of loyalty.

4

Persecution and non-resistance

THE IDEA OF PERSECUTION

The books published in the propaganda campaign of the early 1580s introduced an important new theme in Elizabethan Catholic literature: the idea of persecution. Catholics in England had been discriminated against since the beginning of the reign of Elizabeth, but the Louvainists recognised, quite correctly, that the treatment they received was by sixteenth-century standards extremely gentle. Thomas Harding, writing in 1567, attributed this to the Queen herself: it was she, he said, who protected Catholics from the *yes!* cruelty of the Protestant clergy. He thanked Elizabeth for her 'advised stay from hasty and sharp persecution', while Stapleton praised the Queen for her 'clemency'.[1] The first published complaints about persecution were made by Nicholas Sander after the execution of the Northern rebels and of John Felton, the man who affixed the Bull of Excommunication to the door of the Bishop of London's house. Sander called these political victims martyrs;[2] but he was writing in a crusading, resistant mood, and other Catholic writers in the 1570s maintained a tactful silence on the subject. Gradually, however, the measures taken by the government against seminarists and recusants became more severe, and Catholic authors began to show their awareness of this in the early 1580s.

The first martyrological work produced by an Elizabethan Catholic came (perhaps predictably) from the subtle and prolific pen of Robert Persons: *De persecutione Anglicana*, published in 1581 and translated soon into English, French and Italian. There followed a number of other works describing the persecution in England, written by William Allen, Richard Verstegan, John Gibbons and others, which later became the foundation for other

47

books in foreign languages.[3] These works made England into a show-piece of the Counter-Reformation, an example of the strength of the Church militant and the cruelty of Protestants, a dreadful warning to Frenchmen or Dutchmen not to accept heretic rulers. On a more practical level such books were used to win money and political support for the seminaries abroad from sympathetic continental readers.[4]

At home the idea of persecution and martyrdom was also important. Indeed, it permeated almost everything written in the later Elizabethan period and became one of the most important aspects of Catholic thought. Whether in printed books describing the martyrdom of priests, in other tracts which simply touched on the ill-treatment of Catholics as on other points of controversy, in the private correspondence of the seminarists and exiles, or in the scores of short manuscript descriptions of various aspects of the cruel sufferings of the faithful in Elizabethan England, the constantly recurring theme is that of persecution. The function of the idea of persecution in Catholic literature was to give confidence and encouragement to the faithful in England. The ill-treatment suffered by Elizabethan Catholics helped to prove that their cause was righteous: it connected them in some way with the sufferings of the Israelites, of the martyrs of the primitive Church, of Christ himself. By the same token, the barbarity and cruelty of the English heretics in a way proved their theological falsehood and put them on a level with the persecutors of the ancient Church. Interest in the relics of the executed missioners grew up at once, cults were created and the connection between the new saints and the old was clearly established.

COUNTER-MARTYROLOGY

The persecution of Catholics only proved the truth of Catholicism if one already accepted it as truth. The Protestants themselves had their own martyrs, and they in their turn thought this proved the worth of their heresy. Throughout the reign of Elizabeth Catholic writers found it necessary, in order to vindicate their own suffering and the validity of their own theology, to attack the idea of Protestant martyrdom, and to defend the Catholic persecution of heretics, especially under Mary I. We have, therefore, in Catholic

literature, the theologically sound, but to modern taste rather un-
attractive spectacle of Catholics crying out against their harsh
treatment at the hands of Elizabeth's government, but defending
the persecution of Protestants under Queen Mary. As early as
1563, a Catholic sympathiser in Parliament, Robert Atkinson,
opposing the bill to impose harsher penalties for not taking the
oath of supremacy, described the treatment of heretics by the
Roman Catholic Church as lenient in comparison with the punishments to be imposed on Catholics by the bill. The Church, he
maintained, had only gradually and with reluctance accepted the
duty of punishing heretics with death, and it still allowed them
one chance to recant and conform, only executing them if they
fell back a second time into heresy.[5] The Louvainist, Thomas
Harding, justified the Marian persecution on the grounds that the
Protestants had been executed then as heretics under the law of
the Church. He quoted St Augustine: 'there is an unjust persecution which the wicked make against the Church of Christ and
there is a just persecution which the Churches of Christ make
against the wicked'. Harding accepted that it was true, as the
Protestant martyrologist John Foxe reported, that a pregnant
woman had been burnt for heresy, but pointed out that she could
have escaped the punishment if she had revealed her pregnancy:
she had merely been ashamed to do so because she was unmarried.
He claimed that Protestants were more cruel in encouraging the
Queen to persecute Catholics in Elizabethan England than
Catholics had been in merely implementing the old laws against
heresy under Mary.[6]

By 1581 Robert Persons had a real persecution in England to
complain of. It was far worse, he said, than what Protestants had
suffered under Mary: 'if we confer numbers to numbers, men to
men, prisons to prisons, usage to usage, there is no comparison.'
Even the Elizabethan Protestants, he said, admitted that it was
lawful to burn heretics, since they did so themselves, and under
Mary only the most obstinate, malicious and wilful were punished,
while 'infinite many were tolerated and winked at, although they
were known'.[7] Many of these points were repeated by William
Allen in his *True, sincere and modest defence*, published in 1584.
He stressed that it was not a matter of the numbers executed, but
the legality of their execution. Protestants were punished under

Mary in the same way as all heretics were punished, for having fallen from the old faith. They had promised obedience to the Church and had renounced heresy through their parents and godparents at their baptism. This promise was made, tacitly, even in heretic baptisms, and hence all were, willy-nilly, bound to the Catholic Church.[8]

In justifying the Marian persecution and attacking those who suffered in it, Catholic writers inevitably came up against John Foxe's famous *Book of Martyrs*, first published in 1563 to commemorate the Protestants killed under Mary. The Louvainists attacked the book almost as soon as it appeared, but criticism was encouraged as the persecution of Catholics grew in England.[9] Foxe's 'stinking martyrs', in his 'stinking dunghill' of a book, were in some cases, not only heretics but also rebels, like Sir John Oldcastle and Eleanor Cobham. Some of Foxe's martyrs were fictitious, like 'Sir Roger Only', while others were still alive.[10] William Allen described the Protestant 'martyrs' as suicides, for seeking their own destruction for no reason. Cranmer, he said, was a traitor for his part in the conspiracy to put Lady Jane Grey on the throne. Allen stressed the differences in social status between Catholic and Protestant martyrs: Catholics were usually drawn from the upper class, while Protestants were from the lowest.[11] The lengthiest Catholic critique of Foxe was made by Robert Persons at the very end of Queen Elizabeth's reign, in three volumes entitled *A treatise of three conversions of England from paganism to Christian religion*, first published in 1603. He saw that the real merit of the *Acts and monuments* lay in its historical analysis, and his most original contribution to the Catholic attack on Foxe was to refute this aspect of his work.[12] Persons hoped to show that history proved that the true church was Roman Catholic, while Foxe's church had no link with the Apostles and Fathers, but was a recent creation. If this was the case, Foxe's martyrs were clearly false and Catholic martyrs were authentic. To emphasise this contrast, Persons devoted part of his work to printing a 'double calendar' of Foxe's martyrs and Catholic saints, arranged in parallel columns.[13] His main criticisms of Foxe were similar to those of previous Catholic writers. He praised the 'constancy' of Catholic martyrs who stood firm in a reasonable cause and suppressed their carnal will which urged them to recant, but he described the firmness of heretics under persecution as 'obstinacy', for they wilfully opposed reason,[14] and 'stood in defiance of their lawful superiors, pastors and prelates to their faces, and this upon no other grounds, but only upon their own wills'.[15] Persons also asserted (in company with other Catholic writers) that some of those Foxe claimed as 'confessors' of his church were in fact good Catholics; for example, Marsilius of Padua, William Ockham, Pico de la Mirandola and Erasmus.[16] Foxe's other martyrs were mainly a 'rabblement' of 'artificers, sawyers, weavers, shoemakers, spinsters', and some were 'mad or distracted people'.[17]

Typical of the attack on Foxe is an unpublished tract of 1582, intended by its author to show the difference between Foxe's pseudo-martyrs and Catholic martyrs. It began with a short introduction in which the reader was exhorted 'to win the palm and crown due for patience':

be of good comfort, and be more glad to eat the pure azyme bread of penance with Christ's Apostles than the delicately dipped morsel with Judas the Apostata. Let him and his mates carry the purse covetously. Let us and our company bear the burden of all persecution courageously.

There followed a brief description of the martyrdom of a Spaniard called Peter Elcius which occurred in Morocco in 1580, taken from a Latin book written by a Jesuit, Francis de Castro, and printed at Cologne in 1582. This account was full of encouragement to religious resistance and martyrdom, and Elcius was clearly intended by the translator to represent to English readers the ideal martyr. 'Know ye, my brethren,' he said after his capture, 'that all things are but falsehood and vanity save only to believe and hold that which the Holy Roman Church believeth and holdeth.' While being beaten around the thighs with clubs, and despite the fact that his tongue had been cut out, Elcius told his tormentors: 'think not that you hurt me any thing at all, do unto me what you please, all these things do increase my crown and reward, neither can they ever withdraw me from the true religion.' Whatever gruesome torture he suffered, he continued to speak, confessing the faith, refusing to accept Mohammedanism, and telling his persecutors that he felt no pain. The manuscript finished with a long poem in praise of the Spanish martyr, attacking John Foxe and encouraging the Catholics of England to continue their religious resistance. It began:

> Come forth fond Foxe, with all the rabble rout
> Of monstrous martyrs in thy brainsick book
> Compare them to this glorious martyr stout
> And thou shalt see how lothly foul they look,
>> For black and white compared somewhat near
>> Will cause them both the better to appear.

A full doggerel critique of Foxe's book was given and the usual arguments used to show the worthlessness of heretic 'martyrs':

> For 'tis not pain that doth a martyr make
> Ne glorious sort in which he seems to die,
> But faith, the cause, which thine [Foxe's] did then forsake
> When from Christ's spouse they would so fondly fly;
>> Where truth doth want, to utter wrack they fall,
>> Not martyrs made, but most accursed of all.[18]

THE IDEA OF PERSECUTION AND RELIGIOUS RESISTANCE

The description of the death of Elcius illustrates well the way in which the idea of persecution could be used by English Catholic writers to encourage opposition to the Elizabethan religious settlement. Elcius is presented as an example to inspire English readers to keep firmly to Catholicism and to suffer, if necessary, for it:

> You must, therefore, with patience be content
> In hope the pay will overpass the pain;
> And think each cross is for your merit sent
> If you endure the sour the sweet to gain,
>> As hungry bears, which honey will not lose
>> For all the stings and buzzing of the bees.

Normally it was not necessary to go so far afield for such an example; the English martyrs themselves could be used in this way. As the English persecution was beginning, Catholic leaders were developing their campaign in favour of recusancy and separation from Protestants, and they found in their persecution a valuable propaganda weapon. Thus, in Catholic accounts of the death of English martyrs, there is often an explicit call to 'religious resistance', as we shall term it. The priest may refuse to pray in English on the scaffold with the minister, or the report of the trial of the Catholic may say that he might have avoided death had he consented to go to church, or taken the oath of supremacy. Martyrdom was presented as the reward for Catholicism; a chance to achieve salvation. If the reader did not merit martyrdom himself, at least he could bathe in the reflected glory of those fortunate enough to be martyrs, seek their relics and cherish their memory. It was said at the time, and has been repeated since, that Catholicism prospered more under the late Elizabethan persecution than it did under the leniency of the early years of the reign. If this was the case, it was partly because the persecution helped develop a sense of separateness from heretics and a belief in resistance to their religion.[19]

PERSECUTION AND POLITICAL NON-RESISTANCE

The idea of persecution helped Catholics develop a feeling of alienation from Elizabethan England and to embrace religious resistance more firmly, but what effect did it have on their ideas of political obedience? Did it not encourage political as well as religious resistance to the persecutors? It must be admitted that within a few years of the beginning of the persecution – by 1584 – Catholic authors had dropped the non-resistance which prevailed in the early years of the reign and had begun to express ideas of political opposition to the government of Elizabeth. In such books the persecution of Catholics in England was attacked as the worst aspect of Elizabethan tyranny. After a decade of political resistance, however, Catholic authors returned (as we shall see in subsequent chapters) to loyalism and passive obedience, yet the persecution continued, slightly diminished in its cruelty perhaps, but still fatal to many priests and laymen. The idea of persecution, therefore, could be adapted to an ideology of political resistance, but could equally well be accommodated to one of non-resistance.

Even in the early 1580s, in a period when political non-resistance was in vogue, persecution in England was the cause of a more bitter tone. Simply to describe the treatment received by Catholics, especially for a foreign audience, was, of course, highly offensive to the government, and Persons' *De persecutione*

Anglicana of 1581 was attacked in Parliament by Sir Walter Mildmay who said that it exaggerated the cruelty of the persecution.[20] Allen, in his own martyrological work, *A brief history of the glorious martyrdom of twelve reverend priests*, defended Persons' book which, he said, 'hath not uttered the least part of our daily distresses'.[21] Such books, describing the methods of torture and execution used in England, while maintaining that religion was the only cause for this persecution, were, especially if accompanied by engravings depicting the more gruesome aspects of punishment and interrogation, very good anti-Elizabethan propaganda, even if the ideological background to such descriptions was non-resistance in political matters.

When describing the persecution, language could become immoderate. Thomas Hide called the treatment of Catholics in England tyranny;[22] and Allen called the 'bloody questions', 'antichristian tyranny'.[23] A non-resistant document from the beginning of the next reign protested that recusancy fines were contrary to Magna Carta, which forbade excessive amercement.[24] Political non-resistance did not absolve the persecutor from punishment, only postponed the time of its execution. As Martin said, 'there in the next world...kings and queens come to their accounts as well as you and we poor folks'.[25] Punishment for persecution might even come more swiftly; God could deal with His enemies while they were still on earth. Robert Southwell, in a book written slightly later, still, however, *prima facie* a work of political non-resistance, described several cases where this had happened:

Therefore, you that persecute Catholics in England, consider how easy it is for God to practise the like punishments upon you ... Remember the sudden and horrible death of one Young, an apostate and pursuivant, who pursuing a Catholic at Lambeth fell down on the sudden, ere he could lay hands on him that he persecuted, and foaming at the mouth presently died.[26]

After 'long sufferance' God stretched forth His mighty hand upon tyrants and persecutors, wrote William Harris in his enormous historical note-book: God did not merely shake the 'sword of His justice' over such malefactors, as he did for the 'correction and amendment' of other men, but actually struck them 'in his fury', and wounded them 'often...to eternal death'.[27]

This tendency towards bitterness and away from loyalism – perhaps a natural consequence of the persecution – was usually, however, firmly repressed by Catholic authors in the early 1580s. The anger they felt at their ill-treatment was canalised into religious rather than into political resistance to the Elizabethan regime. Above all, the Queen was not personally criticised for the persecution by the writers of this period. Instead they applied to her a variant of the doctrine of the evil counsellors. Thomas Bourchier was full of praise for the Queen in the book he published in 1582 describing the sufferings of Franciscans at the hands of heretic persecutors.[28] There was not enough time, he said, to list all Elizabeth's individual virtues, but he did mention her famous ancestry, her great wealth, her wisdom, her erudition, her knowledge of Latin, Greek, French, Italian, Spanish and German, her Ciceronian Latin style, her singing and skill with musical instruments, and her astronomical expertise. She lacked one thing, however – faith, a lack which was the fault of her bishops, 'dumb dogs who cannot bark, worse than Cerberus, who not only have not barked but have betrayed the house of God to thieves and brigands'.[29] He attacked the bishops at length, urging the Queen to beware of their flattery, because behind it was the Devil. Bourchier's language was rather more extreme than that of most Catholic authors of this period, and he was unrestrained in his attacks on Henry VIII, condemning him for pride, cruelty, avarice, lust and anger. Most writers were less outspoken. William Allen did not blame the Queen for the persecution; he did not even blame her 'gravest counsellors' themselves, but her counsellors' evil counsellors, and even them 'we do from the bottom of our hearts forgive'.[30] He was careful, while castigating the attempt to set Lady Jane Grey on the throne in 1553, to refer to the Earl of Leicester's father as 'otherwise a right worthy and noble gentleman'.[31] Elizabeth did not know the full extent of the persecution, Allen said, and was inclined rather to mercy than to cruelty.[32] According to Alfield, the Queen and her Councillors had been misinformed by 'some hollow hearted friends and flatterers'; these men had sinister motives for encouraging the persecution of Catholics, and they, rather than the Catholics, were the real traitors.[33]

If the Queen were of a cruel disposition, Persons wrote,

Catholics would be prepared to put up with ten times the persecution they already suffered, but he knew she was not. He blamed
the puritans for inciting the Queen to persecute Catholics, naming
specifically John Field, 'a strange brainsick fellow', of such
'fantastical' opinions that 'he can devise any new religion upon a
week's warning given him at any time'.[34] In another book Persons
mentioned the Earl of Huntingdon as one of the anti-Catholic
counsellors who were leading the persecution, although in the
preface to the same book he excused the Privy Councillors as a
whole from blame.[35] A Catholic poem of this period attacks the
Protestant controversialist, William Chark:

> And Chark for all his chat
>   Should merit neither chalk nor cheese
> But rather ought for his deserts
>   To pay the hangman's fees.

It described Meredith Hanmer, another anti-Catholic author as a
'filthy Sodomite':

> And Hanmer hunteth not right well
>   And yet within his charge
> A flock which fondly he did guide
>   And left them so at large
> Enforced thereto (as some affirm)
>   For lewdness of his life
> And now would be restored again
>   Which makes his pen so rife.

But the Queen was reserved from all criticism:

> God save the Queen, and nobles all
>   Forsooth I do profess
> As well to her as Protestants
>   And Puritans more or less.[36]

Catholic authors in this period of political non-resistance
presented persecution to their readers as an attractive experience,
and not as a cause for rebellion. Robert Persons commended
persecution in his most widely read book: it increases our glory,
draws us from the world, preserves us from sin, prevents the
punishments of purgatory, tests our faith, makes us run to God,
manifests God's love and power in delivering us, and brings us joy
when it stops. In times of persecution and tribulation the Christian
man should rejoice, 'or at leastwise have patience', he should

come to God with fervent prayers, and he should imitate the constancy of the Maccabees.[37] We should rejoice in tribulation, Thomas Hide said, and gave the orthodox Christian reason: 'if we be just, then be we tried, if we be unjust, then be we amended'.[38] God spared no one, said William Allen when speaking of how the plague of heresy affected all: He beat the just man as a son, and punished the unjust man as impious.[39]

Indeed, there was no need for political action or political resistance, because by suffering persecution God's wrath would be removed and the country would, somehow or other, be converted back to Catholicism:

This is the way by which we hope to win our nation to God again. We put not our trust in princes or practices abroad, nor in arms or forces at home.[40]

The number of conversions would increase as the persecution continued; the blood of martyrs, Hide said, quoting the Fathers, is the seed of the Church. Or to extend the horticultural metaphor: 'the Church is like camomile, the more you tread on it, the thicker it weareth'.[41] The conversion of England might be effected, on the other hand, through God's intervention in some way that, at the moment, was not clear to Catholics. The persecution would end and the patient Catholics would be rewarded: 'God dealeth with you as the angry father dealeth with his child, whom after he hath beaten, casteth the rod into the fire, maketh much of him, and leaveth to him his patrimony.'[42] Whether through primary or secondary means, England was to be converted not by political activism but by religious resistance:

> God knows it is not force nor might,
>   Not war nor warlike band,
> Not shield and spear, not dint of sword,
>   That must convert the land,
> It is the blood by martyrs shed,
>   It is that noble train,
> That fight with word and not with sword,
>   And Christ their capitain.[43]

MARTYRS NOT TRAITORS

The idea of persecution was easily accommodated in an ideology of non-resistance, in part because in England the problem of political loyalty was so closely interwoven with the question of the ill-treatment of Catholics. Catholics in England were imprisoned and executed not for religious reasons, the government said, but to protect the state from their political intrigues. Catholics replied to this accusation by denying that they were guilty of treason and by affirming the religious nature of the oppression they suffered. This became one of the most frequently stated controversial points in Elizabethan Catholic literature, and it clearly sorted best with an ideological position which favoured non-resistance.[44] Catholic authors did continue later in the reign to argue in books which also supported the invasion plans of Philip II of Spain that the priests executed in England were not traitors, but there was obviously some difficulty in making such arguments convincing. A Catholic poem describing the martyrdom of Campion well sums up this argument (in a non-resistant framework); the allusion to the persecution of the Apostles is typical:

> They subtly take a further fetch
>   contrary to all reason,
> To say he [Campion] is not Caesar's friend,
>   accusing him of treason.
> But shall we much lament the same,
>   or shall we more rejoice,
> Such was the case with Christ our lord,
>   such was the Jewish voice.
> So were their wrathful words pronounced,
>   so was their sentence wrong.
> For Christ did give to Caesar that
>   which did to him belong.
> So Christ His true disciples here
>   no treason do pretend,
> But they by Christ and Christ His love
>   their faith till death defend.[45]

Perhaps the best vindication of Catholics from the charge of treason was that made by William Allen in his *Apology and true declaration of the institution and endeavours of the two English Colleges*, published in 1581. As the title suggests, he dealt mainly with the innocence of the seminaries at Rome and Rheims, defending them from the accusations made in two royal proclamations of 1580. The colleges were intended purely to train priests and keep learning alive, Allen said. The Bull of Excommunication had not been published at the Rheims College.[46] Catholics went abroad to avoid the laws which forbade their religion and with no rebellious intent.[47] There had been no plotting in 1580 to invade England,[48] and the expedition to Ireland, accompanied by Nicholas Sander, was not connected with the activities of the seminaries.[49] Allen praised the Jesuits, who had been particularly attacked in recent Protestant works, and defended them from the accusation of disloyalty.[50] Robert Persons also vindicated his own society and its famous martyr, Campion, from such charges,[51] especially those of John Nichols, a Protestant propagandist who had first-hand experience of life as an English student on the continent. Having published books against Campion, Nichols went abroad again, and in 1583 at Rouen made a full recantation of what he had written on the Protestant side; this proof of Catholic innocence was quickly printed by Allen.[52] In his refutation of Nichols' reports, Persons said that the students at Rome bore the Queen 'all dutiful good will' and prayed for her quite often (as well as praying for the Queen of Scots, the King of France, the King of Spain, the Emperor and the Pope). He denied that any lecturer in divinity at Rome would, as Nichols had maintained, have spoken in favour of a Spanish invasion of England or of the assassination of the Queen.[53]

The accusation of treason levelled at English Catholics sprang, Persons thought, from a desire of the Protestants to make them hated by their fellow-countrymen. Thomas Hide saw it as a 'Machiavellian policy' to terrify 'the untoward and recusant part'.[54] William Allen agreed with both these reasons and added others. He pointed out that it was difficult for the government to persecute Catholics for religion: there were no laws to make Catholicism heresy, it was difficult to persuade men that to practise the ancient religion of England should be a capital offence, it might be dangerous to persecute for religion openly, and the Protestants liked to claim that they did not punish men for their conscientious beliefs. Finally, Allen condemned the Protestants as worldly men who considered the Catholic religion only as it affected the safety of the state and were more interested in looking for supposed treason in Catholicism than for the truth of its religious teaching.[55] Catholics were treated as scape-goats, Persons complained in his *Epistle of the persecution*, and the most ludicrous events were blamed on them. When St Paul's spire had caught fire a number of spells were found buried nearby and the blame was put on Catholics with an interest in witchcraft. In fact, it was found out later that the man who had done it was the strongly Protestant minister of Newington. When, at Oxford, the judge and jury who had sentenced a Catholic bookbinder to lose his ears, all fell ill and died, Persons said this was also blamed on the sorcery of Catholics.[56]

Catholic writers continued, throughout the reign of Elizabeth and beyond, to claim that they were not traitors, that they were persecuted for religion, and that the priests executed by the government were true martyrs.[57] This point was also frequently made by Catholics at their trials. At the same time the prosecution took the opportunity to stress the traitorous beliefs and actions of English Catholics in order to justify their case, which usually rested technically on one or other of the Elizabethan statutes that simply made Catholic religious activities treason. These trials and even the executions were made the focus of the propaganda efforts of both sides, providing the accused Catholic with the unusual opportunity of speaking to a large audience, and the Protestants with a dramatic spectacle in which the treason of Catholics was exposed. Reports of these trials were compiled by Catholics and circulated, once again carrying the simple message of the arraigned to another audience, while the government also published their own description of some of the more interesting or controversial cases.[58]

In the Catholic accounts the martyr is frequently reported to have made a speech protesting his innocence of treason. 'I am executed solely for faith and religion and nothing else,' said James Bird in 1593 at his trial.[59] 'I am here to suffer for my conscience' he repeated on the scaffold. Two years earlier a priest named Roger Dicconson had said the same, 'I came into the realm, my native country, to give myself to study, to prayer, and devotion, and use my function, and that, I hope, is no treason.'[60] Christopher Bales' words were almost exactly similar:

Good people, you are come hither to see a man die, but why or wherefore you know not. A traitor! But now wherein a traitor? In that I am a priest, and seek to reconcile souls unto Almighty God according to my office and calling; but this word *traitor* is such that you cannot see into the cause. But I would that you might but see the soul and the change it makes, and then I doubt not but that this word *traitor* would take no effect.[61]

Examples of this sort of declaration could be multiplied considerably. Occasionally we read a less stereotyped pronouncement made by a Catholic, but usually they have the same aim – to show the martyrs' innocence of treason. Edward Jones took the opportunity of his trial to defend the Marian persecution in the usual terms (while condemning his own punishment) and threatened his judges with divine retribution: 'Take heed what you do, for quis extendet manum suam in Christum Domini et innocens erit?' The Catholic account of this trial describes how one of the justices, 'an upstart gentleman', wickedly scoffed at this text, and how in the end Jones had to be gagged in order to bring his speech to an end.[62]

TOLERATION

From the beginning of the reign Catholics asked the Queen for mercy and toleration, but such requests became more insistent as the persecution grew.[63] They were made even though, as we have seen, Catholic authors maintained that the persecution of Protestants under Mary had been just, and despite the fact that they still opposed toleration for heretics abroad.[64] The earliest plea for toleration was made in 1563 by a Catholic sympathiser in Parliament, Robert Atkinson, who delivered a very unusual speech calling for national unity through freedom of religion. He suggested that harsh laws against Catholics would lead to sedition and rebellion. It was no part of religion, he said, to hate one another, and he suggested that England should follow the example of Germany, where religious peace had been established on the basis of toleration.[65] In the same year the Emperor wrote to Elizabeth asking her to allow Catholics one church in each city.[66] In 1567, Stapleton begged that Catholics might 'be borne withal' for refusing obedience to the Queen in religious matters.[67] But Catholic requests for toleration begin to be made clearly and repeatedly only in the second half of the reign, after the persecution had begun. They begin with the publication in 1580 of *A brief discourse* by Robert Persons. Here Persons asked Elizabeth

to grant Catholics 'more favour. . .or at leastwise equal toleration'
as the other three religions of England, which were, he said somewhat disingenuously, Protestantism, Puritanism and the Family
of Love.[68] Shortly afterwards, Persons pleaded with the Queen
not to enforce the 'most severe' law by which recusancy was to be
punished with a fine of £20 a month. He called for 'liberty of
conscience', telling the Privy Council that it was good policy to
grant toleration, because in a period of persecution there were
many conversions to Catholicism, and Catholics were confirmed
in their faith – a curious argument! Catholics should be shown
mercy, Persons said, because they were such obedient and well-
behaved subjects; in Japan they had been protected from persecution by the King only for that reason, 'only for the commodity
he feeleth his commonwealth to receive thereof'.[69]

A manuscript draft of a petition to the Queen, connected perhaps with Laurence Vaux and Sir Thomas Tresham, and dating
from 1583, is more specific than Persons was in his printed books.
It asks for six Catholic churches in every shire and two in every
city, with the repeal of all laws against Catholicism. In return
Catholics offer the Queen, for as long as she should require it, an
annual payment based on their assessments for parliamentary
subsidies.[70] This petition was clearly drawn up with French
circumstances in mind, but the state of the Catholics in England
was very unlike that of the Huguenots in France and their attitude
to toleration was also most different. The Calvinist counterparts
of Vaux and Tresham in France (and the Netherlands) had
fought desperately for years for the right to maintain a number of
churches in each district. But English Catholic petitions for toleration request it in the humble language of political non-resistance.
When English Catholics adopted the ideology of political resistance, they dropped their pleas for toleration and fought for the
total overthrow of the Elizabethan regime. The English Catholics
aimed too high: toleration was an interim measure to save life
until divine providence brought the return of the true faith. For
the Calvinists in France and the Netherlands, toleration was an
end in itself, to be fought for.

5

The background to non-resistance

The doctrine of non-resistance was under considerable strain. The medieval foundations of Catholic political thought were not built to maintain a structure of obedience to heretic governments. Loyalty to the Pope, and the theory that all political power lay within the jurisdiction of the Church seemed to pull in the opposite direction. Pius V himself had spoken in this vein in 1570 and protestations of affection for the Queen and of support for her rule were difficult to square with this authoritative pronouncement. Not only did ideas of papal power in temporals open an easy avenue for the development of monarchomachism, but the writings of the neo-scholastics of the period likewise provided another springboard for the exposition of theories of resistance. It was generally accepted as orthodox Catholic theology that ultimate political authority lay not in the hands of the prince, but in those of the commonwealth. The history of centuries of ideological conflict in which papal propagandists had ranged themselves firmly against the doctrine of divine-right kingship and non-resistance, bore heavily on the proponents of Elizabethan Catholic loyalism. Moreover, there was by the early 1580s considerable tension between the ideas expressed in their books by the leading Catholics and their actions. Plans to overthrow Elizabeth by invasion and insurrection had never been far from the minds of some of the exiles on the continent since the late 1560s. Plots, of varying degrees of impracticality, were hatched by the more politically minded of the English Catholics throughout the period, when in their printed books often the same men expressed their devotion to the Queen and their adherence to the idea of non-resistance. It is true that William Allen was not deeply concerned

63

in such stratagems in the 1570s, but after 1581, he and Robert Persons turned their minds again, most actively, to plans involving the support of the Pope, Spain and the Duke of Guise in the military reduction of England to the Faith. Why, in these unfavourable ideological and political circumstances, did the Elizabethan Catholics cling so resolutely to the philosophy of non-resistance?

Despite the plotting, practical considerations themselves perhaps favoured moderation in political thought. As has been suggested above, the decision by William Allen to send seminarists to England was accompanied by an attempt to avoid the dangerous consequences of *Regnans in excelsis*, and to reconstruct a theory of passive obedience which ignored the papal bull. As long as seminary priests remained in England, there was very strong practical reason for Catholic authors to avoid attacking Elizabeth or supporting the policies of her enemies. As the priests, and the laity, began to suffer increased persecution, the strongly argued case that they suffered martyrdom for religion and not execution for treason served to reinforce the practical importance of expressions of loyalty to the Queen and a commitment to political quietism. Appeals to the Queen's mercy and requests for toleration could also only be made against such a background of non-resistance. The theory of persecution which Catholic authors developed also helped to strengthen the belief that 'this was the way' to convert England – by suffering, not by force. From a practical point of view again, the propaganda of ideas of resistance was perhaps seen by Elizabethan Catholic leaders – at least before the 1580s – as a hopeless cause. The smallness of the papist community in England, its concentration away from areas of strategic importance, its failure in 1569 to achieve success through insurrection, all counselled caution. Plots to arouse the interest of European powers in the invasion of England were in order, but the Catholic leaders perhaps realised – though they dared not admit it on the continent – that insurrection by itself would not be enough. Hence there was no reason why political plotting and ideological loyalism need not go hand in hand. Both tended in the same direction – the preservation and eventual recovery of Catholicism in England – but by different routes.

The passive obedience of the Elizabethan Catholics also had

stronger theoretical foundations than the foregoing comments have allowed. It is quite true that medieval Catholicism formed an excellent launching pad for ideas of popular sovereignty and resistance to divine-right kingship. But during the first half of the reign of Elizabeth, Catholicism was in fact singularly unfavourable to the development of theories of resistance. Since the outbreak of the Reformation, the Roman Church had on the whole ranged itself on the side of royal and imperial authority. It was the reformers who in the sixteenth century had been forced to adopt theories of disloyalty: in the Holy Roman Empire at the time of the Schmalkaldic League; in England, during Mary Tudor's reign; and most recently in France, the Netherlands and Scotland, in the era of Hotman, Buchanan and Junius Brutus. In the face of this onslaught, Catholic political philosophy had naturally developed rather unwonted conservative tendencies. Out of the front line, Soto and Vitoria might continue the medieval tradition of theories of popular sovereignty, but the areas which exercised most influence over English Catholic exiles saw the production of a literature more in tune with the needs of the time. The Elizabethan papists, exiled to France or the Netherlands, could not fail to be influenced by the prevalent non-resistance and royalism of Catholic ideology in these places. In the 1560s and 1570s only the Scottish Papists – even fewer and more demoralised than their southern colleagues – found themselves in the same position as the English; elsewhere Catholicism was the religion of kings and majorities. Circumstances, and ideology, changed in 1584, when the great and influential weight of French Catholicism swung suddenly over from the side of order to that of resistance. This, as will be shown, had an immediate impact on English political thought, but this was in the future, and as yet the Gallican Church was still committed to the Valois dynasty and to divine-right kingship.

The influence of continental political ideas on the Catholic exiles in this period is demonstrated well in the works which they chose to translate and publish in England. These books often express their support for the politics of non-resistance which was then the dominant ideological theme in the writings of the Elizabethan Catholics. Peter Frarin's *Oration* of 1566, translated and printed by John Fowler, the principal English papist publisher of the period, was devoted entirely to a denunciation of rebellion. Frarin came from Antwerp and his *Oration*, which was delivered first at the university there, is a vigorously sustained attack on what he took to be the essentially Protestant theory of resistance to legitimate political authority, illustrated from the writings of the reformers and the author's own experiences on a recent tour through France. Fowler printed a number of curious and crudely-drawn cartoons at the end of Frarin's book which served to impress more graphically the message of the book; among them was a representation of John Knox and Christopher Goodman, who had been mentioned in the text as typical Protestant theorists of rebellion. The two advocates of resistance were shown blowing trumpets into the startled faces of two un-named queens, shown seated on thrones. Underneath the simple message of the cartoon was explained:

> No Queen in her kingdom can or ought to sit fast,
> If Knox's or Goodman's books blow any true blast.[1]

Another work translated into English at this time also demon-strates the continental support for ideas of non-resistance: Hieronimus Osorius' *Epistle* (1565). Osorius was a Portuguese bishop and although few exiles penetrated as far as his country, the subject of his work – it was a letter addressed to Elizabeth herself – called for its publication in English. Osorius addressed the Queen most reverently, as the Louvainists chose to themselves, and spoke strongly in praise of monarchical government. The *Epistle* was a mixture of rather heavy-handed Fürstenspiegel good advice and religious apologetic. Osorius condemned Protes-tantism as encouraging rebellion and pleaded with the Queen, for her own safety, to embrace the Catholic Faith which taught obedience and good order. The bishop's book evoked a number of Anglican refutations and in response he published a second work which also appeared in English translation at Louvain in 1568 under the modest title of *A learned and very eloquent treaty*, and reinforced a number of the anti-Protestant assertions of the *Epistle*.[2]

Other translations published by English Catholics touched on political matters more briefly, but usually with the same message. Stanislaus Hosius, the Polish Catholic, expressed the fear in one of his books that it would soon be 'no less ignominious to be called a regist than a papist'.[3] The German, Frederic Staphylus, whose *Apology* was translated by Thomas Stapleton and published in 1565, dealt with the impiety and disobedient doctrine of Luther at some length. Staphylus warned his readers to avoid Lutheran teaching:

I beseech you all, good Christian readers, of whatsoever degree or quality you are, remember your vocation, and suffer not yourselves to be abused of this fond friar, or to be led into his seditious errors and contempt of magistrates from the true belief and ancient obedience of Christendom. For the true gospel of Christ commandeth directly all subjects to obey their lieges, princes and sovereigns in all dread and obedience; not only good, virtuous and merciful, but also froward, wicked and cruel.[4]

From France, the Archdeacon of Toulouse's doctrine, published in England as *A notable discourse* in 1575, was similar. Even a ruler as wicked as Nebuchadnezzar was to be obeyed, he maintained, despite what seditious Protestants taught.[5] To drive home the last point, John Fowler had published in 1568 a proclamation of the French king, Charles IX, in which the Huguenots were accused of wishing 'utterly to overthrow...our religion and estate'.[6]

The traffic in political ideas was not entirely one-way, and English and Scottish writers also added to the literature of continental Catholic non-resistance.[7] In a number of Latin pamphlets published in the early 1580s, Richard Hall urged Catholics in the Netherlands to obey Philip II and to murder William of Orange.[8] In France one of the best divine-right theorists of the period was Adam Blackwood whose Ciceronian *De coniunctione religionis et imperii libri duo* was published with a dedication to Mary Queen of Scots in 1575. His thesis in this work was that political obedience was intimately connected with religious observance, and that all Protestants were rebels and all Catholics were model citizens.[9] He returned to this theme, although he admitted he had dealt with it 'ad nauseam usque' already, in his *Adversus Georgii Buchanani Dialogum* (1580), a Bodinian refutation, page by page, of Buchanan's *De iure regni apud Scotos*, one of the great manifestoes of Protestant resistance-theory.[10] A less well-known Scot than Blackwood is Ninian Winzet, a former servant of John

Leslie's, who found himself by the late 1570s abbot of St James's, Regensburg.[11] The administrative burden of running a community which consisted at first of himself, one monk and a novice allowed Winzet the opportunity to publish in 1582 his *Flagellum sectariorum* and *Velitatio adversus Georgium Buchananum*, dedi-cated to Duke William V of Bavaria. Like Blackwood, Winzet attacked Buchanan's book which he called 'De iure populi in regem apud Scotos',[12] but he also flagellated an unnamed work that seems from his description very like the *Vindiciae contra tyrannos*, another masterpiece of Calvinist sedition, which he said was circulating in Germany at the time.[13]

THE CRITIQUE OF PROTESTANT POLITICAL THOUGHT

The works of Frarin, Osorius, Blackwood and Winzet were typical of Catholic literature of the period not only because they preached obedience to kings but also because they denounced heretics as rebellious and Protestant political thought as seditious. Indeed, this was a principal theme in the political writings of English Catholics throughout the reign of Elizabeth. The function of religion within political society has been one of the most fertile sources of discussion among philosophers since Plato, and in the sixteenth century the appearance of Machiavelli's *Prince* and the growth of religious controversy between reformers and Catholics stimulated a new interest in the problem. While writers on both sides of the religious schism generally agreed in denouncing Machiavelli's thesis that Christianity was irrelevant to the success-ful pursuit of statecraft, they advanced contradictory claims for the political value of their own faith to the prince and his subjects. The Catholic contention, repeated time and again in the works of this era, was that Protestant theology by its very nature under-mined civil society, and that many reformers in addition had preached the dangerous doctrines of resistance and popular sovereignty.

It would be difficult to overestimate the part this critique of Protestant political thought plays in Elizabethan Catholic litera-ture. Their own experience of Protestant resistance to Queen Mary I no doubt added colour to the belief of our authors that reformed doctrine was essentially seditious, and with every year that passed the events in France and the Netherlands, where many of them lived, served to confirm this impression. Insistence on this argument became stronger as Protestant controversialists replied with their own accusations that Catholicism surrendered political power into the greedy hands of the Pope and encouraged economic backwardness with its monasteries, saints' days and wasteful ceremonies. From the point of view of the argument of this present chapter, it seems very likely that the insistence of Elizabethan Catholics that heresy was destructive of political order and due obedience helped to encourage the exposition of ideas of non-resistance by our authors. It was clearly rather difficult to denounce reformers as seditious rebels while at the same time preaching resistance oneself. The denunciation of heretic political thought was an important part of the Counter-Reformation attempt to win support for the Church. What better motive for kings and nobles (especially those seduced by the hope of ecclesiastical plunder and full sovereignty) to remain faithful to the Church than to advertise it as the rock of stability and of conservative order in a world unhinged by schism and revolt? The Church of Rome was represented as superior to the reformed sects in its age, its unity and its God-given constitution, in an era when appeals to antiquity, solidity and divine law carried great weight.[14] Since it was founded on a commission of authority from Christ himself, the Church could claim to be 'the most perfect commonwealth in this world', with the 'most orderly manner of government'.[15] Fifteen hundred years of history and the support of all kings of England since (the mythical) Lucius were appealed to by Catholic controversialists, and contrasted with the novelty and plebeian membership of the reformed congregations.[16] The slogan 'No Pope, no King' might stand as the motto of this aspect of the Counter-Reformation. Of course, it was far more applicable to France or the Netherlands in the 1560s and 1570s than it was to England, but the English Catholics in the reign of Elizabeth tended to cling to their continental intellectual models, and political allies, rather undiscriminatingly (in the same way as their Protestant colleagues did throughout the century).

Condemnation of Protestant political ideas went back in the English tradition to Sir Thomas More,[17] and had continued during the reigns of Edward VI and Mary.[18] Beginning with the

Louvainists, Elizabethan Catholics continued and amplified these arguments, which became a staple element in their controversial writings throughout the reign. From the very beginning heresy and rebellion had been associated, Elizabethan Catholic writers maintained. The first Anabaptist, Richard Hall said, was Judas of Galilee, mentioned in Acts and by Josephus, who had incited the people not to pay taxes and to disobey the Romans.[19] The Rheims Testament referred to the heretics called 'Begardi', 'that took away all rule and superiority',[20] while Stapleton described the Donatists as rebellious.[21] Constantine the Great had opposed the Arians because they aimed to destroy all mankind, and he had refused all service from heretics, arguing that those would never be faithful to their princes 'who had forsaken and betrayed their lord and God'.[22] Wycliff and Hus had held that 'a king or queen committing any mortal sin loseth straight his office and is no longer to be obeyed'. Wycliff had also taught that tyrannicide by a private person was lawful, a doctrine condemned at the Council of Constance, and the Hussites had been responsible for the Taborite Rising in Bohemia.[23] But it was Luther's theology which was most frequently criticised by Catholic writers.[24] Justification by faith alone had pernicious social consequences because it discouraged almsdeeds and good neighbourliness:

Who will give his goods to the poor? his lands from his own kindred, to build hospitals and colleges for strangers? . . . when he knoweth that he shall receive no reward therefor in heaven.[25]

Lutheran doctrines, moreover, fostered idleness because they gave no encouragement to the work ethic.[26] After declaring at the Diet of Worms that he 'came not to send peace, but the sword' Luther had published books 'wherein he did the best he could to abolish all due obedience, to abrogate all policy and civil government, to persuade the people to rebel and forsake their spiritual and temporal rulers and masters, to provoke them to stealing and robbing, to bloodshed and murder, to sacking and burning of houses, of cities, of churches'.[27] Thus, in his *De captivitate baby-lonica ecclesiae*, he had taught that 'there is no respect of persons before God, therefore there ought to be no difference of persons, no magistrate in the Church, but that all Christian men are free, and therefore all other distinct estates, dignities, and qualities as well great as small ought to be one and all alike'.[28] In his *Von weltlicher Obrigkeit* Luther had called kings fools, and in other works he had instructed his followers to wash their hands in the blood of the clergy, and to refuse to go to war against the Turks.[29]

Luther's seditious doctrines had led to rebellion and war in Germany. The Peasants' War of 1524–5 attracted most interest in this respect from Elizabethan Catholic writers. The war, caused directly by Luther's 'disciple' Thomas Müntzer, but fundamentally the result of the master's own theology, had devastated Germany: Persons said that 200,000 men had been killed in one day during the fighting; the figures of casualties given by other writers ranged from 50,000 upwards.[30] Luther was not in the least perturbed by this, a Catholic author reported, and he married a former nun while the rebellion was going on. But once he saw that the peasants had failed, 'out of hand, as the wind and flattering blast of fortune turned, so he turned his sail, changed his style, sung another song', and now wrote a pamphlet against the rebels:

See, I pray you, the evangelical sprite of this apostle, how double it is, how expert and ready in false feigning and dissimulation. All this he wrote to make the world believe that he was none of that pack and wicked conspiracy of rebels, whereas indeed he was the author and grand captain that did set them on, and clapped his hands and egged them forward, as long as they had any hope to have the upper hand.[31]

Later in his life, however, when writing in favour of the Schmal-kaldic League, Luther once again defended the right of subjects to 'take weapon and stand in the field against their liege sovereign', and had also encouraged the uprising of the Anabaptists in Münster, and the rebellion of Protestants in Denmark and Sweden.[32]

Calvin's ideas were criticised in the same way. His doctrine of predestination, it was argued, took from men a sense of respon-sibility for their actions.[33] In the 'Institutes' he had said that civil laws did not bind in conscience, 'but only for external and temporal respect'.[34] This, Matthew Kellison thought, took away the authority of all princes and judges, destroyed all laws, broke all contracts and promises, and destroyed all normal social relationships.[35] Calvin's doctrines were linked by the Elizabethan Catholics with the French Wars of Religion, which were frequently mentioned by the Louvainists.[36] Huguenot preachers were portrayed as 'riding with their pistolettes at their saddle bow', and Beza was said to have carried his gun into a church at Orleans.[37] It was at Beza's instigation, moreover, that the Duke of Guise had been assassinated,[38] and in his dedication of a book to Queen Elizabeth he had described 'those French Protestants who died in war against their king' as 'saints and martyrs'.[39] The exiled Elizabethan Catholics had first-hand knowledge of the troubles in the Netherlands. Stapleton, writing in 1567, described how the Calvinist preachers had encouraged the Netherlanders to rebel against 'a most Catholic, most clement and most mighty prince' and how the 'traitorous brethren in Antwerp have not sticked openly to say "Schijte op die Conning"', which he thought was 'an unmannerly talk meet for so cleanly a gospel'.[40] The Scottish disturbances of the 1560s were likewise blamed by Elizabethan Catholic writers on the Calvinist clergy and their doctrines.[41]

As for the English reformers, rebellious doctrine was even detected in the *Obedience of a Christian man* by William Tyndale. Richard Broughton, writing at the very end of Elizabeth's reign, quoted from the denunciation of Tyndale's doctrines printed in Foxe to show that he believed 'every man is lord of other men's goods' and 'the children of faith are under no law'.[42] But it was the events of Mary's reign – Wyatt's rising and the books published by the Marian exiles – which received most attention from the Elizabethan Catholic writers. Goodman, Knox, Gilby and Whittingham were criticised for having justified political resistance and for having condemned the government of women.[43] One Catholic writer commented that in writing the *First blast of the trumpet against the monstrous regiment of women*, the author (whom he described as Christopher Goodman) 'swerved much from the common and accustomed manner and fashion of his fellows', who were usually most fond of women, especially if they were 'fit and ready to the game'.[44] Thomas Stapleton hinted that others – he mentioned Robert Horne, Edwin Sandys and Calvin himself – had approved of the doctrine that women should not rule. This theory rendered void the government of Elizabeth in England, and of all princes who were women or even ruled by virtue of descent from women.[45]

Despite the writings of the Protestant exiles in Queen Mary's reign, however, the people of England had lived 'in an order' then, according to Abbot Feckenham, and had acted reverently towards God. But since Elizabeth's accession, everything had been 'turned up-side down' by the Protestant clergymen:

obedience is gone, humility and meekness clear abolished, virtuous chastity and straight living denied, as though they had never been heard of in this realm; all degrees and kinds being desirous of fleshly and carnal liberty, whereby the young springalls and children are degenerate from their natural fathers, the servants contemptuous of their masters' commandments, the subjects disobedient unto God and all superior powers.[46]

John Murren, Bonner's chaplain, agreed. 'Sicut populus ita et sacerdos', he said: 'so as the priest be, so be the people'. The Protestant ministers had disobeyed the laws of the universal Church and recently had ignored the Queen's own commandment to fast, eating flesh openly. In consequence the people were also disobedient:

they have set the people in such case that no prayer is used, no fasting, little almsdeeds, all liberty used; what disobedience children be in against their parents! how untrusty servants be! what swearing and blasphemy of God is used of all people! what theft, whoredom, craft, subtlety, and deceit! These be fruits that come of this newfangled doctrine.[47]

The seditious nature of Protestantism was soon manifested, the Louvainists saw, in the Vestiarian Controversy,[48] and the part played by the supporters of the Protestant candidate in the early Elizabethan succession dispute showed that they still sought to 'make kings and depose them' as they pleased, and were trying to persuade the Queen to perpetuate their period in favour.[49] William Allen saw the publication of John Stubbes' *The discovery of a gaping gulf* (1579), written in opposition to the marriage of Elizabeth to the Duke of Anjou, as another example of the seditious behaviour of the Reformers.[50] Towards the end of the reign the puritans tended to become the main object of Catholic attacks; there was now material available for denouncing them in the books of the Anglicans themselves.[51] Robert Persons cited

Whitgift's refutation of Cartwright for evidence that puritans wanted to 'overthrow all governors', and later Catholic authors referred to the denunciations of puritanism written by Bancroft and Sutcliffe.[52]

The rebelliousness of Protestants, shown by historical examples, was the result of their false and harmful doctrines. Catholics, on the other hand, received good moral instruction, based on sound theology. Catholics might be bad, Nicholas Harpsfield admitted, but not as a result of their theological principles.[53] In the Preface to his *An epistle of the persecution of Catholics in England*,[54] Persons went through a list of moral doctrines in which Catholics surpassed Protestants. Catholicism taught that goods taken by theft or fraud had to be restored, under pain of mortal sin, which prevented extortion, theft, bribery and so on. Catholics were ordered to keep their vows, which Protestants were told they could break. The Roman Church did not allow divorce and thus promoted social stability. Catholic theology separated venial from mortal sins and denied that concupiscence was a sin, while the Protestants, by their stricter doctrine encouraged desperation and a feeling that it was impossible to avoid deadly sin. Catholics, moreover, believed in purgatory, whereas by rejecting this doctrine, Protestants once again took away from many the hope of expiation for their sins.[55] The Catholic doctrine of penance and confession was 'the very hedge and wall of all virtuous life, and the chiefest bridle of licentiousness in a commonwealth'. In the confessional servants were made loyal to their masters again, breaches between friends and relations were healed, plots against magistrates and ordinary citizens were prevented from being carried out, proud sinners were brought to hearty repentance, the afflicted were comforted, the desperate were mollified, landlords and masters were made kinder to their subjects, subjects were made obedient, and the restitution of stolen goods effected. Thus, confession, or 'this spiritual court and tribunal of God in earth', was most beneficial to the commonwealth.[56]

For about 160 days a year, Persons continued, Catholics abstained from flesh and this enriched the country. Protestants tried to bring in regulations of this sort, but they lacked the force of religious laws. Catholics also fasted for about 100 days a year, which saved more money.[57] Another Catholic writer, Richard

Broughton, following Persons, worked out the cost of the abolition of fasting in England. He said there were 12,000 parishes in England with about 100 men and women of an age to fast in each; the cost of a supper for them all, at a penny a time, was £600,000 per annum. But Broughton then said that this figure was probably too low: the muster books said there were three million men in England, and if that were the case, with women also included, the cost of abolishing fasts would amount to £3,000,000 a year.[58] Persons described clerical celibacy as another political advantage of Catholicism, on the grounds that it kept the population low.[59] The children of married Anglican clergymen put a strain on the commonwealth, since they were generally idle – 'for so are clergymen's children commonly' – and because the parson usually could not afford to keep them and was thus likely to leave 'a pack of orphans upon the poor parish'. Broughton, writing twenty years later, attempted to calculate how far the marriage of clergymen would increase the population. He thought there were 40,000 priests in England, but admitted that others put the figure much lower, and settled in the end on 20,000 as a rough estimate. To compute how far this number of married men would increase the population he turned to the Bible: there were, according to Genesis, 70 Israelites who went into Egypt (or 75 according to St Stephen). Four hundred years later there were 603,550 Israelites, excluding women, children and the tribe of Levi. If there were 1,000 married ministers for each married male Israelite (Broughton thought there were 20 such in Egypt), in four hundred years the male population of England would have increased, as a result of the marriage of the clergy, by 603,550,000 – 'a greater number to be added in our nation than many Englands are able to maintain'. The only way to keep the population low in the face of such an increase was to fight wars in Europe, but such a policy was 'neither easy nor secure to be maintained' and was anyway 'wholly Turkish and more like to cannibals than to Christians'.[60]

Every aspect of Catholic theology received praise from Catholic authors for its political value; every Protestant doctrine was condemned. Catholic teaching on usury was superior to that of the heretics, Persons claimed in a passage defending the city of Rome from the criticisms of English Protestant authors – a controversial point of some relevance to the wider debate over which religion supported political society best.[61] The use of monasteries was described by some writers as one of the social advantages of Catholicism. Broughton, always attracted by bad statistics, accepted Foxe's estimate that before the Reformation a third of the 'substance' of England was owned by the monasteries. Some of this, he said, was spent by the monks on their simple life, but there was a lot left over, because a monk had no wife to supply with a jointure, no elder son to provide for, and no younger son to help by 'improved rents, toils or turning out of farm'. The wealth of the monasteries was used to benefit the commonwealth: some helped to maintain armies, 'more than all the ministers of England and abbey gentlemen are able or will perform'; some went to relieve the poor, for before the Dissolution 'so many statutes against them and to burden the country were not known'; and with the rest of the money, strangers were lodged, pilgrims entertained, the sick and maimed provided for, orphans kept and widows defended.[62]

In reflecting upon Protestant immorality, Catholic writers tended to romanticise the past, describing in glowing terms the good old days of Catholic observance and of political and social stability, and contrasting them with the disorder of the sixteenth century:

The subject in those days loved his prince with fear, and feared him with love. The vassal was to his lord loyal, the servant to his master obedient and faithful. Every man held him content with his vocation, no man was curious to meddle in another's. Charity, simplicity, sobriety so reigned universally, that of us that time might well be called the golden age of which the poets dreamed.[63]

The reasons for the change ushered in by the Reformation were, as we have seen, to be found partly in the Reformers' doctrine, but also in supernatural causes. The steeple of St Paul's Cathedral was struck by lightning at 3 p.m. on 8 July 1561, and burnt 'terrible and helpless into the night', as a result, John Murren said, of the change of religion. God is merciful, he said, but in the end 'strikes suddenly and sore', as in the case of Sodom and Gomorrah, Pharaoh and the Egyptians, and other unfortunates in the Old Testament. In the old days, there had been matins at midnight, masses in the morning, and all kinds of prayers, anthems and services at St Paul's, but since the accession of Elizabeth this had all changed, 'and it is no marvel if God have sent down fire to burn part of the church as a sign of His wrath'. In the old days in England God was served devoutly day and night, everyone lived in fear of God, 'everyone in his vocation', the commandments were kept, but now 'all is in talk and nothing in living'. Then there was prayer, now prating; then virtue, now vice; then building of churches, monasteries and hospitals, now the destruction of them; 'then was plenty of all things, now is scarceness of all things'.[64] There was great material danger in abolishing the mass, Thomas Fitzherbert maintained: 'nothing is more truly political, nor tendeth more directly to the establishment of common wealth than public sacrifice'. The mass united the inhabitants of a country, but also represented a 'covenant betwixt God and them, whereby they become his particular people, and He their God and protector, without whose particular providence and protection no common wealth can either prosper or stand'.[65] Allegiance to the Catholic Church brought political rewards from God; Catholics were blessed both on earth and in heaven, Richard Broughton said. The international power of the King of Spain and of other Catholic countries proved this:

let any man peruse the state and conditions of those countries of Christendom that are fallen to heresy and become irreligious and he shall perceive them to be in most dishonourable terms, both for temporal and spiritual rule, the jurisdiction of none known or acknowledged out of one little country or province, and those which be the greatest adversaries of religion, to be in the most pitiful, poor and uncertain case of the rest.[66]

This insistence on Catholic strength and on the support the Church of Rome received from God's Providence is rather ironical when one considers the dangers and difficulties faced by the papists in England at the time. But it illustrates admirably their own conception of themselves as members of a vigorous, confident and successful Church which had little to fear from persecution and heresy; an opinion confirmed by exile and a consideration of history. Ideological complacency was encouraged by this view. Rebellion and seditious literature was the work of heretics; Catholics could rest secure in the support they had received from the royal families of Europe for centuries. Indeed, the espousal

The effect of the Counter Reformation Baroque on the exiles

by Protestants of ideas of resistance might provoke (as with other matters of doctrine) a Counter-Reformation over reaction, and acceptance of theories of divine-right kingship and absolute obedience. Such ideas were those most common on the continent when Catholic writers moved into exile at the accession of Elizabeth. While their own circumstances in England were so completely at variance with the position of papists in most other parts of Europe, they nevertheless remained true to the political ideas of their European colleagues. When Elizabethan Catholic authors began to adopt a sterner and more realistic political tone in their books it was once again in response to continental examples. Before considering this development it is necessary to consider at greater length the opposition in religious matters of Catholics to the Church of England under Elizabeth.

Part Two

RELIGIOUS RESISTANCE

6

Recusancy

OBEYING GOD NOT MAN

Elizabethan Catholic writers wavered between loyalty to the
Queen and opposition to her – at certain periods in the reign they
preferred one doctrine, at other times the other. There was, however, no doubt expressed by Catholics that religious resistance
was needed, that the laws enforcing Protestantism should be disobeyed and those proscribing Catholicism ignored.[1] Religious
resistance was usually justified by the use of biblical quotations.
'We ought to obey God rather than men,' said St Peter, and
Christ told his followers, 'Render, therefore, unto Caesar the
things which are Caesar's and unto God the things that are
God's.'[2] The Old Testament also supplied such texts. A Catholic
author quoted Joshua 1. 17–18:

There is an honour and obedience due to princes and civil rulers of
the world. These duties also have their limitation. The children of
Israel said unto their ruler Joshua: 'As we have obeyed Moses, so
will we obey thee, look only to this, that our lord God be with thee
as he was with Moses.' As who would say, we will obey thee so long
as thou obeyest God. God is to be obeyed, and so is Joshua, God
before Joshua, God above Joshua and rather God than Joshua.[3]

The idea of religious resistance was widely accepted by both
Catholics and Protestants and rested upon a deeply held presupposition of sixteenth-century political theology. It assumed
that human law was essentially conditional and depended for its
validation on divine law. If human law conflicted with divine
law, it was necessary to obey God not man. This doctrine appears
highly anarchic, but was itself the basis for the theory of the
divine right of kings. By claiming the legitimation of divine law
for their government, kings had to admit that there was a law

superior to their own. In the case of any disagreement between the two systems of law, the inferior naturally gave way to the superior. Thus it was that virtually everyone in the sixteenth century paid lip-service at least to the principles of religious resistance. What the Elizabethan Catholics saw as ungodly and hence not to be obeyed, however, was hardly likely to be accepted as such by the Protestant government.

HOW TO EXPRESS RELIGIOUS RESISTANCE?

If the right of religious resistance was clear and based on sound biblical principles, what was not so clear to the Elizabethan Catholics was how that resistance should be expressed. Here they found themselves breaking new ground. There was no other country in Europe where the problem existed as it did in England, where Catholicism was proscribed and yet there survived a sizeable minority willing to express resistance to a Protestant settlement. Within the English tradition itself there was the example of More and Fisher, who had refused the royal supremacy and accepted martyrdom, and the case of the exiles who had fled from Henry VIII and Edward VI. On the other hand there was the less glorious path trodden by the majority of the Henrician and Edwardian clergy, who had stayed at home, taken the oath of supremacy, and accepted passively all the religious changes imposed on them. In a sense, the Protestants had in the Marian exiles and martyrs more to offer the early Elizabethan Catholics by way of precedent. Just as Protestant political thought affected the political ideas of the early Elizabethan Catholics, encouraging non-resistance in reaction to heretic rebelliousness, so Protestant religious resistance may have influenced the Catholics, although in this case to emulate rather than criticise its example.

As a result of this lack of guidance and the novelty of their situation, it was only gradually at first that the nature of the religious resistance to be followed by the Catholics in England was decided upon by the Catholic leaders. But by the middle of the reign of Elizabeth a whole system of opposition to the settlement had been devised, which went further than anything practised even by the Protestants of Mary's reign. This resistance provided English Catholics with the activity necessary to give them a proper sense of their religious identity. In the early years of Elizabeth's reign Catholicism disappeared in England, not so much because nobody believed in Catholic doctrine, but because there were no accepted modes of activity by which a Catholic could express his belief nor any way the government could effectively test the papistry of the population. Pure belief was then a small part of religious life: activity – church attendance, the sacraments, the calendar – was in some ways more important. As Robert Persons put it, 'The things that a man hath to believe are much fewer, than the things he hath to do.'[4] The Queen need not make windows into men's souls because for most men there was little there to see. What the Catholic leaders achieved under Elizabeth was to provide those who wished it with a way of expressing their Catholic faith in a positive, active way, where previously there had been none at all.

RECUSANCY

The foundation stone of the religious resistance of the Elizabethan Catholics was recusancy – the refusal to attend Protestant church services. A steady stream of books issued from Catholic presses in the middle and later years of Elizabeth's reign encouraging the adoption by Catholics of this practice, and the surviving Marian priests and returning seminarists reinforced the doctrine of these tracts. Soon the activity – recusancy – signified Catholicism itself: by refusing church attendance a man distinguished himself clearly from Protestants, and showed himself and the world what he was.

It is perhaps not surprising that the idea of recusancy dawned only gradually on the Elizabethan Catholic leaders. This was a complete reversal, but one which reflected admirably the revolution which had overtaken the Church in England. For centuries the Catholic Church had punished those who refused on doctrinal grounds to attend religious services; now the Catholics of England were to be told not to go to church. The early activities of Elizabethan Catholic resistance were renunciation of benefices, exile, refusal of the oath of supremacy, and abstention from communion, but not recusancy. This is shown by an anonymous paper, which was cast abroad in the streets of Chester early in

1562. It was written by John Murren, former chaplain to Bishop Bonner,[5] who was behaving 'very seditiously' in Cheshire, Lancashire and Staffordshire at the time.[6] In this document Catholics are told that they may disobey the Queen in matters of religion, and that it is to bishops that they owe religious allegiance. Above all, they must avoid taking communion in Protestant churches: to do so is to break the profession of faith made at baptism. To enter the 'malignant church of Satan' and leave the Church of Christ is the action of a schismatic. Catholics must not allow themselves to be forced by fear of punishment or of the loss of worldly goods to take Protestant communion. If they cannot receive Catholic communion they should say prayers instead: those who are willing but unable to receive communion in fact communicate with the rest of the Catholic Church as effectively as if they actually took the sacrament in a Catholic congregation. But the tract goes no further: it uses the same arguments as were later used to encourage recusancy, but does not mention attendance at church. This suggests that the refusal to attend church was not considered necessary by a militant Catholic in the period immediately following Elizabeth I's accession.[7]

The campaign in favour of recusancy began four years after the accession of Elizabeth, and rather haltingly at that, with the decision taken in 1562 by a committee of theologians in Trent and repeated by the Pope himself that attendance at Protestant church services was not lawful. It is interesting to note, however, that this case of conscience was presented at Trent and Rome via the Spanish and Portuguese ambassadors in London, and not by way of the English Catholic exiles, that the laymen in England who asked the question expected an answer in favour of conformity at church, and that no effort was made to publish these influential decisions in England at that time.[8] Indeed, Robert Southwell hinted that the Tridentine resolution was hushed up in some way in England.[9] Slowly, however, a change became visible, active propaganda in favour of recusancy dates from 1566 when Laurence Vaux, deprived Master of Manchester College, wrote a letter to England, urging some important laymen of his acquaintance to embrace the practice.[10]

A number of other Louvainists or old Marians followed Vaux in encouraging Catholics in England to refuse attendance at

How effective was this? to be mistaking Clerical Catholics for Popular Catholicism — [handwritten marginalia]

church. Nicholas Sander wrote in 1567 forbidding Catholics to have 'fellowship' with Protestants 'in marriage, in prayer and in all the service of God'.[11] The deprived Master of Pembroke Hall and sometime Professor of Divinity at Cambridge, John Young, was even more severe. He saw familiar daily contact with heretics as the first stage on a slippery slope leading to conformity, communion and finally the 'pit' of heresy itself.[12] The former Abbot of Westminster, Feckenham, also wrote a paper to explain why he refused 'to be present at', 'to receive' or 'to use' the services of the Book of Common Prayer.[13] The campaign in favour of recusancy, although slow in developing, was not, therefore, the work of the seminarists alone. Young, Sander, Vaux and Feckenham – members of a generation of Elizabethan Catholics sometimes accused of laxity on this point – had begun the propaganda before Campion and Persons were even converted to Catholicism and before the first seminary priest stepped ashore in England.[14]

The campaign against attendance at church continued throughout the reign of Elizabeth, gradually gathering speed as the seminary movement became better organised. The subject was touched upon in one of Bristow's 'Motives', first published in 1574 and three times reprinted in various forms before the end of the reign; Robert Persons printed a book on the subject in 1580, parts of which were translated into Welsh verse; a number of explanatory annotations to the Rheims New Testament encouraged recusancy; Robert Southwell, John Gerard, Gregory Martin and Henry Garnet published books against conformity; Thomas Hill and Thomas Worthington touched more briefly on the matter at the end of the century; and there were other shorter writings.[15] At the same time, writers impressed on Catholics, less specifically, the need to confess the faith and the rewards to be gained by suffering for Catholicism.[16]

A large number of different reasons for recusancy were put forward in these books, and each writer sought a new angle on the subject. The basic presupposition of all this literature was, of course, that the Protestant service was heretical and false.[17] We may divide the other arguments used by the propagandists of recusancy into two sorts: first, those of a legal or official sort, second, those of a more practical nature. In the first place it was confidently maintained that to go to Protestant churches was against divine law, natural law and Church law.[18] Examples from the Old Testament were used to show the divine nature of the obligation to avoid Protestants. King Jeroboam's idolatry had been punished, Elijah confounded the priests of Baal and condemned the idolatry of Ahab, and the resistance of Daniel, Shadrach, Meshach and Abednego to King Nebuchadnezzar presented a fine example for Catholics in England to follow.[19] One Old Testament example used by Gregory Martin in his *Treatise of schism* to encourage recusancy led to the execution of William Carter who printed the book in England in 1578. This was the story of Judith who slew the idolatrous tyrant, Holofernes, rather than eat the food he offered her:

whose godly and constant wisdom if our Catholic gentlewomen would follow they might destroy Holofernes, the master heretic and amaze all his retinue and never defile their religion by communicating with them in any small point.

The government took this as an incitement to assassinate the Queen, and, indeed, the text was ideologically ambivalent, although it is quite clear that in this case it was meant to encourage religious resistance rather than tyrannicide.[20]

The New Testament was used to furnish texts where open confession of faith was called for, where Christians were told to obey God not man, and where separation from non-Christians was recommended.[21] Church history was used to demonstrate the acceptance of this doctrine by early Christians in their struggles against various sorts of heretics. One of Garnet's books consisted almost entirely of extracts from the Church Fathers which encouraged 'renunciation' of family for the sake of religion. His other book contained the story of Lucius, the Arian bishop, who was riding through a group of Christian children when the ball with which they were playing rolled between his mule's legs. The children, Garnet reported, refused to continue playing with the ball, thinking it was 'polluted with some great filth', and made a fire to purify the ball in its flames. Garnet concluded that Foxe might be told of the story and should include the ball among 'the number of those who have suffered for the Gospel'.[22]

In the same book Garnet gave the longest list of canons in

favour of recusancy: the forty-fifth and sixty-third Apostolic canons, and the decrees of the fourth Council of Carthage, the Council of Antioch, the Council of Laodicea and the 'great' Lateran Council.[23] He, and all the other writers on the subject, declared that it was schism to go to Protestant churches. Gregory Martin gave a graphic, if traditional, description of what schism involved:

We are incorporate into [Christ's] body as truly as the legs, arms and head are by sinews organically joined to the life of thy soul. So truly are they that have put on Christ in baptism united unto the mystical body of Christ, which is the Catholic Church; the soul or life of which body is the Holy Ghost, like as the life of man is his soul. As long as we remain in this body mystical, in this vine, as true members, as true branches, so long have we life, grace and gifts proportionable unto the part that we occupy in the mystical body. If we cut off ourselves by heresy, by schism, by going into the church where it is, or where any part of the schismatical service thereof is said or preached, we have no more the life, graces and gifts of the Holy Ghost to merit life everlasting than hath the leg or arm cut off from the body the life of the soul, which only remaineth in the body.[24]

Garnet maintained that it was 'exterior' heresy to conform and that exterior heretics were ipso facto excommunicate. Conformity was also, he said, a mortal sin.[25] To go to church was to break the oath at baptism.[26] It was, William Gifford said, forbidden to pray or communicate with heretics under pain of eternal damnation, and it could not be made lawful by any human dispensation.[27]

The canonical position was therefore made to appear very clear. In addition, a number of more practical arguments were used. To go into a Protestant church was alleged to endanger the faith of a Catholic. He risked 'infection' by doing so:

If Dame Eva had not presumed to hear the serpent talk, she had not been beguiled, and if when Luther first began to teach new doctrine, the Catholics at that time had not vouchsafed to give him the hearing, but had avoided his preachings and privy conventicles, there had not been now in the world either Lutheran, Zwinglian, Calvinist, Puritan, Anabaptist, Trinitary, Family of Love, Adamite, or the like.[28]

Catholics should refuse to go to church in the same way as Protestants and other heretics themselves refused to go to Catholic churches. One writer cited Foxe for a story of heretic recusancy under Mary, Robert Persons quoted a recently published account of Calvinist religious resistance in France, and Robert Southwell referred to the doctrine of Calvin himself on this matter.[29] Another argument used was that to go to a Protestant church was the distinguishing mark ('signum distinctivum') of a Protestant and hence a man who went to church declared by doing so that he was a Protestant. This argument was also a clear way of impressing on readers that Catholicism involved practical action, more than mere belief; that a Catholic was known by his actions, not simply by his faith.[30]

'H. B.' (or Robert Southwell, if I am correct) brought all his stylistic ability to bear on the subject.[31] Like other Catholic writers he made the position of persecuted Catholics in England appear glorious and tried to make the recusancy fines seem in a way attractive. He reminded his readers that wealth was considered of little account by philosophers:

O happy poverty that is not forced to make friends in court, to retain counsellors for the bar, to wait upon attorneys, to follow sise and sessions, to make her part strong by banding of men against her adversaries.[32]

The heavenly rewards for recusants were well worth their suffering on earth:

Imitate herein those merchants who are content to have their money transported by way of exchange into such places where they may receive it more commodiously. Your country is heaven, be contented that your goods be transported thither, although by the hands of such as think to spoil you. God Himself will be your assurance for receipt of the whole.[33]

The tables would be turned at the day of judgment:

O dear Catholics, lift up your eyes, and look upon this general day of waking from the sleep of death, see with what constancy you shall stand in that dreadful day if you be now constant against those which have oppressed you and have taken away from you the fruits of your labours. Behold again how your persecutors shall be troubled with horrible fear, and shall wonder at your sudden and unexpected salvation. How they shall say within themselves with much anguish of spirit and groaning: what hath our pride profited us? or what the boasting of our riches availed us? all those things have passed away like a shadow.[34]

Throughout Elizabeth's reign, from the later 1560s, therefore, Catholics were taught in a series of books to regard attendance at Protestant church services as sinful and were exhorted to embrace recusancy, however severe the punishment might be.

7

Opponents of recusancy

ALBAN LANGDALE

The pressure on Catholic laymen to conform was great, especially after 1581, when the act enforcing a £20 monthly fine for recusancy was passed, and a number of the Catholic clergy openly taught that it was lawful, in certain circumstances, to go to Protestant churches.[1] Compared with the books produced in favour of recusancy, these writings are very few, and the men who wrote them were rather undistinguished beside the recusant authors – Persons, Martin, Southwell, Garnet – who were all well known. But the teaching of the anti-recusants was worrying to the Catholic leaders: two books were devoted by Henry Garnet – the one in full, the other in part – to a refutation of this teaching, while John Gerard (I believe) and Robert Persons also wrote against it.

The first opponent of recusancy of whom we have much knowledge is Alban Langdale, the deprived Archdeacon of Chichester and chaplain to Lord Montague, who in 1580 wrote a paper defending conformity which was made public by a certain William Clitheroe and persuaded several prominent Catholics, Lord Paget and Ralph Sheldon among them, to go to church.[2] Langdale's main point was that the 'bare going' to church was not mortal sin and not forbidden by divine law. This point was more or less irrefutable; many of the writers against conformity themselves had been forced to admit it. Persons and Martin allowed attendance at Protestant churches merely for the sake of performing some particular service for the Queen, and James Bosgrave said that he had been to Protestant churches himself, quite lawfully, to see what the services and sermons there were like and to improve his English after years of exile. Henry Garnet admitted that the 'material fact of going to church' was not evil.

He gave several cases in which this was true: going to church with one's prince out of obedience, walking through a church, going to a Protestant church to disturb the service, going as a curious observer, and – a slightly different case – being present bareheaded when heretics said grace at table.[3] Langdale's argument was that, since it was lawful to go in certain circumstances to church, a Catholic who did not pray or communicate with the Protestants and remained seated while they knelt, did not show himself to be heretic by going to church and did not scandalise other Catholics. The sixty-third Apostolic canon did not apply in such a case, he said, because it condemned praying with non-Christians. Attendance at church was only forbidden by the human law which forbade association with excommunicates, but – and here he was following fairly orthodox doctrine – human law could not oblige a man to put his life in danger, unless it was a matter of defending the faith or done in the common interests of all. Necessity permitted a man to break human law, and 'just fear' of death, of loss of goods, or of prison, provided such a case of necessity.

In his choice of examples to justify conformity, Langdale was shrewd. From the Bible he chose the case of Gamaliel, who was a disciple of Christ 'but to the end he might pacify [the Jews'] fury, he remained among them'; Nicodemus, who was not rejected by Christ, despite the fact that he remained a secret disciple of his; Joseph of Arimathea, whom St Luke called 'probus et justus', although he hid the fact that he was a disciple of Jesus out of fear of the Jews; Obadiah, steward to the wicked King Ahab, who had hidden a hundred prophets from Queen Jezebel; and, finally, Naaman the Syrian.[4] Naaman was allowed by Elisha to go with his master the king to the temple and bow down before the idol, Rimmon:

Thus we see that Naaman in that place might exhibit his service to the king, that in his fact he was no idolater nor committed mortal sin, and so by a consequent, it appeareth that the bare local abiding in the profane temple at their time of service was not of itself a mortal sin.

Naaman was an excellent example because Gregory Martin in his *Treatise of schism* had said that although it gave Catholics in England no general permission to attend Protestant churches ('he that is Elizeus now, doth give you no such leave'), yet it did allow a Catholic to go to church to do his lord or king some particular service, 'to bear the sword, the mace, the canopy, verge, train, book etc'. This doctrine was followed by Persons, who made quite a point of it, as well as by Gerard and Garnet and was, perhaps, orthodox teaching under Elizabeth.[5]

The example of Naaman was a stumbling-block for the advocates of recusancy not so much because it was a clear biblical case of conformity as because they were usually anxious to prove in their writings their political loyalty to the Queen. The case of Naaman pinpointed with great accuracy the place where religious resistance coincided with political obedience: Naaman was allowed by Elisha to 'go to church' in order to perform his temporal duty to his sovereign, and a Catholic might do the same in England. If they wished to show their loyalty to the Queen and their acceptance of the doctrine of political non-resistance, the Catholic writers had to allow this exception to the rules of religious resistance. It might be said, however, that the zealous Earl of Arundel would not allow himself to take advantage of this precedent and sought exile rather than accompany the Queen as a courtier, to Protestant services.[6] But Langdale extended the case of Naaman to cover all Catholics in England. He stressed that the Queen required attendance at church as a demonstration of loyalty; it was a 'signum distinctivum', a means of distinguishing 'between a true subject and a rebel', rather than between a Protestant and a Catholic. Catholics in England, he said, should avoid causing trouble and encouraging the Protestants to persecute them. Attendance at church was an action required by the doctrine of political non-resistance; it did not fall outside the limits of what the secular state could legitimately command a Catholic to do. It was true, he said, that in the primitive church men had suffered martyrdom rather than accept heretical beliefs, and in England priests might be expected not to attend Protestant churches because of their vocations, while magistrates should use their power to 'withstand' (whatever that might mean exactly). But the ordinary Catholic need not follow these counsels of perfection:

for seeing the outward face of religion etc. is through God's permission for our sins taken away by the civil magistrate, folly it were for a man to seek to exulcerate that which he cannot heal; and it is not every man's lot to purge the Church of chaff; and for a matter which might be made indifferent, to stir trouble is not the best course to quietness. A man which dwelleth among the wicked must lament the state and prudently avoid the peril of temptation, and as much as he may must withdraw himself from trouble, as a peaceable child of the Church, not seeking unnecessarily to provoke ire.

Robert Persons, who was in England at the time, heard of Langdale's tract by a note written him on 6 November 1580 by Edward Chambers. Chambers arranged to meet Persons and George Blackwell – later the Archpriest – at an inn in London that evening and showed them the pamphlet. The next day Persons and Blackwell went to a merchant's house where they knew Dr John Young (author of *De schismate*, which taught recusancy, and lately dead) had kept his library, but found the books 'old and of evil print and edition' and crossed the River to Southwark, visiting the library of Langdale himself, who was in the country at the time with Lord Montague. With the help of Langdale's own books, Blackwell and Persons wrote a refutation of his doctrine, which, according to Persons, was widely spread among Catholics in the provinces.[7] There is a paper among the Tresham papers in the British Library, headed 'Against going to church', which answers the points made by Langdale exactly and which I am very much inclined to identify with the tract written by Persons with Blackwell's help.[8] This paper begins by denouncing Langdale's pamphlet:

A certain treatise very weak for learning and reason, but yet containing seed of great sedition, with matter of great advantage to the enemy, and with utter subversion of the Catholic cause if it should go forward.

Langdale's work was harmful because its doctrine was so appealing:

And there want not some which having now shrunken from God a good whiles agone in their hearts and seeking only but a probable pretence whereby they might (as they seem) with their credits leave his cause, do lay hands very greedily on this man's new device *ad excusandas excusationes in peccatis* and do seek to set it abroad by all means possible and to draw other men to the participation of their evil resolution.

Persons answered Langdale's arguments in turn. He was prepared to accept, as he did in *A brief discourse* at about the same time, that the case of Naaman proved that a Catholic might go 'with the king to church for a mere known temporal service', but it was no general precedent for conformity. Elisha had not given his approval to Naaman's action, as Langdale had claimed, he had simply tolerated it. The Church might tolerate certain things which were evil in order to procure some greater good or to avoid a worse evil, to use the terminology of Aquinas whom Persons cited, but it did not necessarily approve of them.[9] In answer to Langdale's use of the example of Gamaliel, Persons replied:

a Catholic may be present at the diets of heretics in Germany and at the parliament in England, if he go with the mind of Gamaliel, that is, to consent to no act of theirs but to destroy their devices and mitigate their furies.

Langdale had also used an example from the 'Liber contra Constantiam' of St Hilary, in order to show that the Queen should not be exasperated. Persons declared his approval of the sentiment, but thought the example of Hilary ill-chosen:

albeit I mislike it not in a good sense, yet I see not how it can be taken out of the doings of Hilary, for in that same book he calleth the Emperor, heretical, tyrant, Antichrist, persecutor, enemy to God, fox, wolf, Nero, fiend of Hell, and the like; the which I think might suffice to exasperate a prince.

Finally Persons repeated that attendance at church was a distinguishing mark of heresy by which men were known to be Protestants. But he had to shift his ground a little here. He denied that by not praying, kneeling or taking communion in church a man could show himself to be a Catholic (which was Langdale's chief practical point). It was not possible to tell whether a man was praying or not, he argued; a man might not kneel down through illness, and those out of charity with a member of the congregation were allowed not to take communion. It was true that Protestants knew that many Catholics did in fact go to church, so attendance was not in that way a distinguishing mark of Protestantism, but, he added, Protestants knew the difference between 'dissemblers' who attended church (and who were anyway in a state of schism) and 'precise Catholics' who refused to attend church.

THOMAS BELL

The other important advocate of conformity in the Elizabethan period was Thomas Bell, a seminary priest at work in Lancashire who, in the early 1590s, wrote a number of tracts in favour of going to church. He was for a time a serious embarrassment to the Catholic leaders. William Allen wrote a letter from Rome to England attacking what seems to be his doctrine and telling Catholics that the Pope disapproved of it, while Henry Garnet and a certain 'I. G.' also wrote tracts against him.[10] In October 1592, however, Bell declared his conversion to Protestantism and began a career as a writer of anti-Catholic books; his apostasy no doubt acted as the most effective antidote to his former teaching.[11] While still a Catholic, Bell wrote a number of works: 'A comfortable advertisement to afflicted Catholics', an 'Addition', an 'Answer' to a number of objections (probably those of Garnet), and a reply to the letter of six priests who had written criticising his ideas.[12] None of these tracts has survived but we can reconstruct the main points of his doctrine from the answers made to it by Garnet and I. G.

Like Langdale, Bell said that Catholics could attend Protestant churches if they did not pray or receive communion with the heretics, and if they did not show any reverence for their service, but he added a new element. Before going to church Catholics should make this declaration:

Good people, I am come hither not for any liking I have of any sacraments, service or sermons accustomably used in this place, but only to give a sign of my allegiance and due loyalty to my prince.[13]

Such a declaration removed the danger of giving scandal and of being suspected of dissimulation, and it was as effective a distinguishing mark of a Catholic as recusancy. Bell maintained in fact that attendance at church was justifiable as a way of showing obedience to the Queen. He claimed that the Queen required Catholics to attend church for that reason alone:

Her royal majesty and honourable council understand by name of papist or popish priest one that is an enemy to the state and they charge us to come to church only to show that we are no enemies to their state as the very title of their statute doth insinuate, which standeth thus: 'An act to keep Her Majesty's subjects in their due obedience'.[14]

Does he say anything about how these contra-recusant priests

Hence, he claimed, the case of Naaman justified conformity in England. Bell also maintained (wrongly as his opponents showed) that Gregory Martin had approved of this sort of declaration, and that Persons, the theologians at Trent and the medieval commentator on the Bible, Nicholas de Lyra, supported his view when they discussed the story of Naaman.[15] He used other biblical examples: Shadrach, Meshach and Abednego, who attended the ceremony at which Nebuchadnezzar dedicated his idol in Babylon, although they did not kneel down, and Jehu who pretended to worship Baal in order to arrange the slaughter of the idolatrous priests.[16]

All these points were dealt with – at great length – by Bell's controversial opponents, Garnet and I. G. I. G. said that since Bell's protestation contained an attack on the Prayer Book it was contrary to the Act of Uniformity, and hence would carry severer penalties than recusancy itself. He added that since the Protestants were so harsh in their treatment of Catholics it was hardly likely that they would allow them to escape the rigours of the law by making such a protestation.[17] Garnet and I. G. strongly denied that attendance at church was a matter of political obedience. It was not possible, Garnet said, to have a law which merely tested obedience. He cited Aristotle's 'Ethics' to show that law was a means of directing men towards certain virtues, and that to disobey a law was to sin against the virtue intended by that law. 'For when or in what country was it ever heard of, that there was a law made for no other end but for obedience.' The law requiring attendance at church was no more a test of allegiance than any other law.[18] I. G. said that men owed two sorts of allegiance: 'mere temporal' and 'mere spiritual'. While Catholics were quite willing to give temporal obedience to the Queen, they could not give her their spiritual obedience: 'no mere civil magistrate that is neither priest, bishop, nor within holy orders of clergymen can lawfully usurp or have spiritual authority.' It was true that sometimes some people did have both temporal and spiritual power, like the Pope and Prester John 'who is not only king, but also chief bishop in his kingdoms', but Queen Elizabeth did not.[19] Bell's arguments, both I. G. and Garnet said, seemed to suggest that the government was correct in saying that Catholics were disobedient subjects, and that their motives were political rather than religious.[20] Both opponents of Bell defended the works of the other advocates of recusancy from his misrepresentation and attack, and the case of Naaman was interpreted again in a strict sense. I. G. even went so far as to say that because of the Queen's opposition to the Catholic religion it was probably not lawful for a Catholic to carry her book, sword, train etc. into church at her command, which was what previous writers in favour of recusancy had used Naaman's precedent to allow.[21]

Bell's best controversial weapon, apart from Naaman, was the Extravagant, as he called it, *Ad evitanda* of Pope Martin V. This document declared, to use I. G.'s translation:

For the avoiding of many scandals and many perils and for the helping of timorous consciences we have ordained that no man hereafter be bound to abstain and separate himself, nor to avoid the communication of any, in administering or receiving sacraments, or in other divine offices, or without them, by reason of any sentence or ecclesiastical censure or suspension or prohibition generally promulgate of man or of the law, neither to keep the ecclesiastical interdiction if that sentence, prohibition, suspension, or censure be not promulgate and denunciate specially and expressly. . .[22]

Bell claimed that this applied to the case of Catholics in England and cited in his support the works of Navarre, Cajetan and Sylvester, three respected theologians. This was denied, of course, by both Garnet and I. G. They said that this edict applied to excommunicates coming to Catholic churches and not to Catholics going to Protestant churches. I. G. showed that Navarre did not support Bell's argument and that he seemed to say – Navarre was not in fact very clear – that the Extravagant did not even allow everyday social intercourse with heretics in England. Following Navarre, he distinguished between 'notorie excommunicati' and 'occulti excommunicati'; only the latter came within the scope of Martin V's decree. English heretics were, however, 'notorie excommunicati', by the bull *In Coena Domini* in which Popes annually anathematised all heretics and other evil-doers, and also, I. G. said, 'by a particular excommunication published in England by Mr Felton, from Pius V, as all men know', although, as he admitted, that excommunication was mitigated in respect of 'civil conversation and obedience' for the comfort of Catholics.[23]

Apart from Bell and Langdale we know that Dr Robert

Pursglove, the former suffragan bishop of Hull, encouraged conformity during the reign of Elizabeth.[24] In 1580, apparently, it
was suggested that Catholics might go to Protestant churches if
they made a public statement that they did so purely out of a
desire to obey the Queen. A condemnation of this practice, and
of conformity generally, was made at the time by the famous
Catholic theologian, Franciscus Toledo, after discussions in Paris
with English Catholics, and was brought to England by a certain
Edward Stansam.[25] For a short time in the early 1580s, a 'Mr
Aufild' taught that conformity was lawful in certain circumstances.[26] A Jesuit named Thomas Langdale also allowed attendance at Protestant churches in the early 1580s[27] and Jesuits,
according to their enemies at least, allowed conformity in Scotland.[28] In 1590 it was reported that priests in Cumberland and
Westmorland taught Catholics that they could go to church if
they gave no credit to what they heard.[29] In 1606 Robert Persons
published a book refuting the doctrine of a Jesuit, Thomas Wright,
who had claimed – using the writings of a well-known theologian,
Azor, as his excuse – that a Catholic could attend Protestant
services if he made a prior statement that he did so to obey the
King and to avoid the accusation of treason and disobedience
which was levelled against Catholics. The statement, according to
Persons, ran as follows:

Since both the King himself and the English state or commonwealth
seem to be persuaded that Catholic recusants are of doubtful loyalty,
or rather that they are traitors, because they refuse to go to Protestant churches, we, who do not wish to give scandal either to the King
or commonwealth, have decided to conform to His Majesty's will, as
expressed in his laws, and to be present in the said churches, according to the same laws. We do this only to make plain to His Majesty
and the commonwealth that our reconciliation to the Roman
Church is not prejudicial to the legitimate obedience which we owe
His Majesty. Our attendance at church should not be misconstrued
or misunderstood as if it were done in order to pray or out of
religious devotion.[30]

Later, in the seventeenth century and beyond, there were still
Catholics who were prepared to argue that in certain circum-
stances conformity was permissible, for example in the case of
Catholic servants of heretic masters.[31]

8

Casuistry and recusancy

CASUISTRY AND CONSCIENCE

The decision to obey God not man – to become a recusant, for example – was taken in the conscience, according to sixteenth-century theologians.[1] Conscience was seen then as the mental faculty which arrived at practical moral decisions, as a complex piece of psychological apparatus connecting belief to action. Elizabethan Catholic writers stressed that all matters of religious resistance came especially within its scope. Conscience was described as being both very strong and very weak. On the one hand, conscientious decisions were said to be literally God-given: the conscience was God's legate *a latere* or viceroy, implanted in every man. Whatever it decided was therefore right and obliged the will with supreme force, as if God had himself directly issued a command. Man was seen as God's robot, with a radio receiver (the conscience) accepting the commands transmitted from creator to creature. On the other hand, the conscience could err: the receiver was often inefficient. The complex process of decision-making, which was thought to work by syllogistic logic, could fail, and the conscience could produce the wrong decision. But this decision was still obligatory.[2] This explained why heretics were often quite as fanatical as Catholics. Catholic writers used the idea of the erroneous yet obligatory conscience to defend their religious resistance. Gregory Martin said that a Calvinist would sin damnably if, against his conscience, he adored the Blessed Sacrament – even though this was in itself (as far as Martin was concerned) a most commendable action.[3]

The idea of conscience seems very individualistic and, no doubt, modern ideas of political individualism stem in part from the religious conflicts of the sixteenth century. But, as so often in that era, the authority of the priest stepped in again, as it were, by the back door. If the conscience was so unreliable (and yet so powerful) it needed instruction. The priest, through the confessional, sermons, books, and friendly conversation could bring the erroneous conscience home on his shoulder to orthodoxy. The branch of theology which studied conscientious decisions – casuistry – enjoyed a great flowering in this period of decision and choice. The casuist sought to decide beforehand as many difficult cases of conscience as possible, so that there need be less reliance on the intuitive Aristotelian logic of the untutored conscience. Casuistry was naturally studied at the English seminaries on the continent: it was an ideal way of preparing young priests for the confessional, and of introducing them to the special moral problems that faced Catholics in Protestant England. In order to train their students more effectively the leaders of the English seminaries prepared booklets in which particularly difficult moral cases were solved. These manuals have survived in a number of archives and can be used to show what the moral teaching of the Catholic clergy in the field in England itself was during the reign of Elizabeth, or at least what William Allen, Robert Persons and the teachers at the Rheims seminary wanted it to be. By studying these casuist booklets we can look beyond the printed books – such as those in favour of recusancy which we have just described – to the intimate private instruction provided by the seminary priests for the laity in the confessional, through conversation and preaching; instruction which has in other respects inevitably left no trace.[4]

OCCASIONAL CONFORMITY

The casuist manuals deal with the subject of recusancy in some detail. They are interesting because their doctrine is rather different from that contained in the books written as part of the propaganda campaign in favour of refusal to attend church. The casuists accept the fact of recusancy, but they now confront all the difficult moral problems which the doctrine of recusancy itself created. In the face of these difficulties they decide that in several cases the rules of recusancy can be stretched – that, in short, occasional conformity is lawful. It is safe to assume that the seminary priests in England followed their casuist training and that they themselves in the confessional and in their more informal pastoral advice allowed the laity to practise some measure of conformity. This attendance at church was not to be regular or general: there was no covert attempt to contradict the argument of the many books which encouraged recusancy, only to add one or two casuist footnotes to them.

The earliest collection of English cases of conscience I have found is the record of a discussion held in the refectory of the English College at Rheims before all the students on 13 June 1578 and then continued on 27 January 1579.[5] William Allen mentions this manual in a letter, saying that it was being prepared at the college for the training of priests about to leave on the mission.[6] It came, therefore, from a very authoritative source and since it was used in the training of priests must have left its influence, through the confessional, on the social life of Elizabethan Catholics. It is less explicitly lenient than the other casuist booklets in its discussion of recusancy, probably because it was compiled before the persecution in England began in earnest and especially before the passing of the Act of 1581 which instituted the £20 fine. Nevertheless, it allowed certain acts of conformity. A nobleman or noblewoman was permitted to accompany the Queen to the chapel royal in order to carry books or cushions for her or to bear a sword before her. This, as we have seen, was allowed also by the propagandists of recusancy, but the casuists at Rheims extended this exception to embrace servants who accompanied their masters to church out of civil obedience. They suggested, however, that nobles and servants could find some way to avoid fulfilling their obligation to break the rules of recusancy.[7]

In another case the moral theologians at Rheims decided that a priest could admit to mass those who through fear still frequented Protestant churches. Such men were not excommunicates and could still be described as 'true Catholics'. 'Just fear', the seminarists were told at Rheims, rendered participation with heretics and schismatics excusable, and priests could absolve those who had fallen for that reason. 'Just fear' meant the sort of fear which would deter or affect a man of average courage, the concept was used by Langdale to justify wholesale conformity. One phrase stands out from the discussion of this case at Rheims and seems to sum up the view taken in these casuist manuals of recusancy: the priests were told that 'at present one should use practical considerations to judge the present practice in England'. It was no good clearing the young seminarists' minds of the pre-Elizabethan ideas of what the Catholic Church was – a universal, persecuting, self-confident institution – only to fill them up again with prejudices about underground resistance which were fine in theory and in print, but in practice could not hold. The casuist training was intended to give them a sense of the variety of the problems facing Catholics in England, and the need for adaptability in judging them.[8]

Even more of the wisdom of the serpent is apparent in a document entitled 'Resolutiones quorundam casuum nationis Anglicanae', a work dating from the early 1580s and coming partly from the pens of William Allen and Robert Persons.[9] Here, at greater length and with more style the pragmatic message of occasional conformity is spelled out. It is not clear when this influential booklet was written, but I suspect that it dates from shortly after the institution of a £20 recusancy fine which made the case for irregular conformity almost unanswerable.

The document begins with a preface which laid down the general principles on which the cases in the rest of the book were to be solved. It said at first that when human law conflicted with divine or natural law it was to be disobeyed, and the superior law to be followed instead. This was the usual justification for religious resistance and recusancy, but here the casuists turned it on its head and used it in such a way as to justify conformity. The law of the Church, they continued, was human law and hence was not to be obeyed if it conflicted with the natural law which enjoined self-preservation. In other words, the Church had no right to command its members to risk death or serious inconvenience rather than break the canon law.[10] There had been considerable debate among scholastics on this point, and our casuists here chose the laxer although more modern opinion.[11] They accepted, however, that if the law of self-preservation conflicted with both canon law and another (and superior) divine or natural law, then the canon law had to be obeyed. Thus, a man should give up his life in order to protect the faith or the common good of the Church or commonwealth. But if the faith or common good was not in danger, then a man might break the canons of the Church to save his life, for instance, as Richard Hall noted in a work of 1598, break the Lenten fast or communicate with excommunicates. Although God was to be obeyed before man, the law of self-preservation could be obeyed before the Church.[12]

The theoretical discussion in the preface set the tone for the rest of the document. It was decided that Catholics who frequented Protestant churches out of fear 'are not heretics, are not excommunicated and do not behave like heretics'; they might be admitted to mass. Here the decree *Ad evitanda* of Martin V was cited, the canon allowing contact with excommunicates which Bell had used against recusancy.[13] Another case asked whether a Catholic who was travelling in the company of heretics and did not want to reveal his religion might lawfully join with them in their psalms and prayers, or might accompany them to church. As with almost all the other cases in this booklet there was first a long and detailed discussion of the case and then at the end a short summary of the decision, which was attributed to Allen and Persons. The conclusion of this case said that 'all these things are lawful sometimes', but that it had never been the practice of the Church in the past for Catholics to join heretics in prayer – a somewhat ambiguous answer. But the long discussion of the case which preceded this statement was unequivocally lax. It began by saying that Catholics could kneel and join in the prayers of heretics to avoid capture, and then proceeded to discuss the more serious matter of actually going to church. To go to heretic churches was forbidden by human law and, therefore, the Pope could grant a dispensation, not for general conformity, but allowing travellers in England, and others even when they were not travelling, to go to church if they were insistently asked to do so and did not wish to reveal themselves as Catholics. The document gave a number of arguments which might move the Pope to grant such a dispensation. The first was a sound practical reason – the penalties for recusancy are severe and it is necessary to maintain Catholic strength in England:

This is especially the case in a kingdom like England where it is important to keep noble and rich families in their former positions of honour and dignity, so that, after the death of the Queen, they can stand up for the faith with their full authority and protect it with their strength and power against the audacity of heretics. Moreover, it is incredible how bad it is for the Catholic religion when a noble is discovered to be a Catholic and is punished; for often as a result of his ruin some heretic is advanced and nearly all the Catholic's dignities and titles of honour pass to heretics, to the great detriment of the Church.[14]

Other reasons for a dispensation were given: most people who attend heretic churches will not pay attention to the sermons or services and will not be harmed by them, and if they are, they should, by the law of nature, not take advantage of the dispensation; familiar social intercourse with heretics is permitted (presumably by the decree *Ad evitanda*),[15] and so listening to a sermon should also be lawful; Elisha allowed Naaman to go into the temple; and Catholics do go to heretic churches now with bad consciences and as a result are alienated from the Church by her strictness and slip into heresy. Having given all these reasons why a dispensation should be granted, the casuists then said that a dispensation was not in any case strictly necessary, and that a Catholic might by the law of nature, go without papal licence to heretic churches to avoid danger to his life or fortune, under a number of conditions. He must do it infrequently and only when absolutely necessary; second, he should use prayer to prepare for the temptation he might suffer there; third, he must not pay attention to what he might hear; finally, if he felt his faith had been disturbed he should go to see a priest afterwards.

The last case in the 'Resolutiones quorundam casuum' which is of relevance to the present discussion was one which had been dealt with already in the debates at Rheims: whether a priest should admit to confession Catholics who still went to heretic churches.[16] The final resolution of the case, ascribed to Allen and Persons, simply repeated the brief formula used in the Rheims discussion: 'he may be admitted to confession, but not to absolution'.[17] The longer discussion of the case which preceded this decision was less strict. If such people were in a state of mortal sin, they could be admitted to confession but not to absolution. But it was not certain that they were in mortal sin, and the document referred back to the case which we have just discussed, saying that a man might go to heretic churches to avoid danger, if he did it rarely and under the conditions laid down in that case. The casuist then gave a short encomium of the church-papist:

I think that it is most certain that many of those who go to heretic churches at present in England, not only among the Catholics but even among the heretics, are Catholic and most Catholic and do not show themselves to be heretics by going into these churches, but simply do not reveal themselves to be Catholics, as they are not bound to do, except in cases of necessity.[18]

The discussion ended, once again, with the advice that a papal licence should be sought enabling Catholics to go to heretic churches.

The 'Resolutiones quorundam casuum' of Allen and Persons, and the Rheims discussions are the two most important casuist documents of the period, but their doctrine is confirmed in the other sources of a rather similar sort. In 1578, Antonio Possevino decided, in response to the questions of some Englishmen, that a Catholic nobleman could accompany the Queen to church (he mentioned Naaman), that Catholics could go into empty Protestant churches to pray alone, and finally that to avoid danger it was possible in individual cases, to attend heretic services if one read Catholic prayers during their course.[19] A number of brief cases of conscience were found by government agents in the study of Sir James Hargrave in 1580. In these, it was concluded that Catholics could attend schismatical prayers out of curiosity and that it was only by showing consent in their activities that a Catholic communicated with schismatics in such circumstances.[20] Again, there is in the Bodleian Library a short collection of cases of conscience dating from the second half of the reign of Elizabeth which deals almost exclusively with attendance at Protestant churches. It allows nobles to accompany the Queen to church, citing Naaman (of course) and the more recent precedent of Lord Montague who had apparently escorted Elizabeth to chapel. This aside, it stresses repeatedly that it is quite wrong to go to Protestant churches, even out of fear of death, or to avoid the fine, or after making a protestation, or even if the Queen herself declared that she required attendance at church only to show civil obedience. But while strongly condemning regular attendance at Protestant churches, this document unequivocally supports occasional conformity. If an individual Catholic is required to attend church as a test of his religion, he should refuse, but where (as in England) everyone is ordered to attend Protestant churches, Catholics may in cases of necessity comply, if it can be done without giving scandal or without endangering their own beliefs. Similarly in Turkey Christians may wear Moslem clothes to avoid persecution, unless they are asked to do so as individuals.[21]

The casuist who composed this collection of cases also touched briefly on the allied question of whether it was lawful for a man to deny that he was a recusant, and to claim, contrary to truth, that he had attended church, in order to avoid the penalties of the law. He decided that this was not permissible. But two short documents from the Elizabethan period do allow this sort of deception. The first of these papers maintained that evasive and equivocal answers could be made to 'simple men, or churchwardens or such who go from house to house pro forma, and as it were of custom', but that before a 'public magistrate', 'greater consideration' was to be taken. The recusant could evade the questions asked by churchwardens, by answering, 'think you that I will live like an atheist', 'doubt you not but I will behave myself like a good Christian and dutiful to God and my prince', 'think you I am one of the Family of Love', and so on. He could also say that instead of going to church he had heard service at home (meaning Catholic service, but not saying so) and that he had 'received' at Easter (meaning Catholic communion, it seems). But crude forms of equivocation should be avoided: for example, if asked whether he had 'received', he could not answer 'yes', meaning 'his rents' rather than Anglican communion.[22] The second document said that a Catholic should not help his persecutors by making a confession of his recusancy, but should 'wholly...rely upon the benefit of the statutes either by due proof therein limited to be convicted, without accusing of himself, or that otherwise being not chargeable by law he may rather with great comfort of mind rejoice, rather by will and authority to be punished than by the ordinary means of law, and due course of proof, to be convicted'. The author then went on to show that 'ordinary means of law' could not prove anyone guilty by the Statute of 1581 against recusancy since its wording was too vague, but concluded by saying that it might be best for a Catholic to take the path of perfection and make open profession of his recusancy.[23]

The examples just given have been drawn from the extant Elizabethan Catholic casuist documents of which I have know-

ledge and they do not present an unduly one-sided picture of their
teaching on recusancy. To summarise, it must be admitted that a
general agreement that refusal to attend church is the best policy
underlies the whole discussion of the matter. None of these
casuists suggests that regular attendance at Protestant churches is
anything other than sinful. But these manuals of the confessional
do allow, to a greater or lesser extent, occasional conformity. The
printed books encouraging recusancy and these booklets agree that
recusancy is best for Catholics, but the casuists go on to say that
there may be reasonable grounds for not following this policy at
all times. I would go further and say that since the two most
important casuist manuals are connected with the Rheims-Douai
seminary and with Allen and Persons, it is not too much to infer
that Elizabethan Catholic confessional and pastoral practice was
for priests to allow conformity in certain circumstances.

This is borne out by the open letter which Cardinal Allen
wrote to the English Catholics late in 1592. He told the priests
that it was 'contrary to the practice of the Church and the holy
doctors in all ages. . . to communicate with the Protestants in their
prayers or service or conventicles where they meet to minister their
untrue sacraments'; it was against the law of God to do so and
the Pope himself (Clement VIII) had given this as his opinion
when consulted. But the Pope had added 'that such as of fear and
weakness or other temporal force or necessity should do it ought
to be gently dealt withal and easily absolved'. Allen advised
priests to show compassion and mercy, not to be 'rigorous nor
morosi' in absolving those who conformed through 'fear' or
'necessity', to avoid their own or their families' ruin: 'tutior est
via misericordiae quam justitiae rigoris'. 'No more severity is to
be required of the penitent than in other sins that be subject to the
sacrament of penance and perhaps [less], all circumstances well
and discretely weighed.' There was no doubt, moreover, that
priests in England were legally able to exercise this leniency, since
Allen himself and then the subdelegates to whom he chose to
extend the power had the faculty of absolving in conscience
from all sins, censures, pains and irregularities due to heresy or
schism, even those included in the dreaded bull *In Coena Domini*,
which strongly denounced heresy.[24]

The reason for this laxity in the confessional is not difficult to see. There may have been theoretical doubts about whether recusancy was really enjoined by divine law and whether conformity was mortal sin, but it was practical considerations which must have played the chief part in determining the attitude of the Catholic leaders towards conformity. It was clearly necessary to insist on the separation of Catholics from heretics and to teach that recusancy was a 'signum distinctivum' of Catholicism. Unless this was done, unless Catholics were given some practical duties to perform, then in a very real sense Catholicism would not exist at all in England. But a certain degree of laxity was also required. The laws against recusancy, against Catholic worship and contact with seminary priests, were extremely severe; enforced to the full, they would bring ruin and extermination to the Catholic community in England. It was essential for the priests to maintain this community and so they must of necessity help the Catholic laity to avoid some of the perils of the penal laws. Moreover, in individual cases, laxity could be beneficial: a schismatic who was about to be reconciled to the Church needed encouragement; once a convinced Catholic layman was in touch with a priest, a little prudent laxity need do him no harm, since the fact that he had a father confessor demonstrated his sincerity and devotion. The confessional practice of Elizabethan priests must also be seen in the wider context of the policy of the Elizabethan Catholic leaders. Their aim was the reconversion of England to Catholicism, and the way they hoped to achieve this was political; through conquest, rebellion, succession, or the conversion of the ruling family. They needed a healthy and devout Catholic community in England to form the nucleus of a future Catholic regime in England. In other words, it was more important for them to preserve and augment the numbers of this community, through the careful use of laxity, than to maintain its absolute purity and complete alienation from Protestant England.

9

Casuistry and the resistance of the laity

DIVORCE, EXILE AND OTHER ACTS OF RESISTANCE

The main form of religious resistance dealt with in the printed books of the Elizabethan Catholics is, as has been seen, recusancy. There are frequently also more general exhortations to the 'profession' or 'confession' of faith in the writings of the time, often coupled with some description of the heroic behaviour of a martyr. Sometimes specific acts of resistance – apart from recusancy – are mentioned. Henry Garnet encouraged Catholic women to leave husbands who forced them to go to church or to perform unlawful acts of religion. He maintained that, just as (according to the fundamental principles of religious resistance) a subject did not have to obey his king if he commanded anything against God's law, so in similar circumstances the wife need not obey her husband, the child his parents and the servant his master. He told Catholic women: 'Your husbands over your souls have no authority, and over your bodies but a limited power, but your heavenly spouse can condemn both unto everlasting fire, or reward both with everlasting bliss.' To drive the message home, he filled his book with examples of how religious divisions had broken up families in the days of the Primitive Church.[1]

Garnet's fellow Jesuit, Robert Southwell, intended to write a tract encouraging people to shelter priests, but never got round to it.[2] There were also attacks in Catholic books on the oath of supremacy, especially at the beginning of the reign, stressing the need to refuse it.[3] We sometimes find exile defended as a means of religious resistance. Thomas Hide described exiles as martyrs and warned of the infectious air of Protestant countries.[4] William Allen encouraged his fellow exiles to write letters to academics in England in the hope of persuading them to leave.[5] The vindication of exile spoken at his trial by John Storey was published in several books. He claimed that everyone had the right to 'renounce his naturalisation and betake himself to the subjection of another prince' if his natural prince persecuted his religion, since 'kings were first set up to defend and protect their people' rather than harm them by religious intolerance.[6] Sir Thomas Copley, something of an expert on the subject since he had been exiled as a Protestant under Mary and then again as a Catholic under Elizabeth, said that 'the law of nations permitteth every man as animal liberum to go freely where he list upon the face of the earth, which is to man ut piscibus aequor', and more prosaically that by ancient statute he could travel abroad as a merchant.[7] But Copley's pronouncements were confined to the relative privacy of letters to the Queen, and generally there was little effort by Catholic authors to make exile into one of the acts of resistance required by the Catholic faith. Indeed, it seems that emigration was actually opposed by the leaders because, one must presume, they feared that it would weaken the community at home which eventually might form the nucleus of a Catholic restoration. In 1582 William Allen rejected the idea of transporting Catholics to Terra Florida, suggesting that it would be a better idea to send puritans instead.[8] At about the same time a plan to set up a Catholic colony in America foundered, despite the patronage of a papist with practical transatlantic experience, George Peckham, and in 1605 Robert Persons discouraged a scheme to colonise 'Norimbega' with Catholics.[9]

RESISTANCE AND COMPROMISE: THE DECREE AD EVITANDA

On the whole, however, the printed books are a poor guide to what, beyond recusancy, was required of the Elizabethan Catholics in terms of religious resistance. For this we must return to the manuals of casuistry used to train and guide the Catholic priests who went as missionaries to England. These casuist booklets give a very clear picture of the sort of life the Catholic community in England was expected to lead. Once again, as in the case of recusancy, we see that the casuists expected resistance, but also emphasised the need for caution and compromise. Just as the

He is looking at theory — what were people doing?

casuists allowed recusants to attend church occasionally to avoid capture and to protect the Catholic community, so they would also allow the other acts of resistance they expected of Catholics to be tempered with circumspection.

There is a real tension in these casuist booklets, and elsewhere in the literature of the English Catholic community, between the desire for total alienation from Protestant society, and the need for some contact and compromise with the enemy. According to St John, strictly interpreted, a Catholic was not to receive a heretic into his house, nor to 'bid him God speed', and the Catholic Church had through the centuries taught that the evil limb of heresy was to be struck off from the sound body of the Church. But things were not so easy now. It was natural to wish to preserve the community of the faithful in England, and it was clear that there could be no such preservation unless a certain amount of guile and stealth were employed, unless the doctrine of complete alienation from heresy was abandoned.

We see this tension in the Rheims New Testament of 1582, in the annotation to the important text just mentioned, II John 10–11 ('If there come any unto you, and bring not this doctrine, receive him not into your house, neither bid him God speed. For he that biddeth him God speed is partaker of his evil deed.') The apostles of recusancy, Young and Martin, had interpreted this literally to mean that a Catholic should avoid all contact with heretics, not even wishing them 'Good morning'. Part of the gloss in the Testament puts the same interpretation on the text:

If then, to speak with them or salute them is so earnestly to be avoided according to this Apostle's example and doctrine: what a sin is it to flatter them, to serve them, to marry with them, and so forth?

Indeed, even 'in worldly conversation and secular acts' we must avoid too much contact with heretics, because their errors are 'contagious', especially to the simple. All religious association with them is forbidden: praying with them, reading their books, hearing their sermons, being present at their services, and partaking of their sacraments. But the annotation then admitted that certain contact with heretics was permissible:

In such times and places where the community or most part be infected [with heresy], necessity often forceth the faithful to converse with such in worldly affairs, to salute them, to eat and speak with them, and the Church by decree of council, for the more quietness of timorous consciences, provideth that they incur not excommunication or other censures for communicating in worldly affairs with any in this kind, except they be by name excommunicated or declared to be heretics: yet even in worldly conversation and secular acts of our life, we must avoid them as much as we may.[10]

But this is not what happened!

The decree of council referred to was the decree of Martin V, *Ad evitanda*, which was felt by Elizabethan Catholics to have an important bearing on the question of what contact was lawful with heretics. It had been used by Bell to justify conformity; it was cited in 1578 as a justification for Catholics who had not rebelled against the Queen; and it was discussed at length in the 'Resolutiones quorundam casuum' of Allen and Persons, in the case which dealt with the question of whether a priest should allow those who still attended heretic services to come to mass.[11] Following other writers, the casuists describe it as a canon of the Council of Constance, although it was not. It was in fact part of the Concordat made in 1418 between the Pope and the German nation, and it found its way into a canon made at Basel and into another made at the Fifth Lateran Council, as part of the agreement between Leo X and Francis I of France.[12] As we have seen, it allowed Catholics to communicate with excommunicates in certain circumstances, but the 'Resolutiones' reported that there had been some controversy over the scope of the decree.[13]

The controversy concerned the sort of people who were excepted from its provisions: that is, with which sort of excommunicates it was not lawful to communicate. All agreed that those who had been excommunicated by name were excepted, but St Antoninus of Florence said that only those who were known to have murdered a clergyman were also excluded.[14] On the other hand, 'Panormitanus', the famous glossator of the fifteenth century, along with his contemporary Nicolaus de Auximo and other writers, said that all who committed a sin to which excommunication 'latae sententiae' was annexed (that is, which automatically rendered the sinner excommunicate by the nature of the crime and without any denunciation of the sentence) were also to be avoided.[15] This was the difficulty, as the English casuists explained:

For if we follow the account given Antoninus we are not bound to avoid heretics, whether they are reconciled to the Church or not, since they are not individually declared excommunicate. But if we follow the account of Panormitanus we are bound to avoid any people who were at any time public heretics and who consequently are public excommunicates.[16]

The Spanish canonist Diego de Covarruvias y Leyva had sought to solve the problem by impugning Antoninus's account of the decree, saying that it did not date from as early as the Council of Constance.[17] This was dismissed by the authors of the 'Resolutiones' who decided to accept Antoninus's laxer interpretation. Thus, the Elizabethan casuists used *Ad evitanda* to justify the sort of everyday contact with heretics without which the life of Catholics in England would have been intolerable, but which the strict interpretation of St John seemed to forbid.

BAPTISM, MARRIAGE, THE HOUSEHOLD
AND THE FAMILY

It is interesting to see how the tension between the need for separation from heretics and the possibility of accommodation with them, justified by the decree *Ad evitanda*, was expressed in the casuist booklets. Many aspects of Catholic life in England were discussed in these manuals, and advice given on how the laity should express their religious resistance in baptism, marriage, family life, fasting and so on.

Baptism and marriage were fields in which religious resistance was required of Catholics. It was not lawful, the casuists decided, for a man to allow his children to be baptised by a Protestant minister, even if they were christened by a Catholic priest as well, nor could he deliberately have a layman baptise the children instead. Catholics should not act as godparents at Protestant baptisms, nor should they themselves use heretics as godparents. But there was a certain degree of compromise here, for the casuists accepted that some forms of heretic baptism were lawful, and that such a baptism was always valid.[18] It was clearly dangerous for Catholics to marry freely with Protestants, and this was forbidden by the casuists. Parents should stop their children marrying heretics: indeed, 'it is better to marry someone of an inferior

social class than to marry a heretic'. On the other hand, practice
and commonsense showed that marriage to a schismatic (rather
than a heretic) was not necessarily sinful, and marriage to mild
and simple heretics was excusable, since it might result in conversion. It was wrong to marry in Protestant churches, but there
was no reason why a licence from a Protestant bishop allowing a
wedding without full solemnity should not be used by Catholics as
legal proof of their marriage, even if the licence was not acted
upon. Moreover, if a Protestant wedding had for some reason
been performed, it was to be considered valid and could be blessed
later by a Catholic priest.[19]

The casuists thought that the whole household should be
Catholic. Only Catholic servants were to be employed, and they
ought to be encouraged to recusancy. Similarly, parents should
'labour most diligently' to make their children 'think badly of
heretics and avoid their company'. But if this ideal situation
could not be achieved, then the head of the household would have
to permit his servants and even his older children to go to Protestant churches when it might be dangerous for him to stop them.
In the cases resolved by Allen and Persons a politique text from
Aquinas was quoted at this point, where the Angelic Doctor said
that the secular magistrate could allow sins to be committed if it
was dangerous to stop them. In the same way, a father should
disinherit his heretic children, but only with circumspection, for
'if the heretics ever discovered that Catholics disinherited their
children for religious reasons, it would cause a tragic outbreak of
persecution against Catholics'.[20]

The whole household should fast together, although difficult
servants might be allowed to break the fast. Heretic visitors should
be given the same food as everyone else on the fast day: 'it does
not seem...to be ill-mannered for a guest in a Catholic house to
be expected to eat the same food as the rest'. But, in the spirit of
compromise, one casuist document said that a Catholic could give
powerful visitors, from whom he might have something to fear,
prohibited foods. There was some difference of opinion on this
matter: in the discussion at Rheims, Catholic inn-keepers were
allowed to serve prohibited foods on fast days and the head of a
household was permitted to serve such food out of mere hospitality; on the other hand, Richard Hall expressly opposed this. It

was generally agreed, however, that in the interest of preserving the community in England, a Catholic could break the fast – for example, to avoid capture. A Catholic traveller could also join in a heretic grace at table to avoid detection, and could remain silent even if his fellow eaters started to blaspheme and to rail against the Church.[21] In the same spirit, the casuists taught that a Catholic could entertain heretic bishops, preachers or judges, when they came into his area to preach against the faith, or to persecute Catholics, if he could mollify them in some way by doing so. But generally it was agreed that a Catholic should avoid too much familiarity with powerful heretics, even in the interests of pacifying their persecuting zeal: 'when a Christian wants to treat Jews or Turks with familiarity and it is not absolutely necessary that he should do so, it is considered wrong, but it is much worse with Protestants since they are more grievous enemies of Christ and much more to be hated'. A very strong statement of the need for Catholic alienation from Elizabethan society, and at odds with the spirit of the decree *Ad evitanda* as interpreted by the same casuists.[22]

TITHES AND PUBLIC OFFICES

These two countervailing considerations – desire for separation and need for compromise – were brought to bear by the casuists on the question of the relationship of Catholics to the new Church of England. Plainly Catholics could not pay to provide prayer books and communion tables for the churches, but it was lawful to pay tithes to avoid persecution, since this was a matter of human law. On the other hand, it was 'most lawful and most holy' to defraud the parson of his tithe and to give the money to poor Catholics ('a most holy act and worthy of all praise') or even to keep it oneself.[23] It was also lawful, the casuists decided, to repair the fabric of churches, since they were Catholic buildings and would in a short time, it was hoped, be restored to their rightful owners. There was no objection to Catholics buying the produce of church land or even renting it. Lay patronage posed a problem: obviously, a Catholic should not present a heretic to a benefice, but it was not clear what he should do otherwise when the living fell vacant. It was agreed, however, that if a heretic minister was presented, the Catholic patron could defraud him of his income – 'the more he takes from the minister the better he does, since the minister is not a pastor but a ravaging wolf and therefore no maintenance is owed him'.[24] Finally, the English moral theologians who drew up these cases of conscience forbade Catholics to act as magistrates, as notary to a bishop, as mayor of a town, as bailiff, constable or justice of the peace. Such offices would involve the unjust persecution of Catholics and were therefore unlawful. But in the spirit of accommodation and pragmatism it was decided that Catholics could sign legal documents which carried the royal title, 'Supreme Governor of the Church', at their head. It was wrong for Catholics to show any agreement with this style, but they might lawfully pretend to do so.[25]

The casuists on whom the seminary priests relied, therefore, tried to regulate the lives of the Catholic laity in England quite minutely. Not just recusancy, but other acts of self-denial and religious resistance were required of Catholics. Baptism, marriage, the life of the household, fasting, and relations with the Church of England, the government and with heretics in general were all expected to be affected by a man's Catholicism. But while separation from heresy and resistance to the heretic laws of Elizabeth was expected, the casuists were careful to allow Catholics sufficient laxity and latitude for them to escape persecution, and to continue as far as they possibly could to lead normal lives.

10

Casuistry and the resistance of the clergy

AVOIDING CAPTURE

The casuist documents cast a new light not only on the life of the Catholic laity in England, but also on the position of the priests themselves. Like the laity, the clergy had to adapt itself to a completely new situation. The casuists recognised this and encouraged the seminarists to improvise. Thus, the missionaries were taught that mass might be said without consecrated vestments, and sacraments could be administered without the full vestiarian complement. Tin chalices and old missals could be used, if necessary. A priest could celebrate mass without having confessed, without having recited the morning hours, and without the help of an assistant. Priests might even leave their breviaries behind on the continent to avoid detection when they landed in England.[1] In these and other ways, the seminarists were trained to expect to have to perform their vocational functions in England without the usual equipment of a Catholic priest.

Just as the casuists allowed the laity to avoid the more fatal consequences of their Catholicism, so they permitted the clergy to practise certain subterfuges to avoid discovery and capture. The seminarists were taught that disguise, trickery and (what we would call) lying were permissible in the interests of self-preservation. This was justified by an extension of the principles of religious resistance. By opposing Elizabeth's religious policy, Catholics were obeying God in preference to men, disobeying bad human laws in order to obey good divine laws. It was also lawful, therefore, to disobey good human laws (for example, those which forbade lying and deceit) in order to break the bad human laws which prevented obedience to the commands of God.

In the first place, priests were allowed to disguise themselves in

England. They could grow their hair and beards, and could wear laymen's clothes. The tonsure and clerical dress were matters of human law and hence could be altered in cases of necessity. Several Catholic authors defended the disguises assumed by the seminary priests in reply to the criticisms of Protestant writers. Allen used the example of David's feigned madness, of Nicodemus's secret support for Christ, of Christ's own escape from the Jews, and of the use by the Church Fathers of the catacombs. Southwell added other biblical precedents and said that 'the salvation of souls' was 'much more weighty' than 'the external decency of our apparel'. Decency was 'necessary in time and place, yet is it not so essential a point, as for the care thereof to neglect the charge of God's flock and safety of our own lives'. Persons and Campion, however, were instructed before going on the mission to wear 'modest and sober' clothes and to 'give no appearance of levity and vanity'.[2]

A priest could also change his name to avoid detection. This could be done quite simply since it was common practice when entering religion. For a priest to change his name or appearance was not tantamount to lying, but should rather be described as 'dissimulation', for which there were good precedents: Christ had pretended to his disciples that he would go further than the village of Emmaus; St Paul reported that James and certain Jews had dissembled with Barnabas (although he showed little approval of it); ambushes were allowed in a just war, as Joshua's stratagem at Ai showed; and Pope Adrian VI, in his Commentary on Peter Lombard's 'Sentences', allowed such pretence.[3] The priest could go further: if asked whether he was a Catholic, what his name was, where he came from or who were his friends and family, he could (if no other Catholic, who might be scandalised, were present) reply in a misleading way. The casuists go on to describe how he may do this with a safe conscience. He could, for example, when asked about his name, give the name he assumed on entering religion, which would deceive the questioner, but would be a perfectly honest answer. It was admitted that this amounted to equivocation, but 'it is most difficult to take equivocation out of human intercourse, since we are often asked many things to which it is not expedient to reply and to which it is best to avoid making a reply by using equivocation'.[4] Moreover, in this case the priest did not, strictly speaking, deceive the questioner, but the questioner deceived himself through his own stupidity in misunderstanding the reply. Similarly, if a priest were asked about his parents or whether he came from a certain town, he could deny that the town and his parents were 'his', if they were Protestant, meaning he did not have to recognise them as his, since they were now heretic. This would be 'pious equivocation'. If a priest had lived in two regions and were asked if he came from one of them, he could reply by saying, 'I am from elsewhere – from such a place', naming the other region in which he had lived, just as St Paul said he was a Roman citizen.

What should a priest do if he was asked a question to which it was difficult to make an evasive reply of that sort? Could he directly deceive his questioner? In this case, the 'Resolutio quorundam casuum' decided it would depend on whether the questioner had legitimate authority. The man making the enquiry would be saying, in effect, 'according to the power I have and the jurisdiction I have in this case, I ask you to confess to me as to your superior whether you are Peter'.[5] If he had no legitimate jurisdiction, the Catholic could reply, 'I deny that I am Peter,' adding mentally, '...who is bound to reply to you.'[6] This was a technique of equivocation known as 'mental reservation'. The whole problem, therefore, was whether the ministers of the Queen had the authority to question priests. It seemed to the casuists that they did not:

Firstly, because a heretic queen is not a legitimate queen... Secondly, because in this matter at least she does not conduct herself like a queen but exercises tyranny by persecuting religion. Thirdly, because a clergyman is not bound to answer to a secular judge, but only to an ecclesiastical one. Fourthly, because the judge proceeds in his judgement from suspicion and often from insufficient conjectures which cannot be proved, and often conjectures which he has as a private person and not by the authority which he has as a judge.

But, it was decided, even if the questioner did have the authority to demand truthful answers, a false reply to him would be a venial sin only since it was committed by the priest in the line of duty.[7]

The other important Elizabethan casuist manual, however, adopted a stricter attitude to the question. It was possible, it maintained, to equivocate when answering questions asked by the collectors of tolls at ports, who were interested in money rather than religion, and in replying to the questions of travellers and companions at table with whom the priest found himself, because they were merely curious. But when a priest was questioned by one of the Queen's officials or by anyone whose motive was hatred of religion, he should confess his faith openly.[8] The 'Resolutio quorundam casuum' was less strict: no one was obliged to confess the faith, if it meant endangering his life, but was simply bound not to deny the faith (according to the text Matthew 10. 32–3), and equivocation – deluding the questioner – did not amount to denial of the faith. A priest sent to England should consider whether he was sufficiently brave to withstand torture before he put his life in danger. It might be that the Holy Ghost would move the priest to embrace martyrdom, but on the other hand it might guide him to avoid danger.[9] The lives of saints gave many examples of men who had through the inspiration of the Holy Ghost thrown themselves into mortal danger when there was no necessity to do so.[10] But, the 'Resolutiones' continued, it was notoriously difficult for men to know whether it really was the Holy Ghost which moved them to embrace martyrdom – the Apostle commanded us to test every spirit, to see whether it came from God.[11] On the whole this document seemed to favour the more inglorious path.

Once the Catholic had been captured, the casuists continued to allow him to escape with a clear conscience. He might bribe his guards, his escorts, or the magistrates in charge of them, to let him go free. This was not to encourage the guards to do wrong, because they were under no obligation to carry out the Queen's commands against Catholics, even if they had sworn an oath to do so, since an oath to commit an injustice was not binding, like the oath which Herod made to kill John the Baptist. Even if bribery was considered sinful, a Catholic by bribing his guards was simply substituting a lesser injustice for a greater – bribery for wrongful imprisonment. Technically, moreover, to bribe a persecutor was to 'buy off ill-treatment' (*redimere vexationem*) and was lawful.[12] Finally, these casuist documents discussed whether a Catholic was bound to keep his word when he had promised his heretic captors that he would not run away. He could have made such a promise in two ways, the 'Resolutiones' said. First, with the intention of obliging himself to keep the promise; second, without this intention. It was considered quite acceptable to make a deceitful promise, since the unjust persecution which Catholics suffered in England rendered it just. If, however, the priest made the promise in the first sense, then it was mortal sin to break it. It was true that Thomas de Vio, a respected Catholic theologian of the early sixteenth century, had maintained that to break a promise was merely to lie and, therefore, to commit a venial sin, but a stricter and more commonly held view was that it was a matter of commutative justice and, indeed, the foundation of justice itself. Nevertheless, in certain circumstances, it was possible even to break a promise sincerely made, the casuists decided. The Catholic might, however, have promised deceitfully, saying, 'I will never run away,' but adding mentally, '...in your presence,' or '...if I cannot'. If the 'Resolutiones' followed respectable sixteenth-century Catholic theology, it would have said that such a promise did not oblige the Catholic, but we do not have the decision because the document is incomplete and finishes in the middle of this case.[13]

EQUIVOCATION

The technical term to describe what we would call lying, when used for example by a priest to conceal his identity in the face of persecution, was as we have seen 'equivocation'. The use of equivocation was approved in many works by Catholic moral theologians in the sixteenth century, and it is not surprising to find our casuists recommending it. It was a subject which prompted a number of English Catholics (especially Jesuits) to speak or write in its defence. At his trial in 1595, Robert Southwell justified himself for telling a woman that 'if, upon her oath, she were asked whether she had seen a priest or no, she might lawfully say "no", although she had seen him that same day – keeping in her mind the meaning: that she did not see him with intent to betray him'.[14] John Gerard was examined on Southwell's doctrine while in custody a few years later,[15] and in 1598 the Jesuit superior in England, Henry Garnet, defended Southwell's case in a work entitled 'A treatise of equivocation' (or 'A treatise against lying and fraudulent dissimulation'), but decided not to publish it.[16]

Early in the next century Robert Persons devoted half of his *Treatise tending to mitigation* (1607) to the subject, and to defending Garnet's work from criticism.

Garnet and Persons found biblical justification for equivocation. Their best text was the saying of Christ that he did not know the date of the end of the world. Garnet explained that Christ must have reserved some extra proposition in his mind which would make the whole sentence more in accordance with Catholic theology. Christopher Bagshaw, a Catholic opponent of equivocation, however, suggested that the text was corrupt – an 'Arian foist'.[17] Equivocation had been endorsed, Persons and Garnet said, by Catholic theologians from Augustine to Aquinas, although they admitted that some were happier with it than others.[18] Indeed, Appellant priests like Bagshaw opposed the doctrine, and the English Benedictine, John Barnes, attacked it at length a few years later, while Persons' Protestant controversial opponent Thomas Morton quoted frequently from Sepulveda, a sixteenth-century Catholic who had written against the practice.[19]

There were various sorts of equivocation, Garnet and Persons said. The simplest was the use of ambiguous words; for example to say 'non est hic', meaning 'that he eateth not here', rather than 'he is not here'. More devious was the evasion of the question combined with the 'mental reservation' of an extra phrase, which would, if spoken, make the statement truthful; for example, 'I know not', combined with the internal proposition, 'for to utter it'. Third, there was what Persons called 'amphibollogie', which was a direct spoken lie with the mental reservation of a part of the sentence which would render the whole true; for example, 'non feci', with 'ut tibi dicam' added in the mind. Some respected Catholic moral theologians, including Dominic Soto, had said that this final method was wrong, and Garnet found it rather difficult not to agree.[20] But he decided that he could accept the 'probable' (but not 'certain') opinion of the theologians who supported 'amphibollogie', even in the face of Soto's influential opposition. He appealed, in so doing, to the other doctrine for which Jesuit moral theologians were to be excoriated in the next century, probabilism, and quoted a recently published work on the theory of conscience by the English non-Jesuit, Richard Hall, to justify himself.[21]

Garnet's main practical message was that a Catholic was not bound to reveal where a priest was hidden, even to royal officials. It would be 'manifestly contrary to Christian duty' to do so:

We say that in this case of religion, we are by God's laws exempted from all civil magistrates ... We say that the law which persecuteth Christ's priests doth persecute Christ Himself ... and we persuade ourselves that we cannot doubt of the unjustice of this law except we would withal doubt of the most certain verity of our faith, and live like atheists and infidels in this world.[22]

In his book justifying equivocation, Persons said that in times of persecution Catholics needed to make open profession of their faith, unless to do so was harmful to other Catholics. Thus, a priest taken prisoner should conceal his identity through the use of equivocation, if by confessing his faith he might also reveal the names of the laymen who had harboured him. On the other hand, if a priest were stopped at a port on entering England, he would hurt no one by confessing himself to be a priest, but since he would lose the opportunity to work in England he would also be justified in concealing his identity. In times of persecution, although confession of faith was called for, flight was also permitted, as St Athanasius showed in his 'Apologia de fuga'.[23] But in conclusion Persons exhorted Catholics not to use equivocation, even when it was otherwise lawful, except when 'some urgent occasion' induced them to do so. He stressed that it was not to be employed in everyday conversation and business. Catholics ought to avoid lying of every sort, and should be careful not to cause scandal or to lose the good opinion of others:

in opinion ... and estimation of others ... the word of a Catholic man ought to weigh more than the oath of an other, and the oath or promise of a Catholic more than any band or obligation of an other, which for the most part I doubt not, but is so already taken in England.[24]

Indeed, somewhat ironically, in 1606 it became important to Persons that Catholics in England should not use equivocation in one important matter, that is in taking the Oath of Allegiance, which, in the aftermath of the Gunpowder Plot, had been devised to test the loyalty of Catholics. The oath, which was partly a piece of anti-Catholic propaganda, contained a clause dealing specifically with equivocation, in which the Catholic had to say 'these things I do plainly and sincerely acknowledge and swear, according to these express words by me spoken, and according to the plain and common sense and understanding of the same words, without any equivocation or...secret reservation whatsoever'. Persons and most of the English Catholic leaders rejected the oath because it declared that the notion of papal political power was heretical, and Persons contributed several works to defending this position.[25] He devoted part of one short tract to demonstrating that a Catholic could not equivocate with the oath. Since the oath contained an express denial of this practice, to use equivocation with respect to it was, he said, 'to equivocate upon equivocation procedendo in infinitum: so these men will like eels slip out, how fast so ever you think to hold them'.[26] Since the judges were in this case competent and observed the form of law required, equivocation was not lawful before them. It was not right to equivocate in matters of faith, Persons said (adopting rather a strict line now): 'it is all one in effect to equivocate and to deny' the faith. Since, therefore, papal power in temporals was a matter of faith, a Catholic could not practise equivocation about the oath.[27] Moreover, in religion, and 'in ordinary traffic, negotiation and conversation', if equivocation caused injury to a neighbour 'in soul, body or goods', it was not justifiable. Hence in a matter like the oath which caused damage to the public good of Catholics, it was not lawful.[28] Nor could a man, as Persons said some English Catholics had suggested, read the oath over and only pretend to swear it, but inwardly refuse actually to do so: 'for in man's court we must follow the outward and apparent proofs, tokens and presumptions to judge of men's actions and not the intents inwardly reserved and only known to God, which no way are known to us but by external means'. Neither was it possible to take the oath and then make a protestation (rather like Bell's protestation about going to church) that one accepted the oath as far as it was inoffensive to God. The oath of allegiance was one area of religious resistance in which no compromise in the form of equivocation was possible.

The most important aspect of Elizabethan Catholicism was the active organisation of a system of religious resistance. It consisted of laity and clergy working together harmoniously to maintain the existence of a core of Englishmen who continued, despite all difficulties, to follow the ritual and life of Catholics. The laity sent their sons overseas to be trained in the seminaries, the clergy abroad organised their training, the young men returned as clergymen and ministered the sacraments secretly to the laity, who in their turn sheltered and fed the priests. It was not only necessary to maintain the administration of the Catholic sacraments, but as far as possible to separate Catholics from heretics, especially in worship and religious fellowship. Moreover, such separation was at least the negative definition of Catholicism. A 'recusant' was a Catholic: by not going to the heretic churches, a man showed himself to be a Catholic. But it was essential that some protection be given to both priests and laity, to enable them to survive and to remain as prosperous as possible in the alien environment of heretic England. The Catholicism of the community had to be adapted to an underground existence in a heretic country. A certain degree of laxity about recusancy, about priests and laymen concealing their identity, about contact with heretics was necessary. But the gains to be made from leniency had to be measured against the loss made in terms of separation and of maintaining Catholic identity. 'Now is the time for confession,' the casuists at Rheims said in one case, for open demonstration that one was a Catholic: the Counter-Reformation spirit also required martyrdoms and persecution.[29] The leaders of the English Catholic movement, strongly influenced by European ideas and, of course, with their own English tradition of bigotry (both Catholic and Protestant), tended to draw the line between separation from heresy and accommodation with it for survival's sake rather close to the former. We see in the cases of conscience of the late 1570s and early 1580s the very painful attempt made by the Catholic casuists to wring the last drop of comfort from the dry heart of the Canon Law, Navarre's *Enchiridion* and the *Provinciales* of Lyndwood. Nevertheless, although the concessions made by the casuists in terms of occasional conformity and equivocation were significant, the social doctrine of Elizabethan Catholicism was generally biased towards separation and alienation. This had two consequences: Catholicism remained the faith of a small minority, but this minority clung to it with extraordinary firmness.

Part Three

POLITICAL RESISTANCE

The development and exposition of ideas of resistance 1584–96

IDEOLOGICAL CHANGE: THE INFLUENCE OF THE LIGUE

The non-resistance of the Elizabethan Catholics had always been under strain. The Rising of the Northern Earls and the bull of Excommunication had provided the stimulus for an ideological change in the early 1570s, when political opposition to the government of Elizabethan England had been openly voiced by Leslie and Sander. A decade later similar pressures forced Catholic authors to abandon political non-resistance again. The change came in 1584 with the publication of two important books, *A true, sincere and modest defence* by William Allen, and *Leicester's Commonwealth* by Robert Persons. They signalled the end of the campaign of non-resistance and loyalism which had accompanied the arrival of the early missionary priests in England. For the next twelve years, works expressing criticisms of the Elizabethan government and encouraging political resistance to it were published by the Catholic leaders.

The reasons for this ideological change are to be found partly in the development of plans by the English Catholic leaders for the armed invasion of England by a European power. Persons and Allen were by 1584 totally committed to this scheme and perhaps had reasonable cause to expect its success. There was no need now for hypocritical or cautious assertions of loyalty to the Queen. On the contrary, although the 'reduction' of England was to be the work mainly of invasion, a propaganda campaign might incite rebellion and disaffection, and hence make the task of the invaders easier. Conversely, as the Spanish inability to take England became clear in the mid-1590s, resistance theory disappeared from the books of the Elizabethan Catholics. Connected

with the threat of invasion, and like it conducive to a campaign
encouraging political resistance, was the greatly increased persecution suffered by Catholic priests and laymen in the England of
the 1580s, Persecution could be met with non-resistance, and – as
we have seen – the writers in the first years of its onslaught had
tried to face their ill-treatment in that way, but more understandable was the aggressive and vengeful reaction of those who argued
that force should be met with force. Since, moreover, the persecution had continued despite Catholic protestations of loyalty,
there now seemed no reason for authors to restrain themselves in
order to protect their co-religionists at home.

The most important factor which helped the exposition of
ideas of resistance by Elizabethan Catholic authors in the period
1584–96 was itself, however, ideological rather than political. It
has been argued that the prevalence of ideas of non-resistance in
Catholic Europe acted as a brake on the monarchomach pro-
clivities of Elizabethan Catholic writers in the 1560s, 1570s and
early 1580s. By 1584 this brake was, to a certain extent, released.
In that year the death of the Duke of Anjou left the Catholics of
France faced with the prospect of a heretic heir to the throne.
Their reaction was to revive the Holy League and to prepare to
oppose Henry of Navarre's succession. Very quickly they adopted
political ideas of resistance similar to those which a short while
before their enemies, the Huguenots, had held. The English
Catholics were quickly influenced by this ideological development in France. For the first time in Elizabeth's reign they found
respectable continental support for political ideas of resistance.
Moreover, since the late 1570s, English Catholics had moved into
France in large numbers. In 1578, the seminary at Douai was
evacuated to Rheims where in later years it had close links with
the Guise family and other leaders of the League; other English
exiles also moved at this time from the Netherlands to other parts
of Northern France.[1] The English and French Catholics influenced and encouraged one another in the development of radical
political ideas. Thus, English authors contributed directly to the
propaganda campaign of the Ligue: William Rainolds wrote one
of the most extreme of their tracts;[2] Persons' *De persecutione
Anglicana* and *Leicester's Commonwealth* were translated into
French;[3] and in Rome, William Allen wrote a booklet in which

he argued against accepting the conversion of Henry of Navarre as genuine.[4] There was a two-way traffic of ideas, therefore, and English political thought had its influence on the French Wars of Religion.[5] What the Ligue gave to the development of theories of resistance among Elizabethan Catholics was practical encouragement rather than ideas. For the first time in a major European country there were Catholics in the same position as the English, who were reacting to the situation not by adopting an ideology of political quietism, but by taking up ideas of resistance just as their Calvinist enemies were abandoning them.

THE BOOKS OF 1584: 'LEICESTER'S COMMONWEALTH' AND 'A TRUE, SINCERE AND MODEST DEFENCE'

The change from non-resistance to resistance began in 1584 with the publication of two books, Robert Persons' *Leicester's Commonwealth*[6] and William Allen's *A true, sincere and modest defence*. Allen and Persons, who were by now the leading English Catholic exiles and writers, had in the years before 1584 expressed their loyalty to the Queen in the most courtly fashion and had pledged to her the passive obedience of their followers. Now in these two books there is criticism of the government and a defence of the right of resistance, and in the coming decade Persons and Allen were to prove the most prolific and outspoken exponents of political opposition to the Queen. In *Leicester's Commonwealth* and *A true, sincere and modest defence* we see them make their first essays in resistance theory, while still clinging to some vestiges of their old ideas. Both books are rather uncertainly poised between the two ideological positions, as if their authors were still not completely prepared to take the plunge into out-and-out public opposition to Elizabeth.

In many ways, the arguments used in *Leicester's Commonwealth* and *A true, sincere and modest defence* are reminiscent of the political ideas which Allen and Persons had expressed in the years immediately before 1584, during the period of non-resistance. Thus, neither book contained any personal criticism of the Queen. Allen stressed the loyalty of Catholics in England: they had continued to obey Elizabeth despite the bull of 1570, and were not secretly absolved of their allegiance to her by seminary priests.[7] The papal deposition was not discussed in the seminaries. Only two Catholic authors – Sander and Bristow – had touched on the bull in print, Allen continued, and they had been prevailed upon not to publish their doctrine a second time.[8] The papal faculty of 1580 which allowed Catholics to disregard the bull had been sought by Campion and Persons – proof of their belief in non-resistance. Allen refused to discuss whether the Queen was 'rightly excommunicate', whether she was a heretic or whether her subjects were 'absolved from their oath and obedience'.[9] He tried as far as possible to dissociate himself and his fellow Catholics from the bull: 'we never procured the Queen's excommunication; we have sought the mitigation thereof; we have done our allegiance notwithstanding'.[10]

In these books Allen and Persons also addressed themselves to one of the key controversial issues of the period of political non-resistance – the defence of Catholics from the charge of treason. This accusation had been levelled again at Catholics by Lord Burghley himself in *The execution of justice in England* (1583), and Allen's *A true, sincere and modest defence* was, ostensibly at least, intended as a refutation of this work. Persons himself offered a mild and subtle critique of Burghley's pamphlet in *Leicester's Commonwealth*.[11] There were two sorts of treason, he said: an actual rebellion or attempt on the life of the prince, and a sort of potential treason when a man's religion threatened the state. Burghley, he suggested, was confusing the two and ignoring the fact that puritans were also guilty of treason in the second sense. Persecution, Persons said, often encouraged those who suffered it and won them the support of others. Burghley's ill-treatment of Catholics might be as beneficial to them as the Marian persecution had been to Protestants. Allen and Persons had appealed to the Queen and her government for toleration in their manifestoes of non-resistance; in *Leicester's Commonwealth* and *A true, sincere and modest defence* they continued to do so.[12] Persons put forward a number of arguments for some 'sweet qualification, or small toleration' into the mouths of the characters through whom he spoke in his book. Religious freedom was practised in Germany, Poland, Bohemia, Hungary, France and Flanders; it would remove 'divisions, factions and parties' among Englishmen, thus ensuring peace. During the first twelve years of

Elizabeth's reign, when Catholics were not persecuted, 'all was peace, all was love, all was joy, all was delight'. It was not good policy to allow one religious faction to become very much more powerful than another. The Prince should hold all factions in equality: 'as in a body molested and troubled with contrary humours, if all cannot be purged, the best physic is, without all doubt, to reduce and hold them at such an equality as destruction may not be feared of the predominant'.

So far, these two books appear to be fairly standard productions of the period of political non-resistance. But muddled in with these loyalist arguments is the early expression of the ideas of resistance and disloyalty which were beginning to seize the minds of the Elizabethan Catholic leaders. While it is true that Elizabeth was not directly criticised in Persons' book, her evil counsellor, the Earl of Leicester, was mercilessly attacked. Leicester was accused of having taken control of the court and policy of England – 'a perfect potentate in the court' – and of directing them for his own selfish ends, while the common good of the country and Elizabeth's own safety and interests went by the board. His character was blackened by the judicious use of smut and slander, with stories of plots and poisonings which added to the readability of the book.[13] But the main thrust of Persons' criticism was only incidentally aimed at Leicester himself. Persons and Allen were not ready yet to attack the Queen herself, so Leicester had to take her place. Leicester was in a way a mere symbol of English policy and of the Protestant establishment; in attacking him, Persons was aiming further, but was not prepared as yet to admit it. It is interesting to see Allen in *A true, sincere and modest defence* also briefly insulting the Earl of Leicester, calling Dudley 'a hateful name to England since Henry the Seventh's time, ever aspiring, but still unfortunate to itself and followers'.[14]

Leicester's Commonwealth was as much a succession tract as an attack on the Queen's favourite, and in this respect also it showed a new spirit of resistance. Just as Leslie's books on the succession had been published in the first period of Catholic resistance, so now interest was shown again in this subject, which it was forbidden by parliament to discuss. As before, the claim to the succession of Mary Stuart was defended. But whereas the main rivals to Mary envisaged by Leslie had been the Greys, now

Persons claimed that the Earl of Huntingdon – descendant of the Duke of Clarence – was the real danger.[15] Persons managed to tie Leicester in with the succession question: the Earl had prevented the Queen's marriage to Anjou (a very good match as far as Persons was concerned), and had thus perpetuated the problem, and now he supported the weak claim of the Hastings family while harbouring other more sinister ambitions.[16] Allen also briefly canvassed the claims of Mary Queen of Scots in his *A true, sincere and modest defence*,[17] but the book's main contribution to the development of ideas of resistance among the Elizabethan Catholics was in those chapters where he discussed the crucial issue of papal political power.[18] As we have seen, Allen refused to be drawn on the specific question of whether Elizabeth deserved papal deposition, but he did discuss the Pope's power in political matters as an abstract question at some length and with considerable vigour. Moreover, he also applied his discussion to the concrete example of the recent papal invasion of Ireland, which was bringing things pretty near to home. Allen's doctrine in these sections of the book was closely followed in two of his later books which are unequivocally cast in the mould of political resistance.[19]

THE DEVELOPING PROPAGANDA CAMPAIGN 1585–96

With *Leicester's Commonwealth* and *A true, sincere and modest defence* we are at the turning point. These two books – both excellent examples, it might be said here, of sixteenth-century political writing – still show elements of the old ideology of loyalism and non-resistance, but also clearly express the new political ideas of resistance as well. Within a few years Allen and Persons were publishing books which displayed no such ambiguity and unashamedly expressed a belief in the right of resistance and a detestation of Elizabeth and her government. Allen contributed two more books to this campaign: a work published in 1587 that defended the mutiny of Sir William Stanley, who had betrayed Deventer, which he held as a soldier of Elizabeth, to Philip II of Spain;[20] and the *Admonition* of 1588, a slightly hysterical commentary on the bull *Regnans in excelsis*, written to accompany the Armada.[21] Persons wrote at least five more books before this period of political resistance was over. The first was a long Latin refutation of a royal proclamation of 1591, full of political criticism of the Elizabethan government, which was also published in an English abridgement by Richard Verstegan, Persons' man in Antwerp.[22] Three short printed pamphlets followed this work: one, in Latin, gave a few documents to illustrate the instability of English politics and the cruelty of the persecution there, and another two in English described the seminaries Persons had founded in Spain, praising Philip II and taking the odd sideswing at the Elizabethan regime.[23] Persons' last work in this period appeared in 1595 and was entitled *A conference about the next succession to the crown of England*. If we set Hooker on one side, it is arguably the best political work written by an Englishman between More's *Utopia* and Hobbes's *Leviathan*. The *Conference* is partly devoted to setting out the absurd pretensions of the Infanta of Spain to the throne of England and partly to an exposition of the right of political resistance. It is most interesting because, although the work of a Catholic, it omits all mention of the usual papalist justification for resistance (that is, in the power of the Pope) and concentrates entirely on the rights of the community to overthrow a wicked ruler.[24]

A number of other authors contributed to the anti-Elizabethan literature of this period. The royal proclamation of 1591 also drew replies in Latin from Joseph Cresswell[25] and Thomas Stapleton,[26] and in English from Richard Verstegan[27] and an anonymous writer whose unpublished manuscript tract is among the papers of a prominent layman, Sir Thomas Tresham.[28] Another anonymous pamphlet lamented the failure of the Invincible Armada,[29] and Nicholas Sander's historical work, *De origine ac progressu schismatis Anglicani*, especially in the expanded edition published by Allen and Persons, must also count as a work of resistance.[30] The propaganda campaign against Elizabethan England ends, almost abruptly, in the mid-1590s. Persons' *Conference* was the last work published to express ideas of resistance, and the following year when he wrote his highly political 'Memorial of the reformation of England' he avoided having it printed.

12

The Catholic critique of Elizabethan England

POLITICAL CRITICISMS

The books printed in the period 1584–96 evince a new spirit – a spirit of resistance and opposition to Elizabeth and her government. Yet the reader of most of these tracts has to look fairly closely and carefully before he discovers the defence of the right of resistance or the prolonged discussion of the great issues of sixteenth-century political theology which practically leap at him from the pages of the Calvinist monarchomachs, Beza, Buchanan, Junius Brutus and (with more subtlety) Hotman. The most common way in which these Catholic books express their resistance is in practical and often detailed criticisms of Elizabethan policy. Perhaps this demonstrates that even now the Catholic authors were less firmly convinced of the rectitude of rebellion than their Calvinist counterparts in France and the Netherlands; or perhaps it shows that they had less confidence in the willingness of their followers in England to respond to a call to arms. Indeed, the tone – if I interpret it correctly – of many of these works of resistance seems to be this: look at the mess England is in – it is the fault of Protestantism, a new Catholic ruler would improve matters immensely. To support this simple argument, the whole of Elizabeth's reign is subjected in many of these books to harsh critical analysis. It is not simply the policies of the 1580s which are attacked, but everything of importance since the Queen's accession, because it was with the advent of a heretic government, Catholic writers maintained, that the rot had begun.

Every aspect of Elizabethan policy came under attack, but we can discern three central issues which particularly concerned our authors. First, they continued to denounce the Elizabethan persecution, as they had done in the period of non-resistance (although

now with less restraint) and to refute the allegation that the
seminary priests were traitors.[1] This led in some of their books to a
general denunciation of English justice, to a broad condemnation
of Elizabethan cruelty, or to an attack on the Puritans, suggesting
that they were a greater danger to the country than the Catholics.
Second, and this was a new departure, Catholic authors attacked
Elizabeth's foreign policy as anti-Catholic and defended the papal
cause in the religious wars of the divided Europe of the time.[2] A
number of other issues could then be raised; high taxes, immi-
gration, ex-soldiers roaming the countryside, for example.
Finally, the most important question in domestic affairs discussed
was that of the succession. *Leicester's Commonwealth* and *A true,
sincere and modest defence* had canvassed the claims of the
Catholic, Mary Stuart. After her death, Catholic books expressed
gloomy doubts about the danger of a disputed succession,[3] and
then in 1595 with the appearance of Persons' *Conference* the
claims of the Infanta were first publicly expressed.

The flavour of the detailed political criticism to be found in
Catholic books in this period is given admirably in an anonymous
tract, entitled 'The copy of an answer unto a Protestant's letter'
(a typical title in itself).[4] This short work was written in refutation
of an anti-papist proclamation of 1591, and it is similar in many
of the points it makes to the other Catholic pamphlets which
reply to that royal edict. The tract made two rather contradictory
points: that English Catholics were falsely accused of treason, and
that the Spanish would and should by right defeat the English.
As in a number of other works of this period, it spent a considerable time rejecting the suggestion that English Catholics were
seditious. It spoke in this connection of the 'invisible treasons'[5] of
Catholics in England, meaning that they were not treason at all,
and told a little story to prove the point. The English ambassador
in Turkey had apparently advised the Sultan to prevent a Jesuit
mission being set up near Constantinople to convert some Musco-
vites there, telling him that Jesuits were dangerous men and would
cause great harm to his empire. The Sultan, it was reported, had
been somewhat offended by this advice, asking the ambassador,
'if he carried so slender an opinion of the Turkish Empire as that
six poor priests were able to overcome and ruin' it. The pamphlet
contrasted the attitude of the Sultan with that of the English

government: 'now what an opinion they carry in England of
their well-fortified estate you may well perceive when they think
that a few poor priests and Jesuits sent in among them as lambs
among the wolves are able to subvert and destroy it'.[6]

The seminary priests were defended in various other ways. The
royal proclamation had accused them of being of low birth, and
'The copy of an answer' rejected this calumny. It denied first that
low birth was a disqualification for a priest: 'many of the most
notable popes, emperors, kings and princes have risen of mean
men'.[7] Men of low birth, moreover, were often promoted to high
places by kings, and their families given hereditary honours. But,
the author added tendentiously, it often happened that evil
princes promoted evil men, who later took advantage of the weakness of female or young rulers. He now returned the charge and
declared that many men in authority in England came of families
whose wealth dated back no further than the dissolution of the
monasteries. He gave as an example the Duke of Northumberland,
whose grandfather was a carpenter but whose son had been
nominated a king; Lord Keeper Bacon, whose father was a shepherd; and Lord Burghley, who had tried to conceal his low origins
by employing dishonest genealogists. The accusation made in the
proclamation that Catholic priests were dissolute and ignorant
and that they used spells to win converts was also rejected.[8] On
the contrary, Martin Marprelate was cited to show that the
Protestant ministers of England were themselves unlearned and
profligate, and William Hacket, a madman who had recently set
himself up as Christ, was given as an example of how Protestants
used enchantments.

Catholic priests and laymen were persecuted for their religion
and not for treason, the author of this tract repeated, and he
described some of the anti-Catholic laws, and the way they were
administered, to prove this. He related how at his trial a Catholic
had been called a 'traitorous papist' by the judge and had replied
that 'he was a papist, but traitor was he none', to which the judge
answered, 'I tell thee, to be a papist and to be a traitor is all
one.'[9] The proclamation itself, by giving instructions that stricter
search be made for Jesuits and seminary priests, provided the
author of this tract with more material. He described these instructions as part of an 'English inquisition' and said that they should

be translated into French for the Ligue to use against Huguenots, and into German to be used by the Saxon Lutherans against Calvinists.[10]

The priests, the tract continued, were not Spanish agents. The King of Spain provided their seminaries with money but the King of France had also given alms to the college at Rheims.[11] Moreover, Philip II had no control over priests educated in Spain, since he was not the head of the church there. The seminarists from Spain came to England with the same intention as those trained at Rheims, to convert 'their dear parents, friends and country' from the 'detestable and confused heresy of Calvin'.[12] To accuse the priests of encouraging their converts to support a Spanish invasion by holding out to them the hope of rich rewards was simply a way of winning popular support for the persecution:

to hang priests and Jesuits upon pretence of killing the Queen is for the present laid aside, and this newer invention is now used to decrease the pity and compassion of the case in the eyes and hearts of those that shall see them cruelly killed.[13]

It would not be in character for the King of Spain to confide in English priests:

is it likely that he will communicate his secret designments to young men and strangers, whose wisdom and secrecy is known to be such that he concealeth these from divers of his own privy council?'[14]

It was equally unlikely that priests could persuade men to be converted by holding out to them the hope of rewards if the Spanish invasion succeeded, since the most obvious result of conversion to Catholicism was persecution and the loss of property.[15] The King of Spain and the Pope would not attempt to invade England relying only on the support of the English Catholics, 'whom they know to be disarmed, impoverished, detained in prison and utterly unable to assist them in such enterprise'.[16]

But despite defending Catholics against the accusation that they were traitors and supporters of Spain, the author of this tract justified the Spanish policy of war with England. The English had, throughout Elizabeth's reign, robbed the King of Spain of his treasure, invaded his dominions, supported rebels against him, and occupied his towns.[17] Elizabeth's foreign policy had forced

Philip II into war with her.[18] England was the champion of
heresy:

To whom is it unknown that England of all places under heaven in
this age is become the most capital enemy of Catholic religion and
the greatest labourer to advance heresy.[19]

On the other hand, the King of Spain was 'the chief maintainer'
of Catholicism, and, as the proclamation itself admitted, was
more powerful than any Christian king had ever been.[20] By
attacking Catholic priests, by killing an anointed Queen and by
negotiating with the Turks, the English had called down on their
heads the just wrath of the Pope and the King of Spain. Even if
Philip II were less powerful, the 'equity' of his cause would win
him the victory.[21] It was true that in the past the English had
performed 'most heroical exploits' in France and other countries,
but this was when they were Catholics, and now, like the Germans,
they had declined 'both in faith and fortitude', as was clear by
the results of the present war.[22] The English had lost little less than
thirty thousand men in the wars, 'almost all without battle, but
altogether without effect'. It was English foreign policy which
was chiefly criticised in this tract, but on the domestic front, high
taxes, and the danger which would result from an undecided
succession were mentioned. The proclamation itself was described
as a propaganda device to wring more money from parliament
and the people.[23] The Queen was not attacked personally: the
edict was issued in her name, but she had not been responsible for
it. Everything, including the authorship of the proclamation was
blamed on Burghley.[24] He was above all held responsible for the
persecution of Catholics and was compared with Nero, Decius,
Diocletian, Maxentius, Genseric and Hunneric.[25]

'The copy of an answer' is fairly typical of a number of Catholic
books of the period. It is clearly outspoken and – in Elizabethan
eyes – seditious, but it does not directly attack the Queen, does
not urge Catholics to rise in rebellion, nor does it really deal in
political theories. It assumes a theoretical right of political opposition, but does not discuss it. Moreover, there is in the pamphlet
the curious survival (to be found in other works written at this
time) of one of the principal themes of the period of political non-
resistance – the defence of English Catholics from the charge of

treason. Even after 1584 some Catholic books continued to attack Elizabeth's counsellors rather than the Queen herself. Cecil, above all, was ridiculed and maligned,[26] but Leicester continued to excite interest,[27] as did Walsingham,[28] Hatton,[29] Bacon,[30] and Raleigh.[31] The attack on evil counsellors did not necessarily exclude criticisms of the Queen; Persons compared her to Diocletian, Maximian, Decius and Domitian, while reserving most of his fire for Lord Burghley.[32] Other authors showed no scruples at all about calling Elizabeth names. To Stapleton she was a 'delirious female', exercising a long and barbarous tyranny.[33] Sander in his *De origine ac progressu schismatis Anglicani* (first published in 1585) said she surpassed Athaliah, Maachah, Jezebel, Herodias, Selene, Constantia and Eudoxia.[34] Sander's book also saw the publication of the rather ungallant suggestion that Elizabeth was fathered on Anne Boleyn not by Henry VIII but by Anne's own brother, and further, that Henry – as if in compensation – had 'defiled' Anne's sister and mother before establishing his connection with the Queen herself.[35]

One underlying theoretical presupposition of these criticisms of the Elizabethan regime was that a heretical government was inevitably unprotected by God's providence, and hence subject to dangerous instability.[36] This idea had been expressed, as we have seen, when Catholic authors attacked Protestantism as teaching rebellion and disorder. Now the argument was expressed more directly, and the examples used to justify it were drawn from the events of Elizabeth's reign. Sander's *De origine ac progressu schismatis Anglicanae* shows well the use of history as anti-Elizabethan propaganda. Sander saw his job as historian mainly in terms of the interpretation of God's providence as it manifested itself, in this case, in recent events in England. Thus, Edward VI, Sander showed, died on 6 July, the day of Thomas More's execution:

and so it came to pass that all might see, who rightly consider the course of this world, that Henry paid in the death of his eldest son the penalty of the death of that great man, but yet did not satisfy the divine justice, because he had not done penance for his sin according to the will of God.[37]

During Edward's reign, moreover, the Thames fell and rose three times in nine hours, because of the harassment suffered by Bishop

Gardiner.[38] Meanwhile, Joliffe, head boy of Winchester, was carried away by the sweating-sickness because of his Calvinist beliefs (Sander, like several other Elizabethan Catholic authors, was a Wykehamist).[39] The accession of Mary Tudor was a 'manifest miracle wrought before all the world in favour of the Catholic faith'.[40] But England had not yet paid for her sins:

the sins and sacrilege of Henry VIII and the wickedness of the people were such that they could not be thus lightly expiated, and therefore this calm did not last.[41]

Nevertheless the reign of Mary, in the midst of the schism presided over by her brother and sister, was a 'faithful sign, to the great consolation of the Catholics, that they might not be discouraged and crushed under the burden of heresy'.[42]

The providential theory was a wonderful piece of self-justificatory 'heads-I-win, tails-you-lose' philosophy. Protestant failure showed that God refused to protect heretics, or was actually punishing them for their religious rebellion. But Catholic defeat should be interpreted as a mysterious sign of God's special concern for Catholics, of his desire to try their patience, or as part of some deeper plan beyond human understanding, but certainly not as an indication that he favoured Protestantism. This was the argument of a short book published in 1589, which discussed the defeat of the Spanish Armada.[43] Its author agreed that God had punished Catholics by causing the expedition to fail, but told Protestants that 'the punishment of our faults excuseth not your far greater offence'. He accepted entirely the Elizabethan interpretation of the defeat – that it had been caused largely by the wind – but argued that this should not hearten Protestants, since it showed that Spanish military power was invincible to all but supernatural power. Everything was subject to God's providence: kingdoms rose and fell not according to Platonic cycles, but because of God's will. The Catholic Church showed the sustaining power of providence well, for alone among European states it had remained stable for sixteen hundred years. But even among the nations of Christendom themselves, it was the Catholic countries which survived best and longest. The Armada might have failed once, but it would succeed at its second or third attempts. The author of this work was pleased to end with the recent news – confirming his thesis – that the English expedition to Portugal had ended in disaster.

THE CRUSADE

In their criticisms of Elizabethan government, much weight was given by Catholic authors to the discussion of foreign policy. The defence of Spain and justification of her hostility to England were commonly expressed, and reflected the great hopes Allen and Persons had pinned on Philip II as their saviour and patron. Much of the discussion of European affairs in these books is influenced by the belief that the wars of Spain against England, against the Dutch, and in France, amounted to a crusade. The crusading metaphor is apt. William Rainolds devoted a book of immense size, printed in 1597, to showing the similarities between Calvinism and Mohammedanism,[44] and one aspect of the foreign policy of Queen Elizabeth which was particularly denounced by the Catholics was the diplomatic contact she made during the 1580s with the Turkish Sultan, 'the public enemy of all Christian profession',[45] in an attempt to secure his support against Spain.[46] It was to the leadership of Spain in this crusade that the English Catholics looked. Philip II was told by the English seminarists that he was the 'father of the Catholic world', Abdias to Elizabeth's Jezebel, and that like Moses he would lead the Elizabethan Catholics to their promised land:

at length you will restore this, the scattered seed of Jacob, these, the elect sons of Israel (whom you see before you), these priests, these Levites, these English Catholics: in your lifetime you will achieve this difficult but great and glorious task to which we believe you have been called and preordained by divine providence.[47]

In a book published in 1592, Persons went into raptures when describing Philip II's visit to the English seminary at Valladolid. The sight of the King and his son and daughter made Persons 'imagine that I saw present our noble British Emperor Constantine the Great, with his renowned two Catholic children, Constans and Constantia'. The Infanta caught his eye especially: 'nay the Infanta seemed to resemble not only the piety of Constantia, but even the very zeal, wisdom, fortitude and other virtues of our country woman St Helena herself'.[48] It might be noted, however, that if Philip II was flattered, the English Catholics described themselves in the heroic language of biblical patriotism. Thus, Persons, considering the setting up of the English seminaries on the Continent, quoted the psalmist, 'non fecit taliter omni nationi, no nation in Christendom infected with heresy hath received like favours...as we have done and do daily'. Spanish generosity alone would not have enabled the English to set up their seminaries, God's special providence was also needed. The belief that England was the 'Elect Nation' was not the prerogative of Elizabethan Protestants.[49]

The justification for wars of religion – for a crusade led by Spain against Protestant England, or a rebellion of Catholics against Elizabeth – could be found purely in that religious division between Catholics and Protestants. There was no need for a theory of resistance: Catholics could make war on heretics without any political philosophy to justify it. As Walzer has noted for the Calvinists of this period, the idea of the crusade replaced the idea of the just war – by definition, the crusade was a just war.[50] William Allen was quite explicit: 'there is no war in the world so just or honourable, be it civil or foreign, as that which is waged for religion'. It was the duty of Catholics to punish those who revolted from the Church, by warfare if necessary: 'no crime in the world deserveth more sharp and zealous pursuit of extreme revenge (whether it be in superiors or subjects) than revolting from the faith to strange religion'.[51] The Old Testament provided examples of the form this punishment had taken: those who revolted from God were to be smitten with the edge of the sword, and their city destroyed by fire, as Phinehas had killed those who had committed whoredom with the daughters of Moab,[52] as Abijah had fought and killed the idolatrous Jeroboam, and as Joram had defeated the rebellious Edomites.[53]

In a crusade or religious war, the Christian knight who suffered death was a martyr, William Allen wrote, while those who died on the side of the heretic went straight to hell.[54] No Catholic should serve as a soldier in the army of a heretic: he would hear the blasphemies uttered by the heretic soldiers and would lack the Catholic sacraments in camp, especially the last rites if he fell in battle. Soldiers ought to interpret their commands in the light of the laws of God and refuse to obey irreligious orders; in doubtful cases, they should consult the Pope.[55]

This hostility to heresy and desire to fight against it was in some ways merely an extension of the insistence on the separation of Catholics from heretics and the denunciation of the persecution in England which formed such a large part of the literature of Elizabethan Catholicism. There was no difference in terms of political theory between a call to arms against heresy and exhortations to avoid the religious services of heretics. Indeed, some of the arguments used to encourage religious resistance were adapted to the idea of the crusade. The text II John v. 10, used to justify religious and social separation from heretics, was also used to support the rebellion of Catholics against a Protestant ruler.[56] Heresy itself was sufficient to break the bonds between prince and subject.[57] The Catholic people and their heretic king could be divorced in the same way as the marriage between a Catholic and a heretic was dissolved.[58] It was not a great distance between the aggressive opposition to heresy of a non-resistant writer like Southwell and the idea of the crusade. Southwell wrote: 'Christianity is a warfare, and Christians spiritual soldiers; their conflicts continual, though their enemies be diverse.'[59] He was speaking metaphorically, but the difference between his spiritual struggles and Allen's wars of religion was perhaps not very great.

The strength of Catholic feeling against heretics in the late 1580s is admirably expressed in an oration delivered in 1589 by Thomas Stapleton at Douai University, which bore as its title the very loaded question, 'are the politiques of these times to be counted as Christians?'[60] Politiques came in for Stapleton's criticism because they opposed the idea of a Catholic crusade against Protestants and because they wanted to make concessions to them in order to gain domestic peace. The politiques were those who opposed the 'holy war' of 'our most powerful and most pious Philip II'; in England, more specifically, they were the 'schismatics', the conforming Catholics, who offended against the biblical injunction to obey God rather than men.[61] He found politique ideas best expressed in Bodin's *Six books of the Republic* and summarised his doctrine thus:

The power of the heretics is so great that we cannot force them into order and so we should appease rather than attack them and think of security instead of revenge, considering how to beware of them rather than what we should inflict on them, since we are not strong enough to do so.

Stapleton poured scorn on this 'specious and meretricious' argument; it was 'soft and feminine and not worthy of a man, least of all of a Christian'. The policy of the politiques, freedom of religion and peace with heretics, would lead to the eventual victory of heresy. On the contrary, Stapleton said, Protestantism must be defeated at all costs. 'With David we say, "You heretics come to us with sword, spear and shield, in pride and arrogance, and we Catholics will come against you in the name of the Lord of hosts".'[62]

13

Resistance theory

THE HUMAN RIGHT OF KINGS

Several of the Catholic books published in the period 1584–96 give a more sophisticated explanation for their opposition to Elizabeth than the idea of the crusade afforded. They formulated a theory of resistance – a justification for rebellion and for support of the Queen's enemy, based on a consideration of the fundamental nature of political society and of political authority. This Elizabethan Catholic theory of resistance had two principal aspects, based first on a theory of the rights of the people or political community, and second on the rights of the Pope.

Catholic authors did not rely solely on the power of the Pope to depose kings when they defended the right of resistance. They believed also that the people had power themselves to oppose their king. There were two parts to this idea of popular power: first, a theory of the origin and nature of royal power; second, a belief that the king's coronation oath represented a contract between him and his people. The theory of the origin of royal power used by Catholic advocates of resistance was that the authority of kings derived not from God, but from the consent of their people. There was no divine right of kings, according to this theory. All power came originally from God, it was admitted, but only the priestly office was directly and immediately instituted by him. Royal power came mediately and indirectly from God, by way of the 'commonwealth' or people the king ruled.[1] The king gained his authority from the 'will, decision, designation and free institution of the people'.[2] If kings ruled by divine right (or even derived their authority from nature or the law of nations), Robert Persons said, every nation would be ruled by a king, and history would show no constitutional variety. But since this was not the

case, kingship could not be natural or divine.³ Only sociability
and government itself were natural – one force driving men to live
together, the other enabling them to do so in reasonable comfort.⁴
The choice of which sort of government to adopt – whether by
one, few or many – still lay with the commonwealth and did not
depend on the law of nature or of God.

The doctrine of the human right of kings was an important
starting-point for a theory of resistance. If royal power derived
from the people, the people could withdraw their original consent
from a king who ruled badly. Yet this theory was up to a point
respectable Catholic theology and is to be found expressed in non-
controversial scholastic works in the sixteenth century.⁵ In some
ways the Protestant tradition was more inclined to support
theories of divine right kingship. The Anglican, Jewel, professed
great indignation at the brief denial of the divine origin of royal
power expressed by Harding.⁶ An interesting annotation in the
Rheims New Testament, which firmly taught non-resistance,
shows the strength and respectability of the doctrine of the human
right of kings. The text concerned was I Peter 2. 13, usually a
non-resistant place, which the Rheims translators rendered, 'Be
subject therefore to every human creature for God, whether it be
to king, as excelling, or to rulers as sent by Him to the revenge of
malefactors.' In the margin the translation of this passage made
by Protestants was attacked; they had rendered the Greek κτίσις
(in the Vulgate, 'creatura') as 'ordinance', and not 'creature'.
This was a false translation, the Rheims Testament maintained.
The word 'creature' expressed St Peter's meaning; he wished to
describe rulers as the creatures of their subjects, to give his
approval to the theory of the human (not divine) right of kings,
the theory that kings had received their power from their subjects:

So he calleth the temporal magistrate elected by the people, or holding their sovereignty by birth and carnal propagation, ordained for
the worldly wealth, peace and prosperity of the subjects.

St Peter wished to point out the difference between this sort of
authority and the divinely-appointed authority of priests. This
was not, however, to deny St Paul's doctrine that all power was
of God:

And although all power be of God and kings rule by Him, yet that is
no otherwise but by His ordinary concurrence and providence

whereby He procureth the earthly commodity or wealth of men, by maintaining of due superiority and subjection one towards another, and by giving power to the people and commonwealth to choose to themselves some kind or form of regiment under which they be content to live for their preservation in peace and tranquillity.[7]

It is interesting to note that in his *Conference* Persons interpreted the text in exactly the same way, but now as the starting-point for his exposition of the right of resistance.[8] He even explained Romans 13 similarly: when St Paul said that all power was of God, he meant merely that all power in its 'first institution' was of God, or when it was 'lawfully laid upon any person' by the commonwealth.[9]

THE CORONATION OATH

It is possible to see the doctrine that kings rule not by divine but by human right as involving a belief in a social contract.[10] The other important plank of Catholic resistance theory, which we will now discuss, is clearly a contract of government: it is the oath made by kings at their coronations. The importance of the coronation as a second contract between the king and the Church (the first being his baptism) had been stressed by Sander and mentioned by Harding. Allen and Persons in their works of resistance laid more emphasis than Sander on the actual oath to rule well and to protect the Catholic faith which kings made at their coronation than on the quasi-sacramental nature of the unction. Allen wrote:

And ever sith St Gregory's time, or thereabout, all kings in Christendom, especially those of Spain, France, Poland, and England, take an oath upon the holy Evangelists at their coronation to keep and defend the Catholic faith; and ours of England expressly to maintain also the privileges and liberties of the Church and clergy given by King Edward the Confessor and other faithful kings their ancestors.[11]

Allen pointed out that Elizabeth herself had taken such an oath and had been anointed by a Catholic bishop.[12] William Rainolds gave as a reason for excluding Henry of Navarre from the French throne the fact that as a heretic he could not take the important constitutional step of swearing the oath at his coronation to protect the Catholic Church.[13] The coronation oath was seen by these writers as a confirmation of the power of the people over their king, and of the fact that the authority of the king was bestowed on him by the people. If the oath was broken the people withdrew from the king the power they had given him:

> which oath and promise being not observed, they [kings] break with God and their people; and their people may and, by order of Christ's supreme minister, their chief pastor in earth, must needs break with them.[14]

Robert Persons used the coronation oath as evidence of popular power over kings in his *Conference*, but it is interesting to see how different his treatment of the matter there is from that found in other Elizabethan Catholic books. Persons laid more of the stress on the duty which the oath placed on the king to rule well; since he wished to conceal his religious bias, he did not emphasise the obligation on kings to protect Catholicism. By the oath, Persons said, rulers promised 'that they would rule and govern justly, according to law, conscience, equity and religion', but he did not specify which religion he meant.[15] In the *Conference* the coronation becomes a political contract. Persons gave a whole chapter of examples of coronation oaths used in the Byzantine Empire, the Roman Empire, Poland, Spain, France and England.[16] He stressed the importance of the royal oath to his theory of resistance; the breaking of the oath was 'the ground whereon dependeth the righteous and lawful deposition and chastisement of wicked princes'.[17] The doctrine was important also to his more specific attack on the idea of indefeasible hereditary right. It was not royal blood which gave a king his authority, but the 'agreement, bargain and contract'[18] made at his coronation: 'the commonwealth oweth no allegiance or subjection unto the heir apparent in rigour of justice until he be crowned or admitted'.[19]

The two main secular aspects of the Elizabethan Catholic theory of resistance were, therefore, the belief that royal power was derived from the people, and that kings made certain promises at their coronations. Indeed, the first part of Persons' *Conference* puts forward nothing much more in the way of theoretical argument than this. These two ideas were sufficient to justify the deposition of bad kings by their people and the exclusion of a legitimate heir who seemed likely not to rule properly.

The rest of the first part of the *Conference* was largely taken up with historical examples to show how in the past kings all over Europe had been deposed,[20] and legitimate heirs had been excluded from the succession.[21] Persons used a great deal of historical argument throughout the first part of the book, while the genealogical discussion in the second part also needed the confirmation of historians. This is shown by the tally of the marginal references he makes. Of the 101 authorities referred to in the whole work, that most often cited was the Old Testament, which was largely used for evidence about the history of the Jews. Next came Polydore Vergil; third, John Stow; fourth and fifth, the French historians, Gerard du Haillan and Francis Bellforest; sixth and seventh, the Spanish chroniclers, Estevan de Garibay and Ambrose Morales; and next came Raphael Hollingshed, Aristotle and the New Testament (cited the same number of times each.) Since, according to the theological basis for the Catholic theory of resistance, relations between a king and his people were governed by human law (and not by any higher law), all historical examples of the deposition of kings and exclusion of heirs were precedents which showed the possibility and legitimacy of such action. But Persons was not content to rest there: history was more than mere precedent, it showed the working of providence. Persons claimed that the deposition of kings in the past had received the providential approval of God, because the deposed king had often been followed by a good ruler. He gave examples of this from the history of ancient Israel, ancient Rome, France, Spain, Portugal, Greece and finally England. After John, who had been opposed by his people, came the good kings, Henry III and Edward I; after the deposition of Edward II, Edward III ruled successfully; after the deposition of Richard II, good king Henry IV ruled; after Henry VI, Edward IV; and after Richard III, Henry VII. The kings who succeeded those who had been deposed or opposed by their subjects were all 'most rare and valiant princes'.[22] Resistance to a king and his deposition 'hath fallen out ever, or for the most part, commodious to the weal public', because 'God approved and prospered the same, by the good success and successors that ensued thereof.'[23] The same was true of the exclusion of legitimate heirs: 'God had approved the same with good success.'[24] Persons gave examples from the history of Israel, Spain, Portugal, France and England to show how often the laws of hereditary succession had been broken.[25] If we denied the legitimacy of a king whose descendants had gained the throne without warrant of unimpeachable hereditary right, 'we should shake the states of most princes in the world at this day'.[26]

PAPAL POLITICAL POWER

The *Conference*, although the best work of the period of political resistance, leaves out the crowning glory of Catholic resistance theory, the doctrine of papal political power. In 1596, however, after criticisms of his book, and in order to make it more acceptable in Rome, Persons added a chapter to a Latin translation he made of the second part of the *Conference*, in which he gave a very clear statement of papal political power, and we may take our description of that aspect of Catholic resistance theory from this previously unknown source. Papal political power was defended in several other Elizabethan Catholic books, especially during the period of resistance. We have already described the treatment given it by Sander and Harding in the early years of the reign.[27] William Allen provided a lengthy defence of the theory in his *True, sincere and modest defence*, and later drew heavily on it in his *Admonition*, and to a lesser extent in another work.[28] Cresswell briefly dealt with the topic in his reply to the proclamation of 1591;[29] Persons felt constrained to defend it in two books written against the Appellant priests at the end of the reign;[30] a large number of Catholic books expounded the doctrine in the reign of James I as part of the Oath of Allegiance controversy;[31] finally, it was also dealt with in scholastic non-controversial works written by English Catholics at this time.[32]

According to the theory of papal political power, the Pope had the right to interfere in the affairs of any country, and could even declare its king deposed and his subjects free of their allegiance to him. The doctrine was connected with the other two planks of Catholic resistance theory, human-right kingship and the coronation oath. Papal power was said to derive from God directly – hence the Pope had power over kings who were chosen merely by their people. As for the coronation oath, it was a religious oath, under papal jurisdiction, and administered as part of a solemn religious ceremony by a member of the priesthood. Like the theory of the human right of kings, the doctrine of papal political power was virtually one of the theological tenets of Catholicism, although in the period of political non-resistance Elizabethan Catholic writers had avoided discussing it. A common way of describing this papal power among late sixteenth-century Catholic writers was to call it 'indirect'. This meant that the Pope exercised such power not because he directly possessed political dominion over kings, but because his spiritual authority gave him indirectly the right to intervene in the political affairs of Christian nations. The 'indirect' theory was best expressed by Robert Bellarmine in a work published in 1586, but was by no means his discovery and had been used by theologians since at least the fifteenth century: Bellarmine even claimed Aquinas as one of his authorities, but that was rather far-fetched.[33] After the publication of Bellarmine's book Elizabethan Catholic writers who defend papal political power all follow the indirect theory, while Harding's and Sander's treatment twenty years before had been rather different.[34] Some doubt has been cast on whether William Allen uses the 'indirect' theory in *A true, sincere and modest defence*.[35] I think he does, although it is true that he grants that the Pope may directly intervene in political matters by virtue of the real political power he has as ruler of the Papal States – but this was surely a special case.[36]

In the Latin version of the *Conference*, Persons first entered upon a fairly commonplace discussion of the subject of papal power in temporals. He began by saying that the Pope was not, as some canonists claimed, lord of every nation by virtue of his ecclesiastical authority. Nevertheless he had political power:

the duty of watching over the public good and especially of protecting religion, the ultimate care of which has been given to the Pope, gives him also a supreme right in every kingdom or principality of the Christian republic, to protect religion and see that it suffers no damage.[37]

This was not direct, but indirect and oblique ('obliquum') political power, he said, but it was most necessary and useful for the preservation of Christendom. Persons then gave his arguments to prove that the Pope should have such power. He described the purpose of political society as being twofold: to direct men towards both temporal happiness and eternal felicity. Two authorities in the Christian commonwealth looked after these two human requirements – the civil power and the Church. Christ had exercised the ecclesiastical authority while on earth and had then delegated it to Peter, while he had left political power to kings and emperors; he had shown his disdain for the latter by saying that his kingdom was not of this world. St Paul had taught that those who were least esteemed in the Church of God should exercise political authority, and St Peter had called it a 'human creature', 'because it dealt with human affairs'.[38] Hence, 'spiritual or ecclesiastical power is more eminent and is superior in dignity to civil power, as the soul is superior to the body, the spirit to the flesh, celestial to human concerns, eternal to transient things, the future to the present life, and finally as much as the power of Christ is superior to the power of emperors'.[39]

Because of its inferiority to spiritual authority in the commonwealth, political power is subordinate to it, directed by it, and can be altered by it if this is necessary for the good of the Church and for the salvation of souls, 'which is the chief and supreme end of every commonwealth and government among Christians'.[40] Here Persons referred back to the rest of the *Conference*, to the chapters dealing with coronation oaths, in which, he now said, kings swore 'to procure the public good, but chiefly to watch over and maintain religion, without which it is impossible to achieve eternal life'.[41] Since the Pope has supreme ecclesiastical power,

it follows necessarily that where the public good and especially the well-being of religion requires it, the Pope, with a pre-eminent right, can direct, restrain, check or even correct and punish any civil magistrate whatsoever if he stubbornly strays from the true path of eternal salvation (on account of which all magistracy was founded) or turns others from that path by his government.[42]

If this were not the case, Persons urged, the absurdity would follow that God had not left his Church with sufficient power to protect itself.

The Pope used this power seldom, to settle any serious problems in the Christian world in the interests of the public good and of religion. Persons gave the usual examples: the deposition of King Childeric of France by Pope Zacharias; the donation to Charlemagne of the imperial title by Pope Leo III (who took it from Empress Irene); the transference of the imperial title from the French to the Germans by Gregory V; the removal of the royal title from the kings of Poland for murdering Stanislaus, Bishop of Gniezno; the restoration of the Polish royal title by Pope John XXII to Wladislaw the Dwarf; and the deposition of Sancho II of Portugal by Pope Innocent IV. The Pope should use his authority in England, Persons said, to solve the problem of the succession, because the matter was so complicated, because religion was endangered by it, and 'since it greatly concerns the whole of Christendom who or what sort of prince should next be admitted to the government of England after the present Queen'.[43]

Persons was not, however, content with this conventional justification of papal political power; in the Latin recension of his *Conference* he followed it with a second and far more original argument. The Pope, he maintained, was feudal overlord of England. This idea had been briefly touched upon by Cardinal Allen and other writers a few years before. Stapleton had called John Foxe 'the Pope's privy friend' for printing the 'writing obligatory', or charter, in which King John resigned his kingdom to the Pope. But Persons now set the theory out with a fullness not to be found elsewhere in Elizabethan Catholic literature.[44] England was subject to the Pope not only by virtue of his universal authority, 'but also is bound more closely to him, by the bond of fealty or of a special feudal contract, by which the kings of England have been from the most ancient times the feudal tenants, feoffees, or liege-vassals (to use lawyer's jargon) of the Apostolic See'.[45] The word 'vassal', he said, should not be offensive to kings, since it did not imply subjection and was a title which could have been applied to as mighty a monarch as Charles V, who held Naples and Sicily as vassal of the Pope. Persons next quoted Bodin, who was, as he admitted, 'otherwise not very devoted to Papal majesty', to show the feudal jurisdiction of the Pope over England.[46] Allen, where he had dealt with the matter in *A true, sincere and modest defence*, also cited Bodin and Persons probably found his reference there. Persons made great use of Bodin in this section of the Latin translation of the *Conference*, quoting the *De Republica* verbatim for nearly two pages and cribbing several marginal references from him. Bodin's main point was that in

1212 King John had resigned his kingdom to the Pope, had
sworn fealty to him, and had promised to pay him an annual
tribute.

Persons elaborated and corrected Bodin's narrative. He
described the tribute paid by various English kings before John to
the Pope: by King Ine, King Offa, and 'Edelphus or Adulphus,
whom others also call Adelvulphus, the son of King Egbert'.
William the Conqueror himself had asked for papal support
before invading England. Indeed, 'when great and serious difficulties arise, the English have always been accustomed to have
recourse to the Roman See as to an asylum, and to the Pope as to
the supreme lord of England'.[47] Persons next described the confirmation of papal authority in England by Henry II after he had
repented of the murder of Thomas Becket. The deposition of
Richard II by Henry of Lancaster, which was, in the English
version of the *Conference*, an example of the power of the
commonwealth over its king, now became an example of papal
influence in English affairs. When Richard had shown his failure
to rule properly, had oppressed the commonwealth and trodden
religion underfoot, Thomas Arundel, the Archbishop of Canterbury, went to Pope Boniface IX, and complained to him of the
king. The Pope excommunicated Richard and gave an indulgence
to all who should support the Duke of Lancaster, with the result
that 'in a few days' the kingdom was taken away from Richard
and given to Henry. The same was true of Richard III, 'a wicked
tyrant who had foully killed both his nephews', but who was
deposed by Henry of Richmond after a papal bull had been
obtained by Bishop Morton of Ely in which 'Richard was cursed
and the cause of Henry strongly commended.' Thus the Pope had
been responsible for establishing the Tudor dynasty.[48]

The best example of papal feudal overlordship of England,
however, occurred in the reign of King John, and Persons returned to it. He quoted extensively from Matthew Paris,[49] taking
from this source the document by which John resigned the kingdoms of England and Ireland to the Pope and did homage to him.
A text designed to warm the heart of any papalist:

John, by the grace of God King of England etc., to all Christ's
faithful who may read this charter, greetings in the Lord! To all
you, we wish it to be known by this charter, authenticated by our

seal, that since we have greatly offended God and our mother the holy Church, and therefore stand in great need of divine mercy, and since we can offer nothing worthy to make the satisfaction we owe to God and the Church, unless we humble ourselves and our kingdom; we wish to humble ourselves for Him who humbled Himself for us, even to death; inspired by the grace of the holy ghost, not constrained by force, nor impelled by fear, but of our own good free will, and with the general consent of our barons, we confer and freely grant to God and His holy Apostles, Peter and Paul, and to the holy Church of Rome our mother, and to the Lord Pope Innocent and his Catholic successors the whole kingdom of England and the whole kingdom of Ireland, with every right and all their appurtenances etc. etc...[50]

Persons concluded by repeating that England was the 'fief, feudal dependency and tributary' of the Pope. The feudal right of the Pope was very ancient, but it was, he said, still in existence and probably had increased as a result of the recent defection of English rulers from the Church. The Pope's power should be used to settle the question of the succession, in order to preserve the peace of Christendom and to prevent the rival claimants going to war with one another.

THE POLITICAL IDEAS OF THE COUNTER-REFORMATION

Some historians have perhaps tended to neglect Catholic resistance theory and to dismiss it as rather untypical and perhaps hypocritical. There is still something of a feeling that the Reformers were, deep down, more democratic or liberal in their political doctrine than their opponents. This seems to be the assumption behind an essay by R. M. Kingdon, in which he argued that there was a connection between the ideas of William Allen's *A true, sincere and modest defence* and the resistance theory of the Calvinist monarchomachs of the time: 'polemicists like Fr. Robert Persons and Dr William Allen deliberately crossed lines of confession and nationality in a search for ideas that would advance their cause'.[51] To substantiate this, Kingdon points to those passages in Allen's book where he cites the works of Protestants to demonstrate that they have preached rebellion. It is, indeed, the case that Allen does show a wide knowledge of Calvinist resistance theory, but so, as we have seen, did every Catholic controversialist worth his salt. Nor was Allen's intention in using such material different from that of the other Catholics who had also cited the seditious doctrines of heretics. He gave the usual list of Protestants who had encouraged resistance – Calvin, Beza, Zwingli, Goodman, Knox and Luther himself – and set down some fairly conventional examples.[52] The Latin translation of Allen's *A true, sincere and modest defence* (unknown to Kingdon) improved on this passage, and described the 'frightful lies' and 'horrible and quite Satanic contumely' against kings found in the *Francogallia* and *Vindiciae contra tyrannos*.[53] Allen concluded in sarcasm: 'By all which you see that to resist the magistrate, defend themselves in cases of conscience, and to fight against the superior for religion, is a clear and ruled case and no treasonable opinion at all against the prince, if we will be judged by Protestants.'

By 'using' the extremist political ideas of Protestants like Hotman and Duplessis-Mornay, Allen did not hope to substantiate his own theories of resistance – they would stand alone – but merely to continue a venerable controversial tradition. There was, however, a new twist to Allen's arguments, for by 1584 he was himself beginning to preach resistance.[54] Allen now maintained that Catholics were better at resistance theory than Protestants. Protestants rebelled in a chaotic and seditious fashion, while Catholics did so in a conservative, orderly, respectful way. The key to the difference between Catholics and Protestants, according to Allen, was the theory of papal political power, the special ingredient which made Catholic rebellion so much more respectable. Before rebelling, Catholics appealed to superior and long-established authority, to the Pope, while heretics resisted their kings according to their own whim and fancy. Allen himself, it seems to me, belies Kingdon's thesis that there could be an easy exchange of ideas of resistance between Catholics and Protestants by pointing to one important difference: there was no Protestant equivalent of the theory of papal power in temporals.

In some ways the Catholic tradition was a more plentiful source for resistance theory than the Protestant. Early Protestant leaders had tended to adopt ideas of divine-right kingship to counter papalism, and had often rejected scholasticism wholesale. When the reformers advanced ideas of resistance they tended to look to constitutional law, the Old Testament or humanism for inspiration; reformed theology by itself was not enough. Paradoxically, however, Calvinists and Lutherans needed such a theory of resistance far more than Catholics. It is interesting to note that while Allen and Persons did not (in Kingdon's sense) 'use' Calvinist theories of resistance, Persons' *Conference* and *Leicester's Commonwealth* were republished several times in the next century by Protestants to aid the Good Old Cause of opposition to monarchy. If we are looking for the origins of modern liberalism we cannot leave all the glory to Calvin's Saints.

Although Catholic resistance theory is not a negligible factor in sixteenth-century history, it is not the typical or most important ideological aspect of the Counter-Reformation. Again, some historians sometimes write as if it were. They dwell on the papal bulls which thundered forth against Henry VIII, Elizabeth and Henry of Navarre, on the secret plotting at Rome and the political activities of the Jesuits. We are told that the Counter-Reformation came to England by way of the seminary priests, who were deeply imbued with advanced political ideas and devoted to a sense of 'enterprise'.[55] It would indeed be wrong to deny that sixteenth-century Catholicism had some features which tend to confirm this view of it. It is true that late sixteenth-century Popes were playing an increasingly active role in European affairs. Some of the aggressive forcefulness with which Renaissance Pontiffs had enriched themselves and their dynasties in Italy was now directed to the defence of the patrimony of St Peter north of the Alps. Moreover, there was a strong Catholic tradition of slightly anarchic political theology which flowered most brilliantly in sixteenth-century Spain, in the works of men like Vitoria, Mariana and Suarez. It was also generally considered sound Catholic theology, in the sixteenth century at least, to deny the divine right of kings and to maintain that the Pope had political authority over all nations.

Nevertheless, the ideological achievement of the Counter-Reformation is not best represented in the theory of the Spanish neo-scholastics, nor in the practice of Pius V and Sixtus V. On the contrary, it was the rejection of the doctrine of papal universal sovereignty, the accomplishment of a successful Concordat with the major Catholic powers, and the acceptance eventually of theories of sovereign kingship which were the most significant political aspects of sixteenth- and seventeenth-century Catholicism.

This ideology bore fruit in the absolutism of late seventeenth-century France, Austria and Spain. But we see it developing before, and it is reflected in the bulk of the political works of the Elizabethan Catholics. The seminarists returned to England with no medieval ideas of resistance and with no exaggerated theories of papal power, but with the new Counter-Reformation ideology of non-resistance. When the League and when Allen and Persons preached rebellion in the 1580s they spoke not with the voice of the Catholic revival but in the accents of Hildebrand.

It was indeed difficult, especially in Rome, to accept all the implications of the new ideology. Papal power itself seemed threatened, and some writers continued to speak of an absolute papal political authority over Christendom. But the commonest view of papal political power – the so-called Bellarminian 'indirect' theory – involved very important concessions to the independence and sovereignty of the State.[56] As with so much in the Counter-Reformation, the lead in the adoption of the new political thought came generally from outside Rome. Pius V's indiscretion in excommunicating Elizabeth was condemned by the Catholic rulers of Europe; Bellarmine was put on the Index in Rome. The conflict with heresy put great strain on Catholic non-resistance when there was confrontation between the Pope and a heretic ruler. Here the old medieval ideas tended to come to the fore again, and to replace the new Counter-Reformation political thought. This was the moment of stress which produced the brief period of Elizabethan Catholic resistance theory. But it was an aberration, and within a few years the Catholic leaders were ready to return to the new theories of loyalism and non-resistance.

[handwritten marginalia:] good

[handwritten note at bottom of page:] Commenton the bottom of the previous page – the Some matter was to be attempted by the Pope in negotiation with James I. So how important to resistance theory really & might Eng — how widely was it accepted by the Catholic Community?

14

The end of resistance: Persons' 'Memorial of the Reformation of England'

The most prolific and successful Elizabethan Catholic writer was Robert Persons, and it is not surprising that his was the last word in the period of resistance. In 1596 he wrote 'A Memorial of the Reformation of England', a work devoted to showing how England should be reformed – both in politics and religion – after the restoration of Catholicism. 'A memorial' shows the same interest in political questions as the other works of the period of resistance, and it assumes the sudden conquest of England or the providential succession of a Catholic. But in other respects it displays a definite decrease in ideological fervour, and the very fact that Persons avoided having it printed at the time it was written is a sign of his declining commitment to the propaganda of ideas of political resistance.

Persons' main interest in this book was in what measures ought to be taken immediately after a Catholic recovery of power in England. His principal recommendations in this respect were that a 'Council of the Reformation', composed of clerics, should be set up to supervise the conversion of the country,[1] and that religious toleration should be granted to Protestants for a period.[2] England must be reformed perfectly after the Catholic restoration; the reformation under Queen Mary had not been satisfactory. The decrees of the Council of Trent must be fully implemented, but Trent provided only weakened medicine for a Europe which was then still degenerate, and further measures would be necessary now. England will have to 'embrace also and...put it in ure, where occasion and place is offered, such other points of reformation as tend to the perfect restitution of ecclesiastical discipline that were in use in the ancient Christian Church, though afterwards decayed for want of spirit, and not urged now again, nor commanded by the Council of Trent'.[3] Persons described in great detail various reforms which would be necessary to bring about this perfect reformation, following in some respects the advice of Juan de Avila, a Spanish mystic and reformer.[4]

One very important issue discussed in the 'Memorial' was the question of the ownership of monastic land.[5] Persons criticised the way in which during Mary's reign the holders of this land had been confirmed in their possession by the Pope. This had been done because the Church had been in a weak position then and 'was content to take of her children what she could get, rather than lose all', but it had been the wrong policy and had brought down the wrath of God on England. In the event of a Catholic restoration a different course of action should be followed. However, Persons suggested actually taking back monastic property only from the enemies of the Church – persecutors and those of notorious impiety. Catholics should have their occupancy of such land confirmed, but not it seems their ownership, for they were to pay rent to the Council of the Reformation for it. All monastic wealth would be administered by this Council – a sort of anti-Court of Augmentation – which would use it for various religious purposes, but not restore it directly to the old religious orders to whom it belonged. This last suggestion was interpreted by Persons' enemies as a stratagem of his to increase Jesuit strength in England, and it greatly upset the Benedictines, who sought in the next few years to prove a continuous succession of English monks of their order since the dissolution, and hence ensure that when the faith was restored they could regain their abbeys. Persons also wanted the impropriate patronage which was held by the possession of abbey lands to be resumed by the Church.[6]

In the manuals of casuistry, compiled by the leaders of Elizabethan Catholicism – among them Persons himself – and presumably reflected in the penitential advice of the seminary priests, this attitude to monastic property is also to be found. We see there a firm statement that it still belongs to the Church and that those who hold it must be prepared to do with the property whatever the Pope shall decide when the time comes for a decision. It is suggested by the casuists that Catholics should take an oath at their reconciliation to the Church promising to abide by any future papal pronouncement on the matter. Monastic property is stolen property, they declare, and must be restored to its rightful owners as soon as possible. As with recusancy, however, so with the possession of abbey lands, the position of the Catholic is not made intolerable by the casuists. They will allow Catholics in England to buy, hold, sell and devise such property. They do not encourage possession of it, but say it may be bought for good reasons, for example to stop it falling into the hands of heretics who may spoil it. Catholics may even build on monastic land, but should not erect very luxurious buildings which cannot be re-converted later into habitations suitable for monks, and they should keep a note of what building materials they take from the ruined abbey so that they can repay it later on. A reasonable profit may be made from the land, but anything above ten per cent a year should be given to the poor or returned to the monas-tery. When selling, a Catholic may keep the sum he paid for the land but should give any profit on the sale to the Church, and should make sure that the purchaser understands that the land is former monastic property.[7] But, despite these concessions, it is clear from these casuist documents and from the 'Memorial' that the Elizabethan Catholic leaders had gone back on the Marian decision about abbey land, and that they now reclaimed owner-ship of it for the Church.[8]

Some of the more specifically political reforms suggested by Persons in his 'Memorial' show the enduring influence of the ideology of political resistance which by 1596 was coming to an end. Thus, Persons proposed to increase the role of the clergy in political life: Parliament was to have more representatives of the Church; bishops would play some part in the election of knights of the shire;[9] the prince was to have a Council of Confessors;[10] and the Council of Reformation, composed of clergymen, was to wield great power immediately after the restoration. In the 'Memorial', the clergy are said to be superior to the laity and to fulfil a higher role in the political community, in terms reminiscent of the Latin version of the *Conference*, written at about the same time.[11] The first Parliament after the restoration was to debate whether Elizabeth had been the legitimate Queen of England and whether her first Parliament was lawful without proper episcopal representation.[12] Moreover, in the 'Memorial' Persons said that after the restoration, a Catholic version of the Act of Settlement should be passed, because it was essential to 'link the state of Catholic religion and succession together as the one may depend and be the assurance of the other'.[13] Some of the other political reforms put forward by Persons are also suggested by other Catholic writers of this period, while some are idiosyncrasies of Persons' own, based on his wide experience in exile of foreign methods of government. Like Allen before him he proposes the reform of wardship.[14] He also suggests the drastic step of replacing the common law with the civil law, an idea which Allen had used in 1584 to exemplify the height of radical folly. Like Verstegan after him, he describes the Normans as conquerors who introduced their law to England 'with especial eye to keep down, afflict, and extirpate the English people'.[15] Persons was alone among Elizabethan Catholics, however, in making the novel suggestion, as Harrington was to in the next century, that Parliament should adopt the Venetian practice of voting by the use of coloured balls.[16]

It would be wrong to say that the political reforms proposed by Persons are unimportant; they all demonstrate his shrewd interest in politics and his ability to envisage reform and change. But it must be said that, apart from the degree of power he would grant to the Catholic clergy in matters of state, there is little in his programme of political reforms to suggest that it is a Catholic rather than a Protestant plan. Indeed, there is a good deal of what used to be called 'puritanism' about his reforms: the dress, behaviour and games of the laity are to be kept sober and quiet, and the number of saints' days is to be reduced to avoid wasteful lack of industry. Persons would abolish 'all junkets, all lascivious banqueting, excess of apparel, dancing, fencing-schools and the like' at the universities, and he would 'reduce' the common people 'again to their old simplicity, both in apparel, diet, innocency of life, and plainness of dealing, and conversation, from which heresy hath distracted many'.[17] The 'Memorial' is in this respect instructive about the nature of Catholic and Protestant resistance theory in the sixteenth century. It shows that its aim was purely destructive, to overthrow the existing regime and replace it by one of the right religion. No political reforms of a purely Catholic or Protestant sort were envisaged, because no such reforms existed. Once the restoration of Catholicism, or Protestantism, had been effected, the old political thought of non-resistance, order and degree would apply again, and the life of the country would carry on very much as before. Nevertheless, the 'Memorial' is interesting because it shows a sixteenth-century religious leader reflecting at length on what political changes would be in the interest of his country. Although Persons does not put forward a Catholic programme, at least he does have political ideas. As with the *Conference*, so in the 'Memorial' Persons is stepping outside the sixteenth century into the next era, an era of political rather than religious reform.

The 'Memorial' was the last work of the period of Elizabethan Catholic political resistance. By 1596, when it was written, the ideological climate in Catholic Europe had changed considerably: peace with heretics, divine-right kingship, and non-resistance were now the ideas at a premium in Paris, and soon even in Rome and Madrid. The 'Memorial' is altogether a gentler book, almost a pipe-dream: what to do if the restoration comes rather than when it comes. There is no call to arms, no defence of the right of resistance or of papal sovereignty, no critique of Elizabethan policies or ministers, simply Persons' sober reflections, turned over in his mind (as he says) for some time, and finally jotted down for the use of future generations. It was as if Persons realised that the day of restoration would be after his death. In 1601, almost after all hope had gone, he sent a translation to the Infanta herself – perhaps to stir up memories of her claims to England.[18] But it was a hopeless gesture. The book lived on, however, and when the Catholic restoration finally came in 1685, it was studied, apparently, at the court of King James II.[19]

Part Four

NON-RESISTANCE AGAIN

15

Opposition to the ideas of resistance
1584–96

ROBERT SOUTHWELL

Surprisingly few statements of opposition to the ideology of resistance have survived from the period 1584–96. It is often claimed that the disloyalty of Persons and Allen was unpopular among Catholics in England,[1] but very little criticism of their political ideas appears to have been made at the time. There are the letters of Sir Thomas Tresham to the Queen herself and to various members of her government, which are loyal enough.[2] We know that two dubious Catholic exiles, Edward Grately and Gilbert Gifford, wrote tracts criticising the policy of Allen and Persons: one was an attack on the Society of Jesus – a significant theme in the light of the anti-Jesuitism of the Appellants at the end of the reign – the other a critique of Allen's 'Defence of Stanley'.[3] But neither work survives, and it seems reasonable to suspect that they would have been little more than pieces of Elizabethan propaganda. Both Gifford and Grately were government spies, and Robert Persons said of their books that they 'were so fondly and maliciously written as Walsingham himself was ashamed to let them be printed'.[4] Apart from odd scattered letters, the only Catholic statements of the ideology of political non-resistance which date from the period 1584–96 are to be found in two works, one by Robert Southwell, the other by John Bishop. Both, as we shall see, are in different ways difficult to interpret and hard to accept as evidence of the existence in this period of an alternative Catholic ideology to the political thought of resistance expressed by Allen and Persons.

Robert Southwell wrote *An humble supplication* in 1591. It was his answer to the royal proclamation of that year, but it contrasts strikingly with the works of resistance written by Persons,

Verstegan, Stapleton and Cresswell in reply to the same edict. Southwell addressed the Queen in the most deferential terms, calling her 'most mighty and most merciful, most feared and best beloved princess'.[5] He avoided making any criticism of her chief ministers, with the exception of Walsingham, who was dead.[6] He expressed his belief in non-resistance, saying that 'subjects are bound in conscience, under pain of forfeiting their right in heaven and incurring the guilt of eternal torments' to obey the just laws of princes.[7] He assured the Queen that 'what army soever should come against you, we will rather yield our breasts to be broached by our country's swords than use our swords to the effusion of our country's blood'.[8] His main concern lay in defending Catholics from the charge of treason – a common non-resistant argument.

While his fellow Jesuit, Robert Persons, and the other Catholic leaders were hurling abuse at Elizabeth and inciting rebellion against her, Southwell was praising her and preaching non-resistance.[9] In 1591, he seemed still to hold to the ideology of the early 1580s, of Allen's *Apology* and Persons' *Epistle of the persecution*. In exile they had turned aside into opposition to the Queen; at home under persecution, Southwell retained the old ideology. This appears to be confirmed by certain passages of his *Epistle of comfort* of 1587 or 1588, where (like Allen in what we have termed the 'period of non-resistance') Southwell expresses his faith in evangelical means of conquering England – 'our prisons preach, our punishments convert, our dead quarters and bones confound your heresy' – and gives his forgiveness to his persecutors.[10] Robert Persons characterised *An humble supplication* in this way in 1602: if it sometimes praised the Queen too much, Southwell was only following the example of Cardinal Allen and others, who themselves were permitted to express their loyalty to Elizabeth by the papal faculty of 1580.[11]

The story is, however, rather more complicated, for although *An humble supplication* is a work of non-resistance, a throw-back to an earlier ideological period, there are sound reasons for doubting whether it expresses Southwell's real opinions. Indeed, there is evidence that while Persons and Allen were expressing their ideas of resistance Southwell secretly agreed with such views. One of the most extreme works of the period was Allen's 'Defence of Stanley'. As we have seen, Gilbert Gifford wrote an attack on this work, justifying Elizabeth's Dutch policy and condemning Stanley for surrendering Deventer to the Spanish. We have Southwell's own opinion of Gifford's book. He called it 'quite alien to a Christian sense of justice', a 'vapid production', and 'the work of some atheist or agnostic courtier who is playing at theology and mistaking military precedents for moral principles'.[12]

The best evidence for Southwell's secret acceptance of exactly the ideology which was held in the early 1590s by the Catholic leaders in exile comes from a work he wrote at precisely the time he was composing *An humble supplication*. This tract, 'General heads of the persecution in England', is, as its title suggests, little more than a series of notes, which Southwell perhaps thought of using in a book, but which in the end he sent to Richard Verstegan, who lived in Antwerp and collected martyrological information.[13] It consists mainly of a detailed description of the cruel persecution suffered by Catholics in England, but in Chapter 10 Southwell turned to politics and launched just the sort of attack on English policy which is present in the works of Persons and Allen at this time, but lacking in *An humble supplication*. Southwell began by expanding on the proposition that the whole of England was made by God 'to taste of the same scourges that Catholics are wronged with'. He gave several examples to demonstrate this. In law, he said, no justice is used, but favour and bribery determine most cases; this mirrors the treatment meted out to Catholics by Protestants. Just as Catholics are defamed in England, so England itself is infamous to the rest of Europe:[14]

In France [the English] are counted church-robbers, cruel and unmerciful; in Portugal, cowards and yet bloody, the pirates of all seas, the sowers of sedition in all countries, the maintainers of all rebellions, at home butchers of their own subjects, and persecutors of the Catholic Church. In sum, no nation of Christendom this day so infamous in all countries as the English.[15]

In the same way that Catholics are deprived of their property, the whole population of the country is oppressed by high rents and fines, and by exorbitant taxes: 'No penny being so soon warm in a poor man's purse, but the subsidy-gatherer is ready to fetch it', and all spent 'to maintain the King of Navarre or to help Don Antonio, or to send men into Flanders, to the consumption of English treasure, and disturbance of Christian princes.' The people are impoverished by monopolies, by courtiers who are granted the 'lands of the halls of London, and hospitals, and other places of relief', and by the work of the 'Queen's takers', who requisition as much wood and provisions for themselves as for her and pay only for half their value.[16]

The chief persecutors of the Catholics are hated by all Englishmen, Southwell said. The death of Leicester and of Walsingham caused rejoicing, while Cecil is like a 'storm in the air, that all fear and shun, but none loves'. The country is divided:

Never less neighbourhood among the people, never less agreement in the peers; everyone draweth a sundry way, and standeth in fear of his nearest friends. The whole realm is so full of makebates and factions, that when they begin to work, there can be no invasion of equal misery to the civil mutinies that are likely to ensue.[17]

The liberty of subjects is impaired, so that no one can go abroad without licence. Merchants have lost business. The nobility is reduced to servility under Cecil, 'as if they were perpetual wards', 'like pupils, with a rod', 'like babish fools'. The J.P.s and Lords Lieutenant are subject to the commands of pursuivants and 'promoters'. The commons and 'meaner gentlemen' are in great bondage and are afraid to complain about the heavy taxes they pay. The prisons are full of debtors, thieves and murderers; many are executed 'for vice'; the country swarms with begging ex-soldiers, roaming around causing trouble. Other men, killed in the wars, have left widows and orphans in misery. The loss of so many soldiers makes England an easy prey to its enemies, who are 'justly incensed against us, by our piracy, surprising and invading others' countries'. Great danger threatens the country from rebellion; not against the Queen, 'whose sex is easy to be misled' and who is not personally to be condemned, nor her other counsellors, 'whose wills are violently overruled', but against Cecil, who 'with feigned surmises and odious fictions, hath robbed the commons, dispeopled the country of the best soldiers, kept the nobility in thraldom and the gentlemen in the basest servility that England ever knew – a man that consumeth his prince of more than £20,000 by the year'.[18] England is also in danger because the question of the succession is not settled; this will surely lead to civil war and possibly success for the King of Spain. Southwell ended his tract with a lengthy denunciation of Cecil, who was accused of seeking 'absolute regiment' over the Queen, and with a description of the horrible death of Leicester and of Walsingham, 'the just judgment of God' for their iniquity.[19]

JOHN BISHOP

[handwritten marginalia: Somewhat — He does not preach revolution though!]

It is difficult, therefore, in the light of the 'General heads of the persecution', to see *An humble supplication* as indicative of Southwell's complete commitment to the old political ideas of the early 1580s which his fellow Jesuit, Persons, had by 1591 abandoned. Less difficult to accept as evidence of opposition to the ideology of resistance – although there are interpretative problems associated with this work, too – is John Bishop's *A courteous conference with the English Catholics roman about the six articles ministered unto the seminary priests*, published in 1598 by Robert Dexter of London. Dexter was a respectable printer and had entered the book on the Stationers' Register in November of the previous year,[20] which tells one immediately what sort of political ideas it expresses. In a preface to the reader it is said that the author of the book was John Bishop, a recusant papist born at Battle in Sussex, who lived in London, and whose brother was George Bishop of Northiam in Sussex. The date of its composition has misled several commentators: it was probably written in 1584 or 1585, and it seems to reply covertly to William Allen's *A true, sincere and modest defence* of 1584.[21]

Bishop's *Courteous conference* began by dismissing out of hand the mainstay of the Catholic theory of resistance, the doctrine of papal political power. The Pope and all bishops, Bishop said, were subject to the temporal magistrates of the countries in which they lived. He gave biblical texts showing the power of kings and the necessity of obeying them, and cited Bracton's saying that 'a king cannot be a king if he have any superior in those things that do appertain unto his crown and kingdom, and may not have in his kingdom any equal, much less any superior'.[22] Kings, Bishop said, had power to make 'wholesome laws for the maintenance of the true faith of Christ', and, although they had no power to administer the sacraments, according to Justice Brian under Henry VII, the king was a 'mixed person', 'a person united with the priests of holy Church'.[23] Priests should occupy themselves only with 'saving of souls... preaching, praying, administration of the sacraments, and ecclesiastical discipline.' The Old Testament described how priests were subject to kings; Christ had professed himself not to be an earthly king; and until the year 730, when the 'Papal Duchy' was created in Rome, the Pope had recognised the Emperor as superior.

Bishop attacked the papal power of deposition in various ways, and concluded thus:

> if we do wisely weigh the matter and carefully call to mind all the woeful wars and wastes, massacres, miseries, and calamities that this practice of deposing of princes hath wrought, we shall find that the West Church hath been more wasted and weakened thereby, and that it hath caused the murder of more men than all the cruel persecutions of the heathen and heretics and all the bloody swords of the Turks and Saracens.[24]

The Pope could not release men from obedience to the law of God, which, as the Bible showed, enjoined obedience to kings. Moreover, the Kings of England had never acknowledged themselves to be vassals of the Pope. He proved that canon law was inferior to common law in England by referring to the work of Christopher St German, 'a great lawyer... a good divine and devout Catholic'.[25] Finally, Bishop discussed a canon of the Fourth Lateran Council (1215) which Allen had used in *A true, sincere and modest defence* and which laid down the procedure to be followed when a temporal lord was deprived of his authority by the Church. Bishop denied that it was a matter of faith for a Catholic to obey such a decree and then maintained that since the decrees of this council had not been accepted in England by Parliament, they could not bind Englishmen. To confirm this he cited Thomas More's *Debellacion of Salem and Bizance*, a work written against the 'good divine' Christopher St German, where More said that 'King John could not make his kingdom tributary to the Pope without the consent of the Parliament' and therefore 'much less could he give the Pope authority to give the realm away'. In any case, Bishop said, the excommunication of Queen Elizabeth had not followed the form prescribed by the Lateran Council and hence was uncanonical. All true Englishmen would refuse to accept the bull, Bishop concluded, and would consider it absurd to believe that not to fight against the Queen was to be damned.[26]

Bishop's book is unusual. It is the most extreme Catholic attack on papal political power of Elizabeth's reign; Bishop utterly rejects *Regnans in excelsis* and the theory behind it. The Bishops were a large Sussex clan, with Catholics and crypto-Catholics among them, but I cannot identify John exactly.[27] Could he be the 'small smatterer...in good letters' who published an odd little book in 1577;[28] or the Oxford graduate who was the recusant registrar to the Bishop of Bath and Wells?[29] Without any knowledge of the author apart from what his Protestant editor tells us, it is not easy to form a just estimate of the work. It is possible, of course, that it was a Protestant forgery, but no Catholic author that I know of denounced it as such, and I cannot quite see the point of such a forgery anyway. From the kind of argument he uses, Bishop seems to be a lawyer,[30] in the anti-clerical, but strictly speaking Catholic tradition of St German. Whatever the case, the *Courteous conference* is an intelligent and well-argued piece which gives evidence (if it is genuine) of opposition among Catholics to the ideas of political resistance prevalent in English Catholic literature at the time.[31]

But it claims to be published by a recusant living in England — He undermines his own argument that the exile Catholic leadership was the leadership —

16

The laity

John Bishop's *Courteous conference* is unusual not only in its
outspoken denunciation of the doctrine of papal power in
temporals, but also because it is, apparently, the work of a layman.
The great majority of the books which furnish us with evidence of
the political and religious opinions of the Elizabethan Catholics
were written by the regular or secular clergy. For this very reason,
it is difficult to arrive at a just estimate of the political ideas of the
laity or to discover how far the books written by the priests
represented accurately the views of their flock. It has often been
maintained by historians that the seditious theories and traitorous
political activity of Persons and Allen at the time of the Armada
were viewed unsympathetically by many Catholics, especially
among the laity. The Elizabethan Catholics, according to this
widely-held view, were fundamentally divided in outlook between
those on the one hand who were prepared to suffer persecution
patiently, were loyal to the Queen and in some ways rather poor
papists; and those on the other hand who, better Catholics than
Englishmen, were prepared to rebel against Elizabeth or to plot
with foreign powers the overthrow of her government. Dr Bossy in
his influential essay on the 'Character of Elizabethan Catholicism'[1]
put forward a revised version of this thesis, drawing a sharp distinction between the English Catholic laity and the clergy. The
seminary priests he described as humanists, interested in extremist
political thought, the conquest of England by armed force and
thorough Catholic reformation of the Church (while the old
Marian priests and the Louvainists were more backward in their
political and religious ideas).[2] In contrast to the humanist clerks,
the Catholic laity was in the main composed of 'seigneurial'
gentry whose religious interests were 'survivalist', who had little

concern with the ideals of the Counter-Reformation and who were largely loyal to the Queen. Apart from John Bishop's book (which, as I have suggested, is probably to be treated with some caution), what other evidence is there that the laity were divided from the clergy in their political opinions?

A handful of lay writers contributed works to the corpus of Elizabethan Catholic literature, some of them expressing political ideas. But none provides corroboration for the idea that there existed a distinct layman's ideology. All were intimately connected with the clerical authors who were their contemporaries and associates. Richard Verstegan is inseparable from the other writers of the period of resistance, who were clerks. He acted as Persons' publisher in Antwerp but printed a number of works in his own right, similar in many ways to the writings of his clerical master. Anthony Copley's publications at the end of the century were the work of a man committed to the Appellant cause in the Archpriest controversy, which was almost entirely a quarrel among priests. Thomas Fitzherbert worked very closely with the Jesuit and pro-Jesuit writers at the end of the reign of Elizabeth and in the early years of James I, and he was soon himself to take orders and join the Society. Similarly, the parliamentary speeches made in 1559 and 1563 by Anthony Browne, Viscount Montague and by Robert Atkinson were very little different in tone and content from the orations of Catholic prelates made at the same time.

The evidence of the printed books and parliamentary speeches, therefore, does little to confirm the view that the Catholic laity held political ideas distinct from those of the clergy. In the archives there are, of course, other sources which shed some light on the problem. Sir Thomas Tresham was a prominent Catholic layman in Elizabethan England who has left a few considered statements of his political ideas which have been taken to represent the beliefs of other papist gentlemen at the time. Professor Trimble sees his political thought as 'secular and nationalist...the product of a mind perhaps affected by Gallicanism, but certainly not formed by the currents of opinion exhibited in contemporary Continental Tridentine thought'.[3] In several letters written in the 1580s and 1590s Tresham expressed his loyalty to the Queen, a loyalty which contrasts with the views of the exiled Catholic leaders at the time.

For example, in 1590 he wrote to the Archbishop of Canterbury and others of the Privy Council, expressing his allegiance to the Queen and that of the other Catholics who were also imprisoned:

We all acknowledge ourselves most bounden to Almighty God for His infinite benefits and blessings . . . that He hath bestowed us under the government of so Christian a prince and council.

He went on to remind the Archbishop of the protestations of loyalty he had made in 1588, and his rhetoric shines forth even from the torn manuscript:

As before Your Grace, many months before the invasion, we offered, so did we again to his lordship, at the very instant of the invasion . . . and with importunity begged him that he would obtain [permission of] the lords of Her Highness's Privy Council that we might be employed [*torn*] unarmed in the foremost and before the foremost ranks of our [forces, that] though not able to repulse the enemy, yet to receive the first [*torn*] our naked bodies, thereby to leave undoubted spectacle of our loyalty.[4]

The language of letters to Archbishops and petitions to the Queen tends, however, to be rather high-flown and exaggerated, and there is some justification for wondering how sincere Tresham really was. Among his papers, which were walled up in his house soon after the Gunpowder Treason was revealed in 1605, there is a manuscript tract in answer to the royal proclamation of 1591 which is extremely critical of Elizabeth's government and very pro-Spanish.[5] Tresham's mere possession of the pamphlet does not argue his approval of it, but it would have been a difficult document to explain away, had any government agents come across it. But the best evidence which throws a shadow over Tresham's loyalism is a paper of about 1603 in his own hand. In it he attacks Elizabeth's legitimacy: 'if bastardy and crown right disability were in Queen Elizabeth, then without all exception or question, no sooner was Queen Mary deceased than *in ipso instante* was the crown right of this monarchy in [James I's] mother of most blessed memory, as daughter and heir of the eldest daughter of Henry VII'. The Catholics of England were alienated from Elizabeth from her birth, Tresham continued, while they always favoured the Stuarts, first Mary and now her son.[6] Such statements seem to suggest that Tresham's loyalty was more a matter

of expediency than of deep devotion. Nevertheless, it is clear that
in the 1580s and early 1590s – during the period of political
resistance promoted in the printed books of the Elizabethan
Catholics – Tresham, perhaps as a result of circumstance rather
than from inclination, was loyal and non-resistant.

Tresham's political position was also adopted by other Catholic
laymen at the time. The Catholic gentry seem to have subscribed
the Association in some places (although, on the other hand, so
did Mary Queen of Scots herself).⁷ Sir Thomas Cornwallis is to be
found expressing his disgust at the books written by the Catholic
exiles in which seditious theories were maintained: 'It will but
exasperate matters. In nos cudetur faba. They be out of the way
themselves and therefore do not regard what we endure.' But
Cornwallis was strongly favoured by the Queen, who protected
him from the penal laws; and perhaps he had more reason for
loyalty to her than most Catholics.⁸ A strikingly similar attitude is
to be found in a letter of 1603, in which the writer described
some adventures he had in 1596 when he brought a message to
England from abroad, under instruction to show it to various of
the leading Catholic laity. In this letter the Infanta was extolled
as a worthy successor to Elizabeth, 'for that she was religious' and
because 'she was both strong and mighty and also abounding in
wealth and riches by which means she would be able in a very
short time both to furnish our Church with such things as were
necessary and also to erect monasteries and religious houses',
while the King of Scots was 'debased'; 'such as would consent' to
his succession 'were no good Christians, nay rather they were not
to be accounted Christians' at all. The bearer of this message
found himself most unwelcome in England. He read the letter to
one man and

after that I had read it unto him and others [he] became so dis-
contented that the night following he could not take his rest, as his
bedfellow showed me the next morning; then the party himself afterwards told me that he did marvel much at F[ather] P[ersons] and my
L[ord] C[ardinal] for writing such letters and books as they did,
thereby to disquiet the poor Catholics in England and they themselves to be secure enough and far from all danger.

The reception he received at the next Catholic house at which
he called with the letter was most unfriendly:

from the stable I was preferred to the gate, from the gate to the court, from the court to the hall, from the hall to the kitchen and there was I placed until such time as they had supped, as I supposed; from there at length I was brought to my chamber where I supped and lay that night; the next day I was more liker to depart from thence and not to speak with either P: [the master of the house?] or gest: [guests] than otherwise.

But this letter is perhaps rather too good to be true, being possibly the work of John Cecil, one of the slipperiest Appellants, and it paints just the ideological picture of the loyal laity which the Appellants were anxious to make public.[9]

It is difficult to find the authentic voice of the laity expressing its non-resistance in the 1580s and 1590s. In the same way, we seldom come across Catholic laymen expressing a belief in the right of resistance or other seditious doctrines. One can argue from the plots and rebellions themselves, of course – from the Rising of the Northern Earls, the Babington, Throgmorton, Ridolfi and Gunpowder Plots – that some Catholic gentlemen believed in a right to resist.[10] The Northern Rising and subsequent Ridolfi Plot represented an important threat to the stability of Elizabeth's government and involved a number of Catholics. The latest interpretation of the 1569 rebellion does not dismiss it as a 'bastard-feudal' phenomenon, a throw-back to the past, but sees the ideas behind it as those of the Tudor Renaissance rather than the old-fashioned 'blood ideology' and 'lineage culture' of the late medieval Border. M. E. James stresses the strength of Northumberland's adherence – under the influence of his mentor, George Clarkson – to the idea of 'order' and to the belief – so dear to the Louvainists, as we have seen – that Protestantism was destructive of political and social stability.[11] Northumberland confessed, after the Rising, that he and the other rebels had consulted two priests on the legality of their intended rebellion and had been told that no resistance to the Queen was licit unless she had been excommunicated, but that, by refusing to receive the Pope's ambassadors, she was 'lawfully excommunicate'.[12] Even if (as seems probable) religion was not the major factor in the Rising, there was clearly some connection in Northumberland's mind between his revolt and the main aspects of Catholic resistance theory as set out later in the reign in the works of the clergy; and the mysterious embassy of Nicholas Morton (probably one of the priests referred to by Northumberland) from the Pope to England in 1569 shows contact between the rebels and exiled Catholic divines. The other Elizabethan plots were individually not of great importance and are difficult to interpret properly, but taken together they do give an impression of less than total belief in non-resistance among the laity. *How many of the laity?*

Various scraps of evidence exist to show support among the laity for the ideology of resistance in the 1580s and early 1590s.[13] The paper found in the church porch by the sexton of St Giles-without-Cripplegate, London, at six o'clock in the morning of 6 July 1582 may well have been the work of a layman.[14] It was dedicated to showing that Bosgrave and Orton, two priests who had given entirely loyal answers to the 'bloody questions', had been misreported by their Protestant interrogators. Various arguments were adduced to prove this. The Protestants, the tract said, often calumniated Catholics, and their lies would be difficult to refute in this case since Bosgrave and Orton were kept closely guarded in the Tower and might not be allowed the opportunity to speak at Tyburn. It was possible that the Protestants had tricked the two priests by asking them ambiguous questions. They had perhaps asked them if they accepted that 'the Pope's Holiness cannot depose princes at his pleasure', and when the priest had agreed, they had reported that 'he denieth the Pope's authority in deposing, when just cause is given'. This paper seems to show that its author believed that a Catholic priest ought to declare that he believed in the papal power to depose princes. Similarly, in 1589 Nathaniel Bacon sent Walsingham a fragment of a letter which he said had been found on the high road near Fakenham in Norfolk, close to the houses of some Catholic gentry. The letter mentioned the failure of the Portugal expedition of that year and the large numbers of men and ships which had been lost during its course. It went on to say that the Protestants blamed the loss of life on disease, 'but certain it is that God and the famous Christian Catholic Spaniards put them to the loss of life and goods in cause and defence of God's true religion and virtue (thanks be to God for it). I hope this hath well cooled the Protestants' potage. I marvel they brag not at this with ringing of bells and bonfires, with triumphs and other melodies. Why do they not make another

that does not → support of revolt.

Pope again to burn at Norwich?'[15] This seems to me to have a very authentic ring to it. At a lower level, papists were occasionally involved in riotous behaviour in the darker corners of England. In 1601 or 1602, for example, papists broke into the church at Emborough in Somerset 'and rent and scattered the service book and tore church Bible and register books'. They left some doggerel verse behind:

> The service book here scattered all
> Is not divine but heretical,
> So is the Bible of false translation;
> To cut it and mangle it is no damnation.[16]

The most seditious laymen were in exile, of course, in fairly large numbers and often in the service of the King of Spain.[17]

It seems to me, in short, that the idea that the Catholic laity as a whole were deeply and sincerely loyal to the Queen is short-sighted and romantic. Elizabeth and her government certainly did not share this faith in Catholic jingoism: they locked up Catholics at times of crisis, disarmed them, and banished them from London – surely not entirely out of bigotry or paranoia. Moreover, in the diplomatic memorials they presented to their foreign allies, the Catholic leaders were prepared to describe the Catholic laity as waiting impatiently for the day of deliverance from the Elizabethan tyranny and prepared at any moment to rise up in armed resistance to throw off its intolerable yoke.[18]

The evidence for the loyalism of the Elizabethan Catholic laity is therefore rather slim and can be contradicted from other sources. We are simply not yet in a position to speak confidently on the subject. The historians of Catholicism – often clergymen themselves – have not unnaturally focused their attention on the heroic exploits of the seminarists, and the history of the Catholic laity under Elizabeth remains to be written. Developments in the local field and the gradually increasing availability of printed records make such a task a reasonable possibility now, but until a reliable statistical, biographical and geographical survey of the sunken portion of the Catholic iceberg is available it is probably best to reserve judgement. Nevertheless, it does seem clear that the view that laity and clergy were at loggerheads over politics – or other matters – needs reassessment. Indeed, even if it were accepted that the laity was on the whole loyal to the Queen, this might be

held to reflect the strength of the clerical hold over them. For two
and a half decades since the accession of Elizabeth – with the
brief exception of the years 1569–73 – the message of the clerical
political writers had been clear: resistance to the Queen was not
lawful. By 1577 the crypto-Catholic Earl of Oxford could dismiss
Papists as 'good Ave Mary coxcombs' who were 'content to lay
down their heads till they were taken off'. Twenty years of sermon-
ising on the value of obedience and loyalism had taken their
toll.[19] Is it surprising, therefore, that by the 1580s the laity had
learnt their lesson and that they looked askance at the sudden
ideological volte-face performed by the clerical pamphleteers
during those years? If Allen and Persons found their new resistant
doctrine unpopular in England they only had themselves to blame
for so firmly inculcating the opposite political theory earlier in the
reign.

In the field of religious resistance it is sometimes argued that
there was a division between priests and layfolk: that the priests
urged their flocks to embrace recusancy and martyrdom, while
many of the laymen were less keen and preferred the unheroic life
of the Church papist (as Catholics who conformed outwardly
to the Church of England came to be known).[20] Two answers may
be made to this. First, that in fact the clergy, as is revealed in
their cases of conscience, were quite prepared to allow a certain
amount of latitude to laymen who needed to attend church and
associate with Protestants to avoid capture or ruin. Second, that
many Catholics accepted whole-heartedly the idea of separation
from Protestants and went to great lengths to avoid religious
contact with them.

A tract written in 1601 describes a singularly resolute piece of
religious resistance performed by the Catholic prisoners in York
Castle with very little in the way of clerical leadership. There
were only two priests in the prison at the time, one of whom was
an old Queen Mary's priest, although he was more effective than
his seminarist colleague. The Council at York, under its new
President Lord Burghley, the tract reveals, organised a series of
sermons to be given to the Catholic prisoners in the castle in an
effort to convert them. The sermons began on 9 December 1599
and continued to be preached at roughly weekly intervals for
nearly a year. The prisoners objected to being forced into religious

contact with heretics in this way, and their spokesman, a gentleman named William Stillington, visited Burghley on several
occasions to voice their opposition to his actions. Stillington was a
skilled amateur theologian and he engaged in a number of
lengthy arguments with the President. He denied that Catholics
were heretics with respect to the Church of England, and that
they should be compelled to take part in its services. Even if they
were to be accounted heretics, as Burghley maintained, this
should rather encourage Anglicans to avoid their company and
religious contact with them. Stillington tried to convince Burghley
by using the very arguments that Catholic advocates of recusancy
themselves used:

I said it was a known thing that the Church used always to excommunicate heretics, and to drive them not only from communion
with the faithful in divine things but even also from civil society and
conversation with them.[21]

Despite Stillington's skill at theological argument, the Catholics
continued to be dragged to the sermons. They tried their best to
disrupt the proceedings. Margaret Silvester, one of the prisoners,
was accustomed to speak out against every preacher, and she
amused the audience, which came to see the fun in the hall of the
castle, by addressing Dr Palmer, one of the speakers, as he came
to the pulpit, thus: 'Out upon you, is it you that must preach?
I was weary of you thirty years since at Doncaster.'[22] The prisoners
murmured together to drown the voice of the preacher, and were
commanded to stop. They stopped, and put their fingers in their
ears. The Lord President ordered the guards to hold down their
arms; they murmured again. Discussions were held on the lawful-
ness of stopping ears. Stillington saw Burghley:

I told his lordship we were of another religion, and it was against our
consciences to be present to hear their sermons, and therefore we
could do no less being hailed thither than stop our ears in sign of
dislike.[23]

It also meant, he pointed out, that they did not have to murmur,
which had annoyed the Lord President. The prisoners presented
a petition defending the stopping of ears: the prophet Isaiah had
commended it as a just act, they said, and it had been used by the
Catholics of old against the Arians. 'It was. . .a secure way to

keep their consciences at quiet, and a harmless defence allowed them by God and the law of nations.'

The establishment of a separate Catholic community in England during Elizabeth's reign was the achievement of both laity and clergy, usually working in harmony. The agreement between the two is admirably expressed in a work written by William Wiseman, a Catholic gentleman, at the end of Elizabeth's reign. He described the ideal of the Tudor gentry:

You expect obedience of your subjects, obedience of your servants, obedience of your tenants, obedience of your children, some obedience also of your wives; and if you have it not, they afflict you . . . They must obey you, they must believe you, they must trust you in everything and do every syllable of your biddings, or else you are angry.[24]

But this admirable state of affairs had a price: 'But how should they do this and you subject unto none?' The next link in the chain was supplied by the clergy. Wiseman put these words into the mouth of an angel:

This we find and know to be most sure, and therefore if God should favour you with my presence among you continually I could say no more unto you but *obedite praepositis vestris,* obey your prelates, and not only so but *subiacete illis,* be subject unto them and be directed by them in all your intentions. And why? *Ipsi enim pervigilant,* for if you do so, they shall answer for your souls and not you for yourselves.[25]

It may be that laymen less humble than Wiseman saw the ideal relationship between cleric and gentleman as based on a greater degree of equality than he did, but that there should be agreement and co-operation between the two essential constituents of the Catholic community in England was accepted by all.

17

The Appellants

THE ORIGIN OF THE IDEAS OF THE APPELLANTS

Whilst it may be true that Persons' *Conference* and the other seditious pamphlets of the years 1584–96 did not find favour with the laity in England, reasoned criticism of their doctrine is confined to the works of Bishop and Southwell, which are themselves rather enigmatic and need to be handled with caution. The real opposition to the ideas of resistance came afterwards, at the end of the century, when, ironically, Persons and those who had propagated seditious and extreme political ideas in the 1580s and early 1590s, had themselves also adopted an ideology of loyalism and non-resistance. The foremost exponents of these new ideas were the Appellant priests, who between 1601 and 1603 published eighteen books, many of which contain lengthy discussions of political matters. The reign of Elizabeth ended amid a great anthem of praise and flattery from these authors, who pledged to her their undying loyalty and their opposition to theories of resistance.

The name 'Appellants' is given to a group of priests who appealed to Rome on two occasions at the end of Elizabeth's reign against the appointment of George Blackwell as Archpriest, or superior of the mission. The English Catholic movement – previously fairly well united – divided as a result of these appeals. The supporters of Blackwell were led by the Jesuit Robert Persons, and opposition to the Society of Jesus was a common theme in the writings of the Appellants. The political ideas of the Appellants were important, and the removal of Blackwell, by no means their sole or even perhaps their principal aim, was intimately connected with their wider ideological and diplomatic concerns. But the division between Appellants and Personsites did not have as much ideological significance as many historians have maintained, because by the end of Elizabeth's reign there was substantial theoretical agreement between the two camps.[1]

What was the origin of the new political ideas of the Appellants? Two influences were brought to bear on these writers, one historical, the other geographic. First, the Appellants were responding to the great change which affected the whole of Catholic Europe in the 1590s. The League had been dished by the conversion of Henry of Navarre in 1593, and Catholics in France had hurriedly set aside ideas of resistance and taken up again the slogans of divine-right monarchy. Spain was beginning to withdraw from her Northern European commitments – the wars with France, England and the Dutch. The Appellants recognised these developments and reflected them in the political messages of their books.[2]

France was the key to the changes in political thought which affected Catholic Europe in the 1590s, and it was the country in which the Appellants felt most at home. Many Elizabethan Catholic exiles had returned to France after Henry IV's conversion, and the four priests who went on the second Appeal to Rome in 1602 received the influential support of the French ambassador there. The Appellants accepted the political ideas of the Catholic *ralliement* to Henry IV – divine right, non-resistance, anti-Jesuitism, anti-papalism, rejection of the ideas of the League, even (to a limited degree) a politique desire for peace with heretics. Catholic anti-Jesuitism in France was of particular interest to the Appellants, since their chief enemy was the Jesuit Robert Persons. Two French Catholic books attacking the Jesuits were published in England by the Appellant William Watson.[3] Their main argument was that the Society of Jesus had been responsible for the extremist political ideas of the period of the League. The same theme ran through many of the works of the Appellants: they sought to blame the resistance theory of the period 1584–96 entirely on Persons.

The great ideologue of the *ralliement* was the Scot William Barclay, whose *De regno* was published in 1600. It was a long and learned attack on the theories of political resistance taught both by the Protestants Hotman and Junius Brutus, and by the Catholic Boucher. As Professor of Laws at Pont-à-Mousson, Barclay was following in the non-resistant footsteps of his predecessor as Dean,

Pierre Grégoire of Toulouse, whose own *De republica* had
appeared in 1596.[4] The faculty of laws at Pont-à-Mousson had a
bitter feud with the Jesuits, and Barclay distrusted them in particular for attempting to inveigle his own son John, a promising
Latinist, into the Society.[5] An Appellant author, Humphrey Ely,
lectured in law at the university while Barclay and Grégoire held
sway there; Arthur Pitts, another Catholic with Appellant sym-
pathies, lived close by; and Robert Charnock was banished there
from Rome after the failure of the First Appeal of 1599.[6]

Finally, it must be noted that the Appellants established closer
links with the English government than any Catholics before in
the reign of Elizabeth. This is reflected to a certain extent in their
political ideas: they wrote in part at least to please their allies at
court. Their main contact was with the enterprising Bishop of
London, Bancroft, who himself worked quite closely with Cecil. It
is not entirely clear what the bishop and minister thought they
were up to, but they gave the Appellants far more than passive
support. The presses of London were put at the disposal of the
Appellants, and their leaders were released from prison to conduct
the campaign. It is not surprising that the ideas contained in these
books were favourable to the Queen and in some cases even
adapted arguments which Protestant authors had used against
Catholics earlier in Elizabeth's reign.

The political thought of the Appellants may be described as
having four main elements. They returned to the non-resistance of
the previous generation and they once again asked for toleration.
They presented in their books an often detailed critique (to some
extent on the lines of Protestant propaganda) of the ideas of
resistance expressed by Allen and Persons in the period 1584–96.
Finally, they assailed the key doctrine of the era of resistance, the
theory of papal political power. These four principal aspects of
their ideology will be dealt with in turn.

LOYALTY AND NON-RESISTANCE

In the books they had printed at the Queen's expense, the Appellants proclaimed their loyalty to her and their belief in non-
resistance. Although they differed from the Queen in religion,

they were nevertheless her 'born subjects and vassals', as Christopher Bagshaw declared, and did not refuse to give their 'native country' and the Queen their 'respect...duties, love and allegiance' simply because they disagreed with her religious policy. They would certainly not rebel against her, as the Jesuits did. Catholics prayed to God with all their hearts 'to heap upon Her Majesty all temporal and heavenly blessings and upon our state sufficient wisdom and prudence for the good continuance of it'.[7] 'Why should not we, the Catholics of England,' Anthony Copley asked, 'suit our fidelities and love (I say not our religion) to our Protestant princess as well as the Protestants of France do theirs to their Catholic king?' Copley then contrasted the obedience of Catholics with the rebelliousness of Protestants like Zwingli, the Taborites, John of Leyden and Thomas Müntzer, thus recalling the arguments of Catholic writers in an earlier period of non-resistance.[8] Religion, Bagshaw said, did not meddle with matters of royal politics; it did not seek to diminish or increase the right of a king to his throne, but left such matters alone. If God should return England to the Catholic Church by supernatural means Catholics would be 'joyful men', but if not, they would be 'content to languish still and die in...[their] sorrows' rather than plot to restore the Church by political means.[9] John Cecil expressed his belief in political non-resistance by quoting Tertullian's words to the pagan emperor: 'this then is your safety in very deed, not your persecuting us, but that we are honest, patient and obedient and that it is more lawful in Christian religion to be killed than to kill'.[10] Some of the Appellants suggested that they should take an oath to the Queen in which they would swear:

I do unfeignedly profess and affirm that I will ever be ready with my body and goods to withstand to mine uttermost power and ability any such forcible and violent attempts with the like faith and true allegiance that becometh all dutiful and faithful subjects of any other Christian prince to withstand any enemy that shall seek by force of arms, of malice and without just cause, to invade or assault any of their possessions, dominions or countries.[11]

TOLERATION AND ANTI-JESUITISM

Encouraged no doubt by the Edict of Nantes in France, and avowedly following the example of Allen's *Apology* (1581), the

Appellants appealed once again to the Queen for toleration.[12] Now, however, they claimed that their contacts with the English government gave them greater assurance of success in achieving some relaxation of the persecution. The Appellants offered the government of Elizabeth a plausible arrangement. This was based on the supposition that there were two sorts of Catholics: loyal obedient subjects of the Queen (the Appellants and most of the laity) and traitors (the Jesuits). The secular priests and their lay supporters in England should be granted toleration of some sort in return for protesting their allegiance to the Queen and renouncing political resistance. The Jesuits, on the other hand, should be expelled from England because they were disloyal to the Queen and would not renounce sedition and plot.[13] Let 'the stroke... light where the offence hath been given,' said William Clarke.[14] The Jesuits should be banished in the same way as the Knights Templar had been driven from France and England in the fifteenth century; William Watson said he would write a whole book comparing the Jesuits and the Templars.[15] If the Jesuits really had 'zeal and charity' for their country, an Appellant wrote, they would be willing to accept their own expulsion from England in order that other Catholics might achieve liberty of conscience as a result.[16]

Anti-Jesuitism was crucial to this aspect of the Appellant programme. Just as their friends in France accused the Jesuits of being responsible for the opposition of the Holy League to Henry of Navarre, so the Appellants said the Society in England was to blame for the resistance of the late 1580s and early 1590s. This explained and justified their opposition to the Archpriest, who was very strongly supported by the Jesuits and whose appointment, they said, was part of a plot to further the political machinations of Persons.[17] Opposition to the Society of Jesus would also, they hoped, provide a plausible enough excuse for the government to favour them after twenty years of persecution and anti-Catholic propaganda. The Appellants reinterpreted recent English history in such a way as to explain the persecution of Catholics and yet allow them to retain their loyalty to the Queen. The Appellants' view of history contrasts markedly with the historical argument of Sander and other writers of the period of political resistance. The Queen's government, they claimed, had by and large been 'both mild and merciful' towards Catholics.[18] If there had been any persecution – and this had been exaggerated in Jesuit books[19] – it was due to the plots of the 1580s and 1590s and the war with Spain, both of which were caused by the Jesuits.[20] William Clarke justified Elizabeth's persecution by asking whether there was 'any prince in the world, be he never so Catholic, that should have within his dominions a kind of people amongst whom divers times he should discover matters of treason and practices against his person and state', and whether in such circumstances a king could not justifiably bring in severe laws against such people. Anthony Copley thought that the ill-treatment of Catholics was also partly caused by the Protestant desire to avenge the events of Mary's reign, when in his opinion blood was too profusely shed. He took the opportunity to compare Elizabeth favourably with Mary, who attained the throne 'through the pikes of a competitor', while the present Queen acceded peacefully and with the universal consent of all Englishmen.[21]

If the Jesuits were recalled from England and if the laity and secular clergy dissociated themselves entirely from the Society of Jesus,[22] the government would have no cause to persecute Catholics, and they could practise their religion unmolested. The Jesuits themselves, the Appellants maintained, opposed toleration because it did not fit in with their ambitious plans for domination in England,[23] or because it 'would make the Catholics of England dull and without spirit', as Bagshaw reported Persons had said at the time of the Treaty of Vervins.[24] It was true, one of the Appellant books admitted, that in *A temperate ward-word*, published in 1599, Persons had asked for toleration, but there 'he dissembleth the matter and feigneth', in typical Jesuitical fashion.[25]

When in Rome, the Appellants used rather different arguments to explain their request for toleration. Clement VIII was decidedly cool on the question when it was first broached by the Appellants on their second Appeal in 1602. He asked them whether they could be among thorns without being pricked and told them that toleration was a 'chimera' which would do more harm than good. The memorial in favour of toleration presented by the Appellants in Rome reflects this hostile attitude.[26] It begins by saying that it is, as a general rule, impious to believe that heretics should not be punished, but that in troubled times the question of toleration (for Catholics) can be raised. Catholics in England are cruelly afflicted; infinite numbers of them now go to Protestant churches but would return to the faith if the bloody and capital laws against Catholics were revoked. Many Catholics defect, especially in the North of England, as a result of the persecution; there are few converts these days because of the penal laws; the Catholic laity is poverty-stricken by the recusancy fines, and, as a result, some priests have no residences and are compelled to wander from place to place, lacking the necessities of life. The greater part of the English – even Anglican pseudo-bishops, ministers and academics – are Catholics at heart, and they would revert to Catholicism if the persecution were reduced in severity. The request for toleration is not unprecedented: Justin Martyr, Tertullian and Aristides of Athens; Allen in his *Apology*; Robert Persons in his *Epistle of the persecution*; and Robert Southwell in his *Humble supplication* all sought it. Only a year ago, the memorial goes on, Persons himself entered into negotiations with the King of France in order to secure toleration for English Catholics. If the persecution were ended the Catholic body in England would be increased in strength, in preparation for the Queen's death and the possible need to help a Catholic claimant to the throne – an argument which could, of course, only be used in Rome. The Appellants urged the Pope to act quickly to secure religious freedom for English Catholics and stressed that a papal condemnation of plotting would be necessary.[27]

THE CRITIQUE OF THE IDEAS OF THE PERIOD OF RESISTANCE (1584–96) AND ANTI-JESUITISM

The Appellants did more than return to the well-worn slogans of non-resistance and appeal again to the Queen for toleration. They reinforced these points by attacking the doctrines of the period of Catholic resistance which had recently passed, and by depicting it as the work of their enemies, the Jesuits. They hoped that this would ingratiate them with the Queen and their new-found Protestant friends, who had themselves been critics of these same ideas. The seditious books and plots of the 1580s and 1590s were repeatedly assailed in the Appellant books. The replies to the royal proclamation of 1591, especially Persons' *Elizabethae*

Angliae reginae,[28] his 'Memorial of the Reformation',[29] *Leicester's Commonwealth*,[30] and Sander's books, were all attacked.[31] The Ridolfi Plot, the Throgmorton Plot, the Babington Plot, the Squire Plot and all other attempts to depose the Queen were criticised.[32] Wherever possible the blame for books and conspiracies, and for the attempted Spanish invasion, was put on the Society of Jesus. Persons, it was said, had tried 'to dye his cap with English blood and to enrich the Spaniards with the spoils of our country under pretence of bringing in religion'.[33] The Jesuits were involved with Persons in all the plots:

The old saying was, let the shoemaker meddle with his slipper, the smith with his anvil, and the priests with their prayers; but the Jesuits like frank gamesters are in at all . . . matters of state, titles of princes, genealogies of kings, rights of succession, disposing of sceptres, and such affairs, are their chief studies.[34]

The writings and seditious activities of the Jesuits moved the Appellant authors to prayer: 'God preserve this realm from their Spanish designments; Her Majesty from their Clements, Barrières and Ehuds of the Jesuitical inspiration; the good estate of the Catholic Church from their frantic deformations; us poor secular priests from their malicious practices; and you all true Catholics from the leaven of such Pharisees. Amen!'[35] Bagshaw took up the same strain: 'we will always remember as an addition when we say the litany: a machinationibus Parsoni, libera nos, Domine.'[36]

The Appellants had something of a difficulty when it came to Cardinal Allen. They always expressed their affection for him and looked back to his non-resistant writings of the early 1580s for inspiration,[37] but it was difficult for them to deny that he had played some part in the composition of the tracts which expressed ideas of resistance, or in the plots to overthrow Elizabeth by rebellion or invasion. It was necessary to invent the fiction that Persons had written Allen's most extreme works of resistance, the *Admonition* and the 'Defence of Stanley';[38] or that he had perverted the Cardinal from his former non-resistance.[39] To add to the story it was said that towards the end of his life Allen had seen the light and turned against the Jesuits and Persons.[40] The non-resistant Allen was acceptable to the Appellants, but the resistant Allen had to be seen as a Jesuit perversion.

The book most frequently criticised by the Appellants was
Robert Persons' *Conference*, and the policy most often attacked
was the support Persons had given to the Infanta as a candidate
for the succession on the death of Elizabeth. Criticism of the
Conference and the policy behind it dates back to 1595 when the
book was published. William Gifford, Dean of Lille, who was
later a supporter of the Appellants, denounced it as soon as it was
published as 'the most pestilent that ever was made' and said that
the papal nuncio in the Netherlands, with whom he had considerable influence, had told him 'that Persons had ruined himself and
that the Pope would detest his behaviour and that he could never
have done anything more disgustable to the Pope'.[41] In the English
College at Rome, which was troubled at the time by the sixteenth-
century equivalent of student demonstrations, the dissident
scholars were outraged by the book and its pro-Spanish doctrine.[42]
Even the Scottish Jesuit William Creighton wrote to Persons in
1596 criticising the book and expressing the fear that it would do
more harm than good in England. Creighton's real objection to
the *Conference* was that it was unfavourable to James VI, whose
cause he supported in the succession debate.[43] Creighton published
a short tract in 1598 setting out the claims of the Scottish king to
the throne of England,[44] and within a few years other such works
had appeared, from the pens of John Cecil, John Colville and
William Clitheroe. All these books sought to combine attacks on
Persons' genealogical exercises with denunciation of the resistance
theory to be found in the first part of the *Conference*.

John Cecil exhorted Catholics to follow the model of the
Church Fathers, of Cardinal Allen and of Fathers Campion and
Heywood, and to seek the conversion to Catholicism of King
James of Scotland, not 'in the spirit of contradiction and contention, in the spirit of singularity and ambition, not in the court of
princes, by supplications, memorials, and relations, but in the
court of heaven with prayers, penance, tears and oblations'.
Catholics should use peaceful methods to achieve their political
aims: 'by the Word and not by the sword, by sanctity and not by
subtlety, by painful labours and not by disdainful libels, by sub-
mission and not by sedition, by persuasions and not by invasions,
by requests and not by conquests'.[45] Colville presented his odd
little book, the *Palinod* (1600), as the refutation of a tract that he

claimed he himself had written before against the Stuart claim, and which is described in such a way as to suggest a parody of the *Conference* itself. The foundation of his former attack on the Stuart pretension was, Colville said, that 'by right or law of nature nothing is mine nor thine, but all be common, nothing proper, and no proprietare; ergo, by law of nature no propriety can be acclaimed.' From his former communism Colville had rather over-reacted, and he now maintained that 'the prince is the immediate lord of our bodies, and of all our worldly fortunes, having power to dispose thereupon at his pleasure'. James VI, having read the book, declared that Colville had 'gone mad', and it is hard not to agree with him.[46] Slightly more serious than the *Palinod* was a work by William Clitheroe published in 1600 and entitled *A discovery of a counterfeit conference.*[47] It was entirely devoted to a refutation of the *Conference* both because it opposed the King of Scots' claim to the succession and because it set out monarchomach political thought. The *Conference* was in reality harmful to the King of Spain, Clitheroe said, because it contained seditious political doctrine. It taught, for example, that 'a multitude having once got by any indirect practice a counterfeited name of a commonwealth...may lawfully place and displace kings and sovereigns according to their restless humours and affection', and that 'the sovereign shall be forced to accommodate himself agreeable to the manners and conditions of his subjects'.[48] 'This popular doctrine', the author said, had been first preached in Scotland by George Buchanan, then taken to the Low Countries and next used in Aragon by Antonio Perez against the King of Spain. According to such doctrine a king had to serve his people 'like a lackey or page in a French joupe to run and ride' after them.[49] He said that to endow the commonwealth with the power Persons had given it in the *Conference* was to make it infallible and hence was a blasphemous insult to the Church, and that if rulers were made dependent on the people rather than on God there would be no difference between kings and tyrants. But usually he relied on mockery and bluster rather than reason and argument; on his own behalf he went little further than the commonplace analogical arguments in favour of kingship. His most telling point against the *Conference* was that its author placed too much reliance on history, 'as if right ought to follow possession', and that by stressing what had been done he had failed to comment on whether it ought to have been done or not.[50] The *Discovery* concluded by defending the claim of the King of Scots, saying that he would probably be reconciled to the Church as Henry of Navarre had been and that the best lawyers of England – in opposition to the fictitious lawyers through whom Persons spoke in the *Conference* – favoured his right to the succession.

The Appellants continued to attack the *Conference* and the pro-Spanish policy of Persons in their books, although their negotiations in Rome and England meant that they found it difficult openly to express any opinion on the matter of the succession.[51] William Clarke praised the *Discovery of a counterfeit conference* and said it was a pity that it was not better known since it showed 'what a gallimaufry' Persons would make 'of laws, common, civil and ecclesiastical and of the whole commonwealth'. Like the author of the *Discovery*, Clarke claimed that Persons had taken his doctrine from Buchanan and that he sought to 'set up the people against their sovereigns'. He took the opportunity to affirm his own belief in non-resistance, pointing out that 'in ancienter times', Christians had prayed for the tyrants who ruled them and had asked God that the tyrants' children should succeed them even though they were 'no better than their fathers'. He felt that Persons had not understood the full consequences of the ideology of resistance. The people were 'not easily staid' when they had accepted such a doctrine and, moreover, 'popularity in the civil state doth not well digest a monarchy in the ecclesiastical'.[52] Another Appellant writer saw Persons' use of the ideology of resistance as a mere expedient. Once the Infanta had been made Queen through such a doctrine, the tune would change: 'that done, a new doctrine quite contrary must be delivered abroad, that there was a happy mistaking, which advanced him or her to this throne; but hereafter the people must take heed of attempting the like; some check must be given to the publishers of such documents; a dispensation must be procured and all shall be well hereafter'.[53] Anthony Copley described in lurid terms the danger of Spanish rule in England. It might bring 'Indie gold', but at such a price 'we had better be pleased with our English copper': 'the same when we have it to be forthcoming to the Spanish magistrate's extortion, and perhaps, to every rascal Spanish soldier's rapine; or haply in lieu thereof, the horn to your forehead, or the rape of your daughter, or the buggery of your son, or the sodomising of your sow, with thousands such like insolencies and shames as are all natural to that torrid nation and you had better be dead than endure'.[54]

As part of the arrangement with Elizabeth's government, the Appellants in Rome sought a condemnation of seditious political activity by English Catholics and of the publication of political tracts. They attacked the Jesuits most strongly for meddling in politics in this way and said that priests should avoid political involvement.[55] William Watson quoted Pierre Grégoire of Toulouse where he exclaimed against 'new smattering divines... who falsely pretend that they are led by zeal, who in their pulpits and lectures cast out not words of modesty or of the word of God, but lightnings and thunderings; who as outrageous men in railing, utter nothing but taunts, scoffs, swords, fires, rages, furies of hell, matters of blood and murtherings'.[56] John Mush answered the accusation that the Appellants themselves were as deeply involved in political matters as the Jesuits because of their support for James VI's title to the succession. He said that this could easily be disproved by considering 'that we are highly favoured by the state and maintained by the Council and magistrates'; they would not have found such favour had they been Scotists. But this simply begged the question of their contacts with the government of Elizabeth.[57]

William Watson gave a much more honest description of how the Appellants looked upon the political activity of priests. He said that the clergy had perforce to deal in matters of state. Bishops might need to engage in the work of statesmen, while the lesser clergy had a political role to perform by instructing their flock 'how they are to behave themselves to God, their prince and their country; when and in what cases bound to acknowledge obedience to the one or the other... and what is to be done in times of persecution, civil wars or foreign invasions and the like'. This, Watson said, was done in the confessional and by means of books. But the Catholic clergy in England should not do the following: 'take upon them by word or writing to impugn the Parliamental laws and statutes made'; meddle in matters of succession; 'control' the actions of the government or 'impeach' the activities of the Council; or publish books which might exasperate the government. They should work to secure toleration, oppose libellous books and 'admonish all good Catholics to bear Christ His cross with patience'.[58] Thus, 'not meddling in politics' meant to Watson teaching reconciliation to the Protestant government and non-resistance. It would have been unthinkable for a cleric in the sixteenth century not to play a part, broadly speaking, in politics. The function of the clergy in political society was to act as an organ of propaganda, to give ideological instruction and advice. The Appellants did not object to priests fulfilling this function, only to resistance.

CRITICISM OF JESUIT IDEAS OF EQUIVOCATION AND OF RELIGIOUS RESISTANCE

Any stick would serve to beat the Jesuits. Like their Protestant allies, the Appellants also criticised the Jesuits for their use of equivocation, which Bagshaw described as 'in plain English, lying and cogging'. He said it harmed Catholics because it gave the government justification for not trusting them:

For example, they may ask us whether we have taught or affirmed that Her Majesty hath no interest to the crown of England, and we answer that we never have either so taught or affirmed. 'Tush,' say they, 'you equivocate with us, you keep this in your minds, viz., "as long as the Bishop of Rome will suffer her", or some such like point.' We answer that we do keep no such thing in our minds. 'Oh,' say they, 'you keep no such thing in your minds "to tell us"; we know your shifts.'

Bagshaw said he preferred the strict doctrine of Soto with regard to equivocation.[59]

Presumably more for their own satisfaction than to impress the Queen, the Appellants occasionally also attacked the Jesuits for being too lax in their doctrine with regard to religious resistance. The Jesuits, it was maintained, had allowed occasional conformity in Scotland, where they had taught that recusancy was only necessary 'if one were a notorious known Catholic where he came' to church, for 'then they taught it to be unlawful in that place to go to church by reason of scandal, and no otherwise'. In

England the Jesuits Garnet and Southwell (Robert Charnock wrote) had held that Catholics could engage in religious debates with Protestant churchmen to avoid imprisonment, but had been corrected on this point in 1591 by the seculars, Colleton and Charnock himself. The Jesuits had taught in the Roman College that it was merely unlawful to go to church in so far as it was a 'sign distinctive' of Protestantism; Frs Bosgrave, Langdale and Kirkham (it was reported) had gone to church in England; and the Society was generally lax on this point.[60] John Mush said Jesuits had allowed mixed marriages, and had taught that a gentleman might 'have licence to eat flesh in Lent, and in all fasting days, among Lollards and Protestants, that by so doing he might live without suspicion of being a Catholic and escape danger of the laws'. Mush attacked this doctrine and said that it was either mortal sin or very close to it to do so; it was scandalous and prejudicial to the Catholic religion in England; and, moreover, he said, 'the opinion of all the learned [was] that no man ought to do anything, either scandalous or prejudicial to the faith of the Church, for to save himself from a temporal harm'.[61]

CRITICISMS OF THE THEORY OF PAPAL POLITICAL POWER

In the books they published in England the Appellants also attacked the linchpin of Catholic political resistance, the doctrine of papal political power. In this respect their political thought represents a distinctly new phase in the history of Elizabethan Catholicism, because with the exception of John Bishop's book – itself an enigma – no other Catholic writers had opposed the doctrine openly. There is, however, an interesting paper attributed to a priest called Thomas Wright, and dating from probably shortly after 1594, which foreshadows the doctrine of the Appellants. The paper is strongly anti-Spanish, in the spirit of the changed outlook of Catholics at the end of Elizabeth's reign, and it opposes violent methods of restoring Catholicism to England. It was written to prove that it was lawful for English Catholics to take up arms against a Spanish invasion, even if the Spaniards had papal support. Wright did not deny papal political power, but circumscribed it considerably. The Pope might err in supporting Spain; he was only infallible in matters of faith, not in matters of fact. It might not be to the benefit of the Church for the Spanish Empire to be enlarged, since if the Spaniards fell into heresy or reverted to Mohammedanism their great Empire would be lost to it. Finally, the Pope had to use his temporal power with the support, and at the instance, of the 'whole community or the chief heads' of the country concerned.[62]

The same attitude to papal political power is evident in the work of the Appellants. The Appeal to Rome against the authority of the Archpriest, who had been appointed by a papal official and confirmed by a Pope, indicates in itself a certain amount of cisalpine independence on the part of the Appellants, even without any discussion of the temporal power of the Holy See. They showed little respect for the Cardinal Protector who had appointed Blackwell; his protectorship, they said, gave him no jurisdiction over the English clergy.[63] The Pope himself could err in matters of fact, one Appellant said, and it was not necessarily disobedience to resist the Pope's will 'proceeding from false information': 'for often times the error of his understanding procured by false surreption is such that it maketh his decree a determination unvoluntary, in which case to obey it were to gainsay his absolute will and truly to disobey him'.[64] Humphrey Ely adopted the same tone. 'The Pope is a man,' he wrote, 'and as a man may err and sin, for he hath his passions of love and dislike...he may be ill informed and by that information do wrong and injustice to another.' Ely asked whether the Pope was better than St Peter to whom he had succeeded. As far as his spiritual authority was concerned he was 'God on earth', but in other respects he might sin. Ely believed piously that all Popes were in heaven, but, he said, it was no article of faith so to hold.[65]

It would be wrong to see the Appellants as fully-fledged Gallicans, but they were prepared to press their case, despite the failure of the Appeal in Rome, and they tended in their English books to be rather outspoken. It is interesting to note that although on occasion they attacked the Jesuit opposition to the Appeals as the erection of a new Praemunire and used the precedent of Thomas Becket to justify freedom of appeal to Rome,[66] yet at other times they opposed the appointment of the Archpriest on the grounds of Praemunire itself, because it might offend the

State. Many princes in Christendom had made laws similar to the Statute of Praemunire, Mush wrote, to ensure that whatever came from the Pope had been 'seen and approved by men appointed for that purpose', that it had been 'rightly obtained', was 'authentical', and was 'without injury or prejudice to any'.[67]

In attacking the doctrine of papal political power itself most of the Appellants showed a certain degree of theological restraint. They tried to criticise certain aspects and manifestations of papal power in temporals, without totally renouncing the doctrine. There is a good deal of slipperiness about the passages in which the Appellants discuss the matter. On the one hand they wanted to impress the Queen with their boldness; on the other they hoped to avoid giving too much offence to the Pope. Anthony Copley said that papal bulls against Elizabeth had been 'surreptive' and 'granted forth by them as men, and not as Popes', and hence Catholics could oppose them, just as Charles V had fought against the Pope in similar circumstances. This was exactly the line taken by the Appellants over the papal brief confirming the Archpriest's appointment, and Allen himself in his *A true, sincere and modest defence* had defended Charles V in the same case.[68] In a later book Copley said that the Pope could not command the Appellants to stop writing patriotic books preaching non-resistance. He went on to say that Popes had been 'I will not say to blame', but 'overseen', in their policy towards Elizabeth. They should have followed a policy of 'lenity and oil' rather than one of 'bulls and censures of excommunication and deprivation'. Copley now repeated the point his colleagues had made with reference to Blackwell's appointment: 'His Holiness's infallibility is only peremptory through the Holy Ghost in matters merely of faith and not of fact.' In questions of state the Pope might easily err, since, as a priest, he had no experience of such affairs. Times had changed; this was an age of 'discession' from Rome and of 'Antichrist's antelope'. Kings were no longer willing to submit to the temporal sovereignty of the Pope. He for his part should move with the times and 'shift the reins into his left hand and benignly, though somewhat sinisterly to retain Christian princes' by using gentler tactics. Popes had shown lenity in the past with the House of Austria and French kings; why, Copley asked, had they been so severe with the Tudors? Finally, he denied that the Pope had 'implicite nor explicite, as Christ's Vicar other commission out of Christ's own words than that which Christ said himself to have, viz., no kingdom of this world, but merely pastoral' authority:

No no ... Saint Peter had no keys commissioned him by Christ as Caesar, but as a shepherd, as appears plain by the words of his commission, Pasce oves meas, pasce agnos meos. Neither is His Holiness at this day a temporal prince, but only in little Romania and that by the bounty (as ye may read) of our countryman Constantine Caesar.[69]

This looks pretty anti-papal at first blush, but is in fact no more than Bellarmine admitted; it is simply a denial of *direct* papal political power.

The furthest any of the Appellants went was to say that it would be right to oppose an invasion of England which had the approval of Rome. This was maintained by Bluet briefly and then at more length by Watson and Clarke. The two latter also said, however, that despite this they accepted the doctrine of papal political power, while Bluet was very short and said that 'our purpose is not to dispute this point'.[70] Watson reported with approval what two prominent Catholic laymen, Viscount Montague and Lord Dacre, had said:

That if the Pope himself should come in with cross, key and gospel in his hand, he would be ready with the first to run unto [him] ... in all humbleness of heart, and what not, to show himself a dutiful child. But if instead of coming in solemn procession with cross, book, prayers and preaching, he should come in a sounding royal march with heralds of arms ... then would he be the first man in the field ... to resist him in the face with all his might and power ...

But in another section of the same book Watson spoke of papal political power in terms which show he accepted its theological basis, even if he disagreed with its use. He quoted St Paul: 'All things are lawful unto me, but all things are not expedient', and he blamed the English Catholics who had asked Pius V to issue *Regnans in excelsis*, rather than the Pope himself.[71] Clarke also maintained that it was lawful to resist a papal invasion, but explicitly said that the Pope had indirect power in temporals. He tried, rather unsuccessfully, to draw a distinction between such a power and the implementation of its sentence, which he said was a matter to be left to God. Heretics should be reconverted by evangelical and not violent methods. The subject was bound by the law of nature to resist the invasion of his country, and in a defensive war of this sort priests themselves could take part. Even if the Pope had a just cause to invade, it would also be just for Catholics to oppose him: 'many times the invader or oppugner hath just cause to invade with arms and therein doth no injustice and yet for all that, on the contrary side, the defendants may justly by force of arms keep and defend themselves'.[72]

Despite the caution the Appellants showed when attacking papal political power, it must be admitted nevertheless that to criticise the doctrine at all was a new departure in the history of Elizabethan Catholic political thought and one which might have made possible the establishment of better relations between the Protestant government and English Catholics. The Appellants were important in three respects. First, the Appeals represented a serious rift in what had hitherto been an almost undivided movement; they were, moreover, significant from the point of view of the organisation of the mission. The disagreement between the heirs of the Appellants and the heirs of Robert Persons continued into the next century, and with great passion shown on both sides. Second, the Appellants had a plan; to secure toleration and favour from the Protestant government in return for a sort of Concordat with Rome and the expulsion of the Jesuits. This failed both in Rome and England. Third, the Appellants expressed political ideas of non-resistance with more clarity and less ambiguity than ever before. But a certain amount of caution should be exercised when considering these political ideas, which were designed at least partly to win the favour of the government.

When in Rome and faced with the accusation that their books had gone too far in praising the Queen and attacking papal power, the Appellants renounced all but the three dullest (in political terms) of the tracts they had printed. Moreover, several of the more senior Appellants wrote to Watson criticising his *Decacordon*, which was one of the more outspoken writings in its expression of loyalty to the Queen.[73] The way in which they treated Southwell's *Humble supplication* (printed in 1600) shows the opportunism of the Appellants.[74] This book expressed ideas of non-resistance and loyalism similar in many ways to those held at the time by the Appellants themselves. Yet, because it was written by a Jesuit, far from accepting it as a work which supported their

cause, they used every means to criticise it. They attacked it for
its flattery of the Queen (especially in Rome),[75] but they also
excoriated Southwell for the disrespect he had shown to Walsingham (especially in England).[76] Only Copley had a good word for
Southwell, his cousin.[77] The non-resistance of the Appellant
authors is in two cases belied by their actions. In 1603, William
Watson and William Clarke, two of the most eloquent pamphleteers, were executed, along with Anthony Champney, veteran of
the first Appeal to Rome, for their part in the 'Bye Plot', their
exasperated reaction to James I's failure to live up to their
expectations. Furthermore, most of the Appellants opposed the
Oath of Allegiance, the oath framed by James I after the Gunpowder Plot which in part derived from the earlier oaths and
protestations suggested by them under Elizabeth, while, ironically,
their greatest enemy, George Blackwell, the hated Archpriest, lost
his nerve and took the oath. But what puts the political ideas of
the Appellants into perspective best is to compare them with those
expressed by their opponents in the Archpriest Controversy,
Robert Persons and his supporters, because they had also returned
to political non-resistance.

18

Robert Persons and non-resistance
1596–1603

THE RETREAT FROM RESISTANCE

The retreat from political resistance which is so evident in the
work of the Appellants embraced the whole English Catholic
movement. William Rainolds' career illustrates this well. In 1590
he published the *De iusta reipublicae...authoritate* at Paris, one
of the most extreme expressions of resistance of the League.[1] In
1592 it was republished at Antwerp, probably for an English
audience, with a chapter on tyrannicide omitted.[2] The following
year Rainolds returned to theology, writing a defence of the
Catholic doctrine of the mass, to which was added a preface in
which the rights of James VI of Scotland to the English throne
were briefly set out and the king was warned of 'the very bane and
pest of well ordered commonwealths', Calvinists, who taught men
that they might 'live how they please against the magistrate and
his civil laws'.[3] Before he died in 1594, Rainolds had completed
his *Calvino-Turcismus*, which his friend William Gifford published in 1597. There was no sign in this book of a slackening in
Rainolds' religious fervour; it was written, as its title suggests, to
show the similarities between Calvinism and Mohammedanism.
But the political zeal of four years before had evaporated. At one
point Rainolds nearly discussed politics, but decided against doing
so. He quoted two texts, Exodus 22. 28, 'thou shalt not revile the
gods, nor curse the ruler of thy people', and Proverbs 20, 'the fear
of the king is as the roaring of a lion'.[4] Private persons should not
meddle in politics, 'because in subjects it is a sort of arrogance'.
Men who could not even rule their wives or households should
not discuss the affairs of princes, because these were quite beyond
their grasp. Travellers in strange countries – as Rainolds had been
in France – should especially avoid political discussion, and he

told a cautionary tale of two Florentines who visited Ragusa. They were overheard chatting about the possibilities of a Venetian conquest of the city, were arrested, imprisoned and finally executed. Rainolds commented: 'it is very dangerous to talk about matters which concern princes even in a joking fashion or in familiar conversation'.[5]

Rainolds' abandonment of resistance in the 1590s was part of a movement which affected even Robert Persons and his supporters. The Appellants and later historians were wrong in portraying Persons as still holding to the ideology of political resistance, as still being opposed to toleration for Catholics in England, and as still hoping to effect the conversion of England by Spanish invasion. In most respects Persons and his supporters had gone as far from the positions of resistance they had held in the late 1580s and early 1590s as had the Appellants, although some elements of the earlier ideology remain in their writings at the end of the reign of Elizabeth, and Persons' diplomatic activity suggests that he was not yet fully resolved to follow the path of political non-resistance.

Persons' *Conference* was published in 1595, two years after it was written and right at the end of the period of Elizabethan Catholic resistance. Persons' sensitivity to criticism of the book and the measures he took to defend it in Rome in 1597 indicate a realisation on his part that the prevailing Catholic ideological climate was now antipathetic to such books. After the *Conference* he published nothing for four years. His 'Memorial' was written in 1596 and not printed at the time.[6] This book represents a retreat from the ideas of the *Conference*; it does not set out resistance theory or discuss the conquest of England, and a large part of it is concerned with matters of religious reformation; on the other hand, of course, it does assume the sudden Catholic 'conversion' of England, and perhaps for this reason Persons did not have it printed. Before publishing his next work, *A temperate ward-word*, in 1599, Persons circulated a short memorial in Rome describing the pamphlet by Sir Francis Hastings to which his book replied and drawing attention to the need to refute it, presumably to forestall criticism.[7] In *A temperate ward-word* Persons set out for the first time his new political thought of non-resistance. He and his supporters – and other Catholic writers not associated with either the Jesuits or the Appellants – continued to express such ideas in the books they published in the remaining years of the reign.

LOYALTY AND NON-RESISTANCE

Persons expressed his loyalty to the Queen and belief in non-resistance eloquently in *A temperate ward-word*:

Unto our temporal prince and head of our earthly commonwealth whereof we are citizens, we owe all temporal obedience in civil matters according to the law of God, nature and nations, and according to the particular ordinances of the country wherein we dwell; and so we are to serve him with our bodies, goods, life and whatsoever other earthly means or commodity we have besides in all just causes. And this with all honour, fidelity, readiness, alacrity and promptness of mind, as to the minister of God, ordained ... for punishing of the wicked and comforting the good. And this obedience was due also unto heathen magistrates in Christ's time, for in this temporal government Christ altered nothing at all, but left it as he found it.[8]

In political matters Catholics were taught non-resistance, Persons said; they only refused to obey the Queen in religious affairs, which was lawful and had no effect on their political loyalty.

Writing at the same time, Richard Broughton spoke of the Queen as 'my Catholicly christened, anointed and crowned Queen Elizabeth to whom I wish both as much spiritual benediction and terrene honour as any subject may to his temporal sovereign, or as I would if she were of my own religion'.[9] Thomas Fitzherbert praised the Queen for 'her many princely parts, her power by sea and land, her peace at home, her prosperity abroad, her long life and reign'.[10] Robert Chambers called her 'the glory of England, the gem of all the world', expressed the hope that she would reign forever, said that no one was worthy to pronounce her name, and praised her gracious government of the country.[11] With a few exceptions, Persons said, Catholics 'have lived with that dutiful obedience to Her Majesty in all temporal matters which to any of her Catholic ancestors hath ever been exhibited by their dearest people'.[12] Catholics were loyal and obedient in all countries where they were in a minority – in Saxony, Denmark,

Switzerland, Greece, Hungary, Turkey and Persia.[13] Puritans, on the other hand, had shown themselves to be disloyal. Persons drew a picture of England divided into three religions – Catholics, Puritans and Protestants – and urged the Queen not to listen to Puritans who told her to persecute Catholics, but on the contrary to keep the two factions balanced so as to preserve the politico-religious equilibrium of England. This argument he had used before, notably in *Leicester's Commonwealth*. In attacking Puritans and praising the Queen, Persons was even drawn to speak of 'the valour and prudence' of the Protestant party in England which had kept puritanism in check.[14] While some Catholic authors preferred to continue attacking the politics of all Protestants, others criticised the Puritans alone; thus, one author (possibly Verstegan) described them as teachers of democracy and communism.[15]

The country was to be converted to Catholicism, these writers maintained, by non-violent means. Persons wrote in one of his replies to the Appellants:

There is no doubt or question but that the dutiful manner of carriage hitherto used by our English recusant Catholics in all humility, patience, longanimity, obedience and true spirit of Christian sufferance, ... is absolutely the best way and most pleasing in the sight both of God and man and the principal means whereby we may hope that God will one day have mercy upon us and our country and inspire the hearts both of our prince and state to deal more mildly and mercifully with us.[16]

This was the language of the early 1580s again. Thomas Fitzherbert, a protégé of Persons, repeated the formula: 'this then is the conquest that we desire and expect in England, to wit, a conquest of souls to God, with the suppression of heresy and iniquity'.[17]

The Bull of Excommunication of 1570 was treated in the same way as it had been by Bristow in 1574 and by other Catholic writers in the early 1580s after the papal faculty given to Persons and Campion. In *A temperate ward-word* Persons did all he could to make the bull seem innocuous. The Pope had waited 'a dozen' years before taking any action after the Queen's accession. He had been moved to promulgate the bull by the action of the Protestants in England who had attempted to root out

Catholicism, had slandered the Pope, calling him Antichrist, and had helped heretics all over Europe to rebel against their princes. The Pope would not have acted in such a hostile way towards Elizabeth if the English had 'taken that course which Protestants did in Germany', which was 'to follow...new opinions without galling of others'. Above all, the bull had little to do with the Catholics of England. They had not been consulted by the Pope about it and could not express their approval or disapproval of it to him. Even after the bull, the subject could continue both to reverence his 'natural prince' and to respect the Pope, and 'rather ...commend the matter to almighty God, which is the only thing that resteth for a pious and dutiful subject to perform in such cases, when two superiors shall disagree, until God by his goodness shall determine the controversy and bring all to some happy end as he hath done of late in France'.[18]

In their books published at the end of the reign of Elizabeth Persons and other authors continued to defend English Catholics as martyrs for the faith and to refute the accusation that they were traitors against the Queen. Such a line of argument served to underline their belief in non-resistance, but also to refute the Appellants when they argued that the Queen's government was 'mild and merciful' and when they accused Persons and the Jesuits of plotting the death of Elizabeth and the conquest of England by Spain.[19] Thomas Worthington published a book in 1601 briefly discussing the divisions between Jesuits and Appellants and describing as an example of the Queen's mild mercifulness how sixteen English Catholics had been martyred in the previous twelve months.[20]

Two books were written in 1599 by protégés of Persons – Martin Aray and Thomas Fitzherbert – to deal with the Squire Plot, an alleged attempt on the life of the Queen in which Jesuits were accused of having some part.[21] These authors protested the innocence of the Jesuits of any involvement in plots to assassinate the Queen or other princes. Jesuits, above all men, Aray said, 'detest such bloody means in all their speeches, doctrine and proceedings, leaving them to the adversary spirit of Protestants, Puritans and such other like teachers, who both preach and practise such attempts'.[22] The Squire Plot, and other conspiracies in which Catholics had been involved, were contrived by the government 'for holding Catholics in hatred and suspicion' or 'for better continuing of our breach with Spain'.[23] The reality of the matter was that Catholics executed for a part in such supposed plots were 'innocent servants of God', 'whose glory both in heaven and earth will be the greater in that their pains are inflicted with double wrong'.[24] The common people in England, seeing Catholics put to death as traitors, were brought by the government to imagine 'that all Catholics are perturbers and enemies of the commonwealth' and that their doctrines, far from being the 'common and general religion of Christendom' and the faith of their forefathers, were the 'pestilent opinion of some sect sprung up of late that cannot stand with the safety of kings and princes, nor with the quietness of their states'.[25] Fitzherbert described the ill-treatment of Catholics in England and how for many years they had been accused of treason and unjustly tortured. Like Allen in the early 1580s, he excused the Queen and her councillors from blame for the persecution,[26] placing it on evil councillors who, to extend their own power over the Queen, tried to keep her constantly in a state of fear, at war with Spain and suspicious of Catholics in England.[27]

In reply to both Appellants and Protestants Persons and his supporters defended the Jesuits from criticism. The Jesuits were bound by a rule 'not to meddle in matters of estate' and had played no part in plots to murder princes. Persons said that he himself had actually dissuaded Catholics who wanted to assassinate the Queen.[28] He defended his own books and political activity from attack, saying that he and other Jesuits had taken no part in the various conspiracies against Elizabeth and had not been directly involved in the preparations for the Armada.[29] The suggestion that William Allen was prepared to accompany the Armada into England was strongly denied.[30] Thomas Fitzherbert said that he, Sir Francis Englefield, Persons and Cresswell had advised Philip II in the early 1590s that 'it was not convenient for him to seek the conquest of England, nor probable either that he could conquer it, or yet if he were able to do it that he could long keep it in subjection'. They had all hoped that if the King were successful in conquering England – and they suspected that he would not be – the liberties of the English would be respected, and generally they preferred more peaceful ways of converting the country.[31] More recently, Persons said, English Catholics had played no part in the Spanish support for the Tyrone Rebellion.[32]

Persons pointed out that it was unfair of the Appellants to attack his books and not those of other Catholics who had written about politics during the period of resistance. He mentioned the works of Sander, Bristow and Cardinal Allen and asked 'how then is Father Persons only named...as though his writings only were the cause of all exasperation?'[33] In the *Ward-word* Persons had defended the books written by such men as the judgement of older children on a quarrel between mother (Elizabeth) and father (Pope), given while the younger children (the Catholics of England) kept themselves out of the argument.[34] Persons also said that some of the Appellants themselves had been advocates of political resistance a decade before. He chose an old enemy of his, William Gifford, a supporter of the Appeals, as an example. Gifford, according to Persons, had delivered violent political sermons at the seminary of Rheims before the Duke of Guise; he had also shown his belief in resistance in letters to Allen and Englefield. Finally Persons adduced as evidence of Gifford's former resistance the *De iusta reipublicae...authoritate*, saying it contained 'violent matter against all princes', especially against the Catholic King of France.[35] This book is now usually attributed to William Rainolds alone, but since Gifford is also credited by a contemporary with a Ligueur tract, and since he probably acted as Rainolds' literary executor in the case of two of his other books, perhaps he had some part in this one as well. Persons' attack on Gifford is perfectly accurate, however, in suggesting that the political resistance of the 1580s and 1590s was not simply the work of Persons and the Jesuits.[36]

TOLERATION

In the English Catholic literary tradition, statements of loyalty to the Queen had, since 1580, been accompanied by the request for toleration, and this tradition continued in the works of Persons and his party in the last years of Elizabeth's reign. At the end of *A temperate ward-word* Persons expressed the hope that the Queen and her Council would, like Henry IV of France, be converted to Catholicism. But, if this was impossible, he expressed the wish that Catholics might 'have the same liberty and favour in England for their consciences as Protestants have in France and in other states of the Empire at this day under Catholic kings and emperors'. He then described the dangerous consequences of not granting toleration; 'English natures are vehement, as all men know', he said, and he predicted that the religious differences of England might have lamentable political consequences. After this threat he painted a happy picture of England united by religious toleration:

all sorts of people merry, contented, loving and confident within the realm; all to laugh and sing together; all to pray to God most heartily for Her Majesty's health, wealth, and prosperous long continuance; all to be united in defence of the realm; all made friends and familiar together, as in Germany and other places men be, notwithstanding the differences of religion, which more easily perhaps would be taken away and union brought in, when freely and confidently men might confer, and each man show his reason without fear and hear another man's arguments without suspicion of fraud or violence to be used.[37]

Another Catholic author asked specifically for the freedom to set up seminaries in England and to have bishops to ordain the priests. In return, he said, Catholic exiles would give up the pensions and allowances they received from foreign princes which aroused the suspicion of the English government.[38]

There were even some suggestions in the works of the Catholics at the end of Elizabeth's reign that they themselves were becoming less intolerant towards heretics. Thomas Worthington put forward a rather startling argument for the toleration of recusants in England. He said that the Catholic Church 'is so far from urging or forcing those that be not Catholics to be present at mass, matins, or at any public office in the Church that she alloweth none such at all to enter in, nor abide there, though they should desire it' and even had a special order of clergy, the 'ostiarii', whose job it was to stop non-Catholics coming into church.[39] This was perhaps little more than a controversial point, but Persons, in a book published just after James I's accession, showed a very tolerant attitude. At one point in his monumental *Treatise of three conversions,* he returned to the theme of the inadequacies of the Marian Catholic Reformation which he had touched on in his

'Memorial'. Was it expedient, he asked, to burn so many heretics under Queen Mary? Persons, like previous Elizabethan Catholic writers, did not deny that the persecution of heretics was just, nor did he accept Foxe's claim that it was cruel, but he did question whether it was expedient. He cited Augustine's exposition of the parable of the tares, which showed, he said, that 'prudence and circumspection is to be used in rooting out as well heretics as other malefactors, and not to adventure upon it rashly or violently, when they are so many, or so strange, or so evil disposed as great perturbation and peril of the commonwealth might be expected thereby and so the good wheat pulled up with the darnel'. This is hardly better than a politique argument. If Catholicism were to be restored now, Persons went on, 'a far different course were... to be taken' from that pursued under Mary; there would be disputations, conference, 'mansuetude and longanimity' to per-suade men to be converted rather than fires to force them.[40]

The Appellants accused Persons of not wanting toleration in England, and there are reports dating from 1597 and 1598 which tend to confirm this.[41] But what he did not want was a toleration negotiated by his enemies, the Appellants or their associates, especially if the Jesuits were to be expelled as a result. As his books show, he was not on principle opposed to religious toleration for English Catholics, but he wanted it on his own terms. Thus, when in 1598 negotiations were taking place at Vervins for peace between France and Spain, the possibility of a general peace which they seemed – a little prematurely – to suggest moved Persons to urge, through Roman diplomatic channels, that any conference between Spain and England should include a discus-sion of the problem of the English Catholics. He was, on the one hand, anxious to counteract Charles Paget's proposals, later to be reflected in the policy of the Appellants, that toleration for Catholics might be given in return for the expulsion of the Jesuits; but, on the other hand, he seemed genuinely interested in the hope of freedom of religion which the peace negotiations seemed to hold.[42] He made a list of the terms under which he would accept toleration, which while being perhaps rather too hopeful might have served as a basis for discussion. Catholics in England and Ireland, he proposed, should have the same liberty of conscience as heretics enjoyed in France and as they would be given in the

Netherlands when peace was made there. All laws against Catholics in England ought to be repealed. No Catholic should be accused of treason on account of his religion, or forced to go to Protestant churches. Catholics should be allowed one church in each county, or, if this was impossible, freedom to celebrate mass in their own homes. Exiles ought to be allowed to return, and free passage of students and missionaries to and from the seminaries should be permitted. Nothing came of these suggestions in 1598, but in 1600, when discussions for peace between England and Spain were held at Boulogne, Persons once again urged that the question of toleration in England should be discussed there.[43]

The memorials submitted at Rome in 1602 by Persons' party against the Appellants' plan for toleration in England also showed the same fundamental acceptance of the propriety of seeking liberty of conscience for Catholics. Persons' objection to the proposals of the Appellants were not based on principle; he simply did not trust the Appellants, or, in this case, the Queen. He saw the scheme as a plot by Elizabeth to reduce Catholic strength in England. It was always in her interests to keep Catholics weak; she had made herself 'Antipope' by claiming the royal supremacy in the Church, and she would never consider herself safe while there were Catholics in England. She therefore followed the advice of Machiavelli – 'which is followed by the heretics in everything' – and kept Catholics 'low and oppressed' so that she should have nothing to fear from them. The support she gave to the Appellants was part of this policy, since they were proposing the expulsion of the Jesuits and their Appeals were dividing the Catholic movement and contributing, therefore, to its weakness. Persons said that he would accept only the widest sort of toleration: the revocation of all laws against Catholics and permission to have churches, bishops, and colleges in England. But the Queen, he said, could not make such concessions, since it would arouse too much opposition among Protestants in England. Nevertheless, despite all this, he concluded that the Jesuits and the Archpriest 'greatly desire that the Catholics should gain liberty of conscience'.[44]

VESTIGES OF RESISTANCE THEORY

Although the books written by Persons and his associates at the end of the reign of Elizabeth generally preach non-resistance and ask for toleration, they still retain some elements of the ideology of resistance. Indeed, there is evidence from diplomatic sources that during this period Persons was still engaged in negotiations with the Papacy and Spain which presupposed a belief in resistance.

This diplomatic activity found expression in an interesting manuscript tract, which survives in several English archives, entitled 'A discourse of the providence necessary to be had for the setting up the Catholic faith when God shall call the Queen out of this life'.[45] It appears to be an English translation of a memorial presented to the Pope and dates from about 1598–1601. Bishop Bancroft mentioned it in a letter of late 1602, ascribing it partly to Robert Persons.[46] The 'Discourse' gives a master-plan for an uprising in England to set up a Catholic ruler on the death of the Queen. It does not specify who is to be the Catholic successor, but warns of the dangers to be expected from the Scots and French and suggests that support from Spanish Flanders would be useful. It is optimistic about the possibility of success and paints in glowing terms the advantages to Catholicism of the reconversion of England to the faith; it would lead to success in Scotland and the Netherlands, the decline of Denmark and the defeat of the Turks by an English navy. In order to make the Catholic coup d'état successful the tract urges that it is necessary for the Pope to give his support to a specific Catholic claimant or to issue a declaration of the rewards he would give to those who supported the Catholic successor. This declaration would be made public in England by the Jesuits or the Archpriest and would, it was hoped, attract two-thirds of the nation to the Catholic side. The first reward to be held out in the papal edict as part of this 'policy of promises' would be to confirm supporters of the Catholic claimant in their possession of monastic land, in return (as Persons' 'Memorial' had proposed) for a small rent. Other rewards were suggested: the monastic lands of men who helped the heretics after Elizabeth's death were to be divided among their younger brothers; all usurious debts would be repudiated; and for the benefit of nobles the tyrannical Court of Wards would be abolished. To attract the common people, the Pope should promise 'to restore unto the realm all ancient privileges, and namely to the Parliament the ancient privilege of free speech, freely to accord, or freely to deny whatsoever is there proposed and not to be forced or violated by the will of the prince, and no subsidies or imposts to be laid upon the people but by such free and common consent in Parliament'. Common people who supported the Catholic cause should also be promised freedom from payment of subsidy and from military service abroad, the restoration of common land and an end to enclosure, and the reformation of the legal system, reducing the fees of 'advocates', creating more local courts and providing free legal aid for poor people. Finally, to encourage 'franklins' to support the Catholic side they should be promised advancement to the rank of gentleman and a share in the estates of those of their landlords who supported the heretics. This harsh treatment of the upper classes was justified, the tract said, 'for that (in the constancy of the English clergy in the beginning of this Queen's time, impugning her will in altering religion) this nobility did notably fail of their faiths to God and of their obligation to their own honours, weakly yielding to the Queen's will'. The 'Discourse of the providence necessary' seems to be a bridge between Persons' *Conference* and his 'Memorial': the means of securing the insurrection in favour of a Catholic successor justified in the former work and of instituting the political reforms suggested in the latter. It is addressed to the Pope and uses an argument for papal action in England drawn from the Latin translation of the *Conference*, mentioning the 'authority and prerogative which his Holiness hath over all kingdoms in the world, and particularly over England by grants of kings, and special cession and renunciation made by King John unto the See Apostolic, which the English chronicles printed by permission of this Queen do lay open to women and children that can read'.

The question of the succession, discussed without reference to a specific candidate in the 'Discourse of the providence', continued to exercise Persons and other English Catholic exiles at this time. Between 1598 and 1600 attempts seem to have been made to publish a new and clearer statement of the rights to the throne of the Infanta, the heroine of the *Conference* in the heyday of political resistance.[47]

The policy of conquest and war was, however, gradually becoming less and less practical as Spain disentangled herself from war with France and began negotiations with England. The leaders of Elizabethan Catholicism, especially those like Persons who were closest to Spain, soon realised that this was the case. The 'Discourse of the providence', for example, argues that it is not safe to rely on Spanish help to secure a Catholic succession in England because of the 'natural tardivity of the Spanish provisions; never complete, but ever defective either in men, shipping, victuals, mariners, or money, so as all these hardly concur together in any exploit intended'.[48] The failure of Spain forced the Catholic leaders to reject the policy of conquest. This is seen in a short printed declaration in Spanish dating from 1600 which was later translated into English and incorporated into a Catholic book.[49] This document defends and explains the King of Spain's reasons for supporting the English seminaries, giving reasons of 'piety', or 'honour' and finally of 'temporal utility'. This last section begins by saying that the 'infinite wisdom of God' has joined the affairs of England and Spain together in such a way that 'the security, peace and prosperity of Spain depend upon the conversion of England'. But, 'not without mystery', the conversion of England by force had proved impossible and 'such powerful Armadas...have not had any success'. The maintenance of the English seminaries, training priests as missionaries for England, was justified because they would, it was hoped, accomplish the conversion which the Armadas had failed to effect. The missionaries in England had already had great success in reconverting men to Catholicism and it was confidently expected that they would soon win back the whole island. The complete conversion of England would result in a resumption of trade with that country, the end of vast military expenditure and the collapse of the Dutch rebellion.

This faith in evangelical rather than military means is seen also in a memorial of about the same date written by John Sweet, who was described by the Appellant John Mush as one of Persons' 'parasites'.[50] His paper may perhaps be a reply to the 'Discourse of the providence'.[51] He began by stating the dilemma faced by the leaders of Elizabethan Catholicism: 'the whole debate about the reconversion of England to the orthodox faith consists in this – whether it should be accomplished by force or by preaching the Word'. Sweet was very doubtful about the possibility of success by the use of armed force. An uprising by Catholics was not likely to succeed, he said; the English Catholics were few in number, geographically divided, and without leaders, arms, plans, or even political ambitions. It was probable that a Catholic rebellion, so far from being supported by heretics (as the 'Discourse' had suggested) would be opposed by both Protestants and those not committed to either religion, since as a result of Mary's reign they believed that Catholics were naturally cruel and would put England under Spanish rule. The same soundness of argument Sweet applied to the question of Spanish invasion. The size of the Spanish empire had overstretched Spain's resources; she could not maintain sufficient military forces to keep all her provinces in subjection, let alone conquer England. The English, on the other hand, were skilled in maritime warfare, and the position of England, set in a very dangerous sea, rendered it easily defended from attack. Sweet's good sense deserted him when he came to consider the second method of converting England, preaching the Word. Various reasons made him see this as a very easy task: the devotion of the English in the past, the superiority of Catholic to heretical doctrine, and the recent success of the missionaries. In the past four years, he claimed, ten thousand English Protestants had been converted and probably about the same number had been secretly won over to Catholicism; the spark would soon grow into a great fire.

The idea of resistance, therefore, still influenced the policy of Robert Persons and his supporters at the end of the reign of Elizabeth, although they had doubts about how much they could count on Spain, and generally placed far less reliance on this method of recovering England than they had done a decade before. In the same way, there are still present in the books of Persons and his supporters at the end of Elizabeth's reign some elements of the ideology of political resistance, although the dominant theme in these books is usually that of non-resistance.

In *A temperate ward-word*, Persons was replying to a work by Sir Francis Hastings in which the latter had denied the right of resistance and had said that it was not 'in the power of any one mortal child of man to dispose of kingdoms, to depose princes, or to dispense with subjects for not only disobeying but rebelling against their lawful sovereign'.[52] Persons in reply defended

English Catholics from the accusation that they were rebellious
and said that they had been right to ignore the Bull of Excommunication. Nevertheless, he maintained that the general denial
of a right of resistance made by Hastings was wrong, and proceeded 'not only of deep ignorance both in reason and story, but
of so base a breast also and servile a cogitation, as if temporal
kingdoms were matters of Godhead and immortality'. Hastings
was a 'Prince-idolator', Persons said, to hold such a doctrine;
he should look at the Books of Samuel and Kings to 'see how
many kingdoms were disposed of and princes deposed by mortal
children of men, and the same allowed also by God Himself'.
English history also showed many such changes of royal government, 'made by mortal children of men – seeing they are now
dead that made them – which yet he must approve for good and
lawful, except he will impugn the succession of Her Majesty that
now is, which is not likely, seeing the poor man flattereth so
seriously with all the art and power he can'.[53] In the same book
Persons also briefly alluded to the proposition that it was in some
cases lawful to kill a tyrant; this was 'allowed by all learned men
both heretics and Catholics and read publicly in all famous
schools'. He cited Cicero, St Thomas and the sixteenth-century
Catholic theologians, Thomas de Vio Cajetan and Dominic Soto
in support. This is interesting as the only defence of tyrannicide in
the work of an Elizabethan Catholic (although Rainolds, for a
French audience, dealt with the matter in his *De iusta reipublicae
...authoritate*), but read in context it is extremely innocuous,
contained as it is in a passage which denied that Jesuits had any
connection with plots to assassinate princes.[54]

In the *Ward-word* and in other books, Persons and his friends
also continued the minor, detailed political criticisms of the
Elizabethan government which had been part of the ideology of
resistance. The persecution of Catholics was attacked as cruel and
dangerous to the political stability of England.[55] Persons pointed
out the benefits which would have resulted if Elizabethan had, at
her accession, proclaimed herself a Catholic, and he denied, in
opposition to Protestant writers, that England was a happy and
prosperous country. On the contrary, as a result of Protestantism
it was weak, divided, highly taxed, poor and threatened by foreign
enemies.[56] Persons conceded to his controversial opponents that

the population had increased, even perhaps sevenfold, as they maintained. This was to be expected in Protestant countries, where sexual licence was so common; 'but whether this be a blessing or a cursing, a benefit or a burthen to the commonwealth, let the parishes and parishioners of England be asked, who by statute are bound to maintain their brats, when the parents are not able'.[57] The power and wealth of Catholic Spain was contrasted with the weakness and poverty of Protestant England.[58] Philip III was described as the 'most happy monarch of the world, who hath joined piety with power and so great zeal of religion with so large dominion of so many kingdoms'.[59] At the same time, however, Persons expressed the hope that England and Spain would make peace.[60] Just as Spain was more successful than England, so, Broughton maintained, Protestant individuals were less fortunate than Catholics, and he described the unpleasant deaths of several leading heretics. He went as far as to mention the Earl of Leicester, who died 'terrified with monstrous visions of devils', and Sir Francis Walsingham, who died saying 'lay me aside and let me be forgotten', and whose corpse had such a 'filthy stink' that he had to be buried without a funeral and at night. Abroad, the Prince of Condé, Admiral Coligny, the Prince of Orange, and the Earl of Moray had died unpleasantly. English history furnished examples of kings – William I, William II, King John, Henry III, Edward II, Richard II and Henry VIII – who had opposed the Church and had died miserably or had called down great natural disasters on the country.[61]

In two of his books at the end of the reign Persons attacked the Appellants for denying the theory of papal political power, and in Rome he denounced them to the Inquisition on this count.[62] It was 'fond' and 'impious', he said, to deny a doctrine which was held by 'all the Catholic learned men of Christendom', and in confirmation he gave a great list of authors who supported the theory, including a reference to William Allen's *A true, sincere and modest defence*. Even Jews and Turks agreed, he wrote, 'that for defence and conservation of religion any prince may be restrained that goeth about to overthrow the same'. Persons maintained that the Pope had no 'temporal dominion or jurisdiction over Christian temporal princes that are supreme in their own states', but that indirectly, to defend religion, 'he may...

use the sword or help of temporal forces...either immediately
from himself or by other princes at his direction'. He gave two
reasons, which he had also used in his Latin version of the
Conference. First, civil 'magistrates' are subordinate to ecclesiastical 'magistrates' because they look after the temporal welfare of
the people rather than their eternal salvation; second, God would
not have left his Church without the ability to defend itself.
Persons' defence of papal political power here looks forward to the
attitude taken by Persons himself and most Catholic writers in the
Oath of Allegiance Controversy, when they defended the doctrine
while protesting their complete loyalty to King James I.[63]

In his anti-Appellant works, moreover, Persons defended some
other elements of the policy and ideas of the period of resistance.
He tried, as best he could, to make his political activity at that
time seem innocent, but did not totally deny the ideology behind
it. He made an attempt, as other writers did, to explain Sir
William Stanley's surrender of Deventer and Allen's defence of it.
It was 'evident in conscience and true divinity', Fitzherbert said,
'that Sir William was bound under pain of damnable sin to
deliver it [Deventer] to the King who was the true owner thereof,
and from whom it was wrongfully detained by his rebels'; Stanley
was the 'true mirror of a Christian soldier'.[64] Worthington said
that what Stanley did was 'just, lawful and necessary by the laws
of God and nations', and, moreover, that the Earl of Leicester
had given Stanley permission to leave his service.[65] Persons also
took pains to vindicate his 'Memorial' and other of his books
from the attacks of the Appellants.[66] It was the *Conference* which
Persons expended most energy on justifying, partly for the benefit
of James VI, who it was gradually becoming clear would succeed
without opposition. The book was defended by Persons in print,
and he also sent a number of more or less open letters to England
and Scotland in which it and the policy behind it were justified.[67]
He was careful not to acknowledge his authorship of the *Conference*, and stressed the approval which Allen and Englefield
had given to it.[68] He claimed that the first part of the book showed
'that in all pretence and pretenders to reign over Christians and
succession to crowns, the consideration of true Catholic religion is
the principal point to be respected', which was certainly something the *Conference* had not done. The second part of his book,

Persons stressed – perhaps partly in the hope of placating James VI – was an 'indifferent' description of the rights of the various pretenders to the English throne. In the *Manifestation* Persons went on to examine Clitheroe's *Discovery of a counterfeit conference*, a 'little barking pamphlet' which, he claimed quite fairly, was no match for the *Conference*. He dealt reasonably fully with Clitheroe's book and was anxious to answer its accusation that his own book 'containeth popular doctrine, perilous to princes, states and commonwealths'. In reply he stated what might be called the moderate or constitutionalist case for a right of resistance:

there is no reason why the lawful, grave, just and orderly proceeding of true subjects and moderate commonwealths against pernicious or unlawful princes should be stained or their just authority left them by all law, both divine and human, should be denied for that some wicked and troublesome subjects have, against law and order, misbehaved themselves against their lawful princes.[69]

The *Conference* was now made to sound quite conservative.

In 1602, Persons and the Appellants were much closer in their political thought than might appear at first glance, although they were, of course, bitterly opposed in other ways. Persons, it is true, wished to keep a number of political alternatives open to him; Spain was not much help now, but it would be foolish to abandon the last hope there was for the complete restoration of Catholicism – a disputed succession and a Catholic pretender. Nevertheless, in the political ideas he expressed in his printed books Persons was nearly as far from the position of the heyday of resistance as were the Appellants. Vestiges of the old ideas of the late 1580s and early 1590s remained, and in the face of the Appellant campaign they were inevitably brought into the open. But all that really survived of Catholic resistance theory was the doctrine of papal power in temporals.

This position – loyalty to the Crown combined with a defence of papal temporal authority – remained under James I the most common ideology, repeatedly defended during the Oath of Allegiance Controversy. It is true that there were still a few 'Appellants' about, who were ready to accept the oath and defend in print its rejection of the Pope's power to depose princes, but these were not the ex-Appellants themselves: they refused the

Oath. The paradox is that, for most of Elizabeth's reign, Catholic authors expressed complete loyalty to her in their printed books and refused to discuss papal power in temporals, despite the fact that she had been excommunicated by a Pope; now, under James, who was not excommunicated and whose succession to the throne many Catholics had supported, they published book after book defending the purely theoretical matter of papal power over princes – a doctrine which the King himself found deeply worrying.

Notes to the text

Introduction

1 M. Luther, *Works* (ed. H. T. Lehmann & W. I. Brandt, Philadelphia, 1962), vol. 45, pp. 60–3; C. Ginzburg, *Il Nicodemismo* (Turin, 1970); J. Calvin in *Corpus Reformatorum*, xxxiv (Brunswick, 1867), 537–644.

2 *Sermons or homilies appointed to be read in churches in the time of Queen Elizabeth of famous memory* (London, 1833), 114–27.

3 W. P. Hudson, *John Ponet, advocate of limited monarchy* (Chicago, 1942), esp. 47–78, 98–126.

4 A. F. Allison & D. M. Rogers, *A catalogue of Catholic books in English printed abroad or secretly in England 1558–1640* (London, 1968).

5 The work of the Scolar Press in producing facsimile reprints of many of these tracts has made access to the rarer examples far easier; many are also available through the efforts of University Microfilms. For Latin works the bibliography in J. Pits, *Relationum historicarum* (Paris, 1619) is still useful; cf. the lists of T. Worthington in Westminster Cathedral Archives, MS. AIV, fos. 179–230.

6 J. N. Figgis, *The theory of the divine right of kings* (Cambridge, 1896); *idem, Studies in political thought from Gerson to Grotius* (Cambridge, 1916); *idem*, 'Political thought in the sixteenth century', *Cambridge Modern History*, iii (Cambridge, 1907), 736–69; C. H. McIlwain, *The political works of James I* (Cambridge, Mass., 1918), Intro.; C. Morris, *Political thought in England, Tyndale to Hooker* (Oxford, 1953); J. W. Allen, *A history of political thought in the sixteenth century* (London, 1961); Q. R. D. Skinner, *The foundations of modern political thought* (Cambridge, 1979), esp. vol. ii.

7 T. H. Clancy, *Papist pamphleteers* (Chicago, 1964); A. Pritchard, *Catholic loyalism in Elizabethan England* (London, 1979).

8 J. H. Pollen, *The English Catholics in the reign of Queen Elizabeth* (London, 1920); A. O. Meyer, *England and the Catholic Church under Queen Elizabeth* (London, 1967); A. J. Loomie, *The Spanish Elizabethans* (London, 1963); J. Bossy, 'The character of Elizabethan Catholicism', *Past and Present* 21 (1962), 39–59.

9 W. R. Trimble, *The Catholic laity in Elizabethan England* (Cambridge, Mass., 1964); J. Bossy, *The English Catholic community 1570–1850* (London, 1975); J. C. H. Aveling, *The handle and the axe*

(London, 1976); C. Haigh, *Reformation and resistance in Tudor Lancashire* (Cambridge, 1975).

1 Half-hearted non-resistance: the Louvainists 1558–68

1 J. Bossy, 'The character of Elizabethan Catholicism', in T. Aston (ed.), *Crisis in Europe* (London, 1965), 229–32; *idem, The English Catholic community* (London, 1975), Part 1; P. Hughes, *The Reformation in England*, III (London, 1954), Part II, chap. 1; P. McGrath, *Papists and puritans under Elizabeth I* (London, 1967), chap. 4; A. Morey, *The Catholic subjects of Elizabeth I* (London, 1978), chap. 3; J. C. H. Aveling, *The handle and the axe* (London, 1976), chap. 1; A. Pritchard, *Catholic loyalism in Elizabethan England* (London, 1979), 3–5. For a different view, however, see C. Haigh, *Reformation and resistance in Tudor Lancashire* (Cambridge, 1975), chaps. 13–16; *idem*, 'The fall of a Church or the rise of a sect? Post-Reformation Catholicism in England', *Historical Journal* 21 (1978), 181–6.
2 Strype, *Annals*, I, ii, 399–407. For the vague possibility of a speech expressing opposition to the Queen at the time, see J. E. Neale, *Elizabeth I and her parliaments 1559–1581* (London, 1953), 118–20.
3 Strype, *Annals*, I, ii, 408–22.
4 *Ibid*, 431–8.
5 Strype, *Annals*, I, i, 442–6; cf. T. J. McCann, 'The parliamentary speech of Viscount Montague against the Act of Supremacy, 1559', *Sussex Archaeological Collections* CVIII (1970), 50–7.
6 *Ibid*, 446–55.
7 Bodleian MS Tanner 302, fos. 1–13^v.
8 Pilkington, *Works*, 617–39.
9 Fowler in Frarin, *An oration*, sig. A6^v; cf. Rastell, *A treatise*, sig. A8.
10 Hosius, *A most excellent treatise*, sig. a4–4^v.
11 This point is discussed separately in chap. 5.
12 Hosius, *op. cit.*; Martial, *A treatise*; Harding, *A confutation*; Stapleton, *The history*, sigs. * 2, ▽ 1^v; cf. Bodleian MS Tanner 302, fo. 13^v.
13 Dorman, *A disproof*; Stapleton, *op. cit.*; Harding, *A confutation*; cf. C. G. Bayne, *Anglo-Roman relations 1558–1565* (Oxford, 1913), 221.
14 Martial, *A treatise*, Dedication.
15 In Horne, *An answer made*, 5.
16 Evans, *Certain tables*, sig. E5–5^v; cf. Frarin, *An oration*, sig. A5^v.
17 Dorman, *A disproof*, sig. * 3.
18 Stapleton, *A counterblast*, sig. *** 4–4^v, fos. 14^v–15.
19 *Ibid*, fo. 21.
20 Martial, *A reply*, sig. ** ^{v}.
21 Harding, *A detection*, 85^v–8; Jewel, *Works*, III, 172–3.
22 See chap. 5.
23 J. H. Pollen, *The English Catholics in the reign of Queen Elizabeth* (London, 1920), 45–6; C. G. Bayne, *Anglo-Roman relations 1558–1565* 53.
24 Pollen, *op. cit.*, chaps. II, III, IV.

25 Jewel, *op. cit.*, III, 73–5.
26 Harding, *A detection*, 18.
27 Harding, *A confutation*, 178–9.
28 *Ibid*, 318ᵛ–19.
29 *Ibid*, 179–89ᵛ; *idem*, *A detection*, 11ᵛ–18ᵛ.
30 Harding, *A confutation*, 178ᵛ; *Corpus Iuris Canonici*, Extra. Comm. i. 8. 1; cf. Bodleian MS Tanner 302, 1–1ᵛ.
31 Harding, *A detection*, 11ᵛ–12; St Bernard, 'De consideratione', *Opera*, III (Rome, 1963), 454.
32 Rastell, *A confutation*, 104ᵛ–10ᵛ.
33 Strype, *Memorials*, III, ii, 536–50.
34 *Ibid*, 538–9.
35 *Ibid*, 541; Numbers chap. 16.
36 Strype, *Memorials*, 542; H. R. Trevor-Roper, *George Buchanan and the ancient Scottish constitution* (*English Historical Review* Supplement 3, London, 1966), 8, 14–15; cf. Persons, *A conference*, I, 79.
37 Strype, *Memorials*, 543.
38 Martial, *A treatise of the cross*, 137–8. Heastes are hests, behests or orders (*O.E.D.*).

2 *Resistance and the return to non-resistance*

1 A. F. Allison & D. M. Rogers, *A Catalogue of Catholic books in English printed abroad or secretly in England 1558–1640* (London, 1968), 822 and index.
2 *Ibid*, 827.
3 There are three editions of this book, two dated 1569 and one published by Fowler in 1571 as *A treatise*, which I use here (see Allison & Rogers, *op. cit.*, 214).
4 *D.N.B.*; A. C. Southern, *Elizabethan recusant prose* (London, 1950), 442; cf. Persons, *A conference*, II, 3; M. Levine, *The early Elizabethan succession question 1558–68* (Stanford, 1966), 92–5, 111–15; Leslie, *A treatise* (1584), 7ᵛ; Marie Axton, 'The influence of Edmund Plowden's succession treatise', *Huntington Library Quarterly* XXXVI (1974), 209–26; G. de C. Parminter, 'Edmund Plowden as advocate for Mary Queen of Scots', *Innes Review* 30 (1979), 35–53.
5 Leslie, *A treatise* (1571), Part III.
6 *Ibid*, 8ᵛ.
7 T. Clancy, *Papist pamphleteers* (Chicago, 1964), chap. II.
8 A. C. Southern, *op. cit.*, 444–7; Allison & Rogers, *op. cit.*, art. 454; D. M. Lockie, 'The political career of the Bishop of Ross, 1568–80', *University of Birmingham Historical Journal* IV (1953–4), 111, note 53; J. Bossy, 'The character of Elizabethan Catholicism', *Past and Present* 21 (1962), 40, 49; cf. Christie, *Letters of Copley*, 39–40, note.
9 Leslie (?), *A treatise of treasons*, sig. ā3–4, fos. 19, 23ᵛ; Southern, *Elizabethan recusant prose*, 444–7.
10 Cf. Christie, *loc. cit.*
11 Leslie, *A treatise of treasons*, sig. I3ᵛ.

12 *Ibid*, 146.
13 *Ibid*, sig. ā3ᵛ.
14 *Ibid*, 103ᵛ.
15 *Ibid*, 169ff.
16 Kervyn de Lettenhove, *Relations politiques*, VII, 470; T. M. Veech, *Dr Nicholas Sander* (Louvain, 1935), 90–1; Christie, *loc. cit.*
17 Tierney, *Dodd's Church history*, III, App., pp. vii–xi.
18 Sander, *De visibili monarchia*, Book VII, 686–738.
19 *Ibid*, Book II, chap. 4, pp. 77–92.
20 Sander, *The rock of the church*, 82–8.
21 *Ibid*, 101.
22 Allen, *A true, sincere and modest defence*, 122–3; T. M. Veech, *Dr Nicholas Sander*, 103; Gibbons, *Concertatio*, 412ᵛ.
23 Sander, *De clave David*, see esp. 95ff.
24 Leslie, *Pro libertate impetranda oratio*; Lockie, *op. cit.*, 111, note 5.
25 'Animadversiones in Epistolam et orationem Ioannis Leslaei', in Pollen, *Memoirs of Persons*, II, 164–76.
26 *De titulo et iure serenissimae principis Mariae* (1580); and later English and French editions, *A treatise touching the right, title and interest* (1584), and *Du droit et titre* (1587).
27 Tierney, *Dodd's Church history*, III, App., pp. v–ix; cf. Burghley, *The execution of justice*, 38.
28 Bristow, *A brief treatise*, 72ᵛ–3.
29 *Ibid*, 31ᵛ.
30 *Ibid*, 153–5.
31 *Demands to be proponed of Catholics to the heretics* (1576); cf. Allen, *A true, sincere and modest defence*, 122. The passages reappeared, however, in *A brief treatise* (Antwerp, 1599).
32 A. F. Allison & D. M. Rogers. *op. cit.*, 176.
33 *A brief form of confession*, 229–30; Canisius, *A sum of Christian doctrine*, 79–80; *idem*, *Certain necessary principles*, sig. C5–5ᵛ; Lanspergius, *An epistle*, 53ᵛ–6ᵛ; Loarte, *The exercise of a Christian life*, 177ᵛ–8; Vaux, *A catechism*, 36–8.
34 Allison & Rogers, *loc. cit.*

3 Enthusiastic non-resistance, 1580–83

1 P. Hughes, *The Reformation in England*, III (London, 1954), 305.
2 Hicks, *Letters of Persons*, 317.
3 Allison & Rogers, *op. cit.*, 176.
4 Hicks, *Letters of Persons*, Intro., xxii.
5 *Ibid*, 38; Campion's 'Letter to the Lords of the Privy Council', in Southern, *op. cit.*, 153–5, quoted in T. Clancy, *Papist pamphleteers* (Chicago, 1964), 48.
6 Hicks, *Letters of Persons*, 38–9.
7 Allen, *A brief history*, sigs. c2–3.
8 *Idem, An apology*, 12ᵛ–13.
9 *Ibid*, 51.

10 *Ibid*, 93–4.
11 *Ibid*, 101ᵛ.
12 *Ibid*, 105.
13 Persons, *A brief discourse*, sigs. $+$ 3, $+$ 6ᵛ.
14 *Ibid*, sigs. $++$ 2ᵛ, $+$ 6ᵛ–7.
15 *Ibid*, sig. $+$ 8.
16 *Ibid*, 70ᵛ, cf. 1–3.
17 Persons, *A brief censure*, sig. D8ᵛ.
18 Persons, *An epistle*, 8.
19 *Ibid*, 45–6.
20 Alfield, *A true report*, sig. G1–2.
21 Southern, *op. cit.*, 231–62.
22 *The New Testament*, 64 (Matt. 22. 21), 121 (Mark 12. 17), 197 (Luke 20. 25), 609 (Heb. 5. 1), 639 (Heb. 13. 17).
23 *Ibid*, 415–16 (Rom. 13. 1–6).
24 *Ibid*, 658–9 (1 Pet. 2. 13).
25 *Ibid*, 47 (Matt. 16. 19); cf. also 364 (Acts 25. 19).
26 A. O. Meyer, *England and the Catholic Church under Queen Elizabeth* (trans. J. B. McKee, London, 1967), 138; Appendix, 487.
27 Hicks, *Letters of Persons*, 318 and note 19, 361–3; Meyer, *op. cit.*, 142–3; cf. Persons, 'Of the life and martyrdom of Fr Edmond Campian', *Letters and Notices*, xi (Roehampton, 1877), 332, where Persons, writing in 1594, says that their Jesuit instructions told them not to indulge in politics except where they were closely connected with religion, and admitted that a 'store' of cases came into this category.
28 See above, pp. 29–34.
29 W. R. Trimble, *The Catholic laity in Elizabethan England* (Cambridge, Mass., 1964), 63.
30 Burghley, *The execution of justice*, 18–19; C. Read, 'William Cecil and Elizabethan public relations', in S. T. Bindoff *et al.* (eds.), *Elizabethan government and society* (London, 1961), 37–8; cf. Meyer, *op. cit.*, 138–44.
31 W. Creighton, 'The excommunication of Queen Elizabeth', *E.H.R.* vii (1892), 84–8; Meyer, *op. cit.*, 136, note 1, 140; J. H. Pollen, *The English Catholics* (London, 1920), 294, note 1. If Possevino did write the answers and did so in Rome, they probably date from between late September and early December 1578; when he was there; see O. Garstein, *Rome and the Counter-Reformation in Scandinavia* (Bergen, 1963), 159, 169.
32 Lambeth Library MS 565, fo. 53ᵛ.
33 Douai MS 484, pp. 423–4; Bodleian MS Rawlinson D 1351, fos. 13–14.
34 Cf. the description of the answers of Campion as having been made 'sophistically, deceitfully, and traitorously' by a government propagandist in *A declaration of the favourable dealing*, in Burghley, *The execution of justice*, 47; cf. G. R. Elton, *England under the Tudors* (London, 1969), 306–7.
35 'Quid ad vos, qui constituit vos iudices super eam; quamvis tenetur

quis accusare vel denunciare haeresim, vergentem in detrimentum Ecclesiae . . . tamen non teneor vel accusare vel denunciare quemquam homini nullam habenti iurisdictionem; si vos dicitis eam esse haereticam, legem habetis, et secundum eam iudicate. Si quis eam sic a me appellatam esse dicat prodeat et accuset', Douai Municipal Library MS 484, p. 423; Bodleian MS Rawlinson D1351, fos. 13–14.

36 'si vultis particulatim inquirere debetis probare contra me infamiam precedentem . . . interim sinite me vivere in pace', Douai MS 484, p. 424.

37 'Huic questioni non possum satisfacere nisi prius sit determinatum apud vos, si committat crimen depositione dignum, quem habet iudicem, et quae sunt illa crimina, vel quod rex vel regina non possunt deponi ob ullum crimen nisi haec sint certa questio erit captiosa, quia non proponitur super re certa', *Ibid*, p. 424.

38 Tierney, *Dodd's Church history*, III, App. xi; Allen, *A brief history*, sig. A1–4 (2nd set of sigs.); *idem*, *A brief history* (ed. J. H. Pollen, London, 1908), Intro., xvi. At his execution Briant was asked what he felt about the bull and he replied that 'he did believe of it as all Catholics and the Catholic faith doth', Alfield, *A true report*, sig. D2ᵛ.

4 Persecution and non-resistance

1 Harding, *A rejoinder*, 187ᵛ; *idem*, *A confutation*, sig. * 3; Stapleton, *The history*, sig. * 2ᵛ.

2 See above, p. 27.

3 Allen, *A brief history* (1582); Gibbons, *Concertatio Ecclesiae Catholicae* (eds. of 1583, 1588); R. Verstegan, *Theatrum crudelitatum haereticorum* (eds. of 1587, 1592, 1604); T. Bourchier, *Historia ecclesiastica* (1582, and 7 other eds.); *Ecclesiae militantis triumphi* (1585). Cf. H. C. White, *Tudor books of saints and martyrs* (Madison, 1963), chap. vii; A. G. Petti, 'Richard Verstegan and Catholic martyrologies of the later Elizabethan period', *Recusant History* 5 (1959–60), 64–90; T. H. Clancy, *Papist pamphleteers* (Chicago, 1964), chap. vi.

4 Hicks, *Letters of Persons*, 340–7; cf. A. J. Loomie, 'Spain and the English Catholic exiles 1580–1604' (London Ph.D. thesis, 1957), chap. 6; J. A. Bossy, 'Elizabethan Catholicism, the link with France' (Cambridge Ph.D. thesis, 1960), 114–23.

5 Strype, *Annals*, I, i, 450–2. On Atkinson see G. de C. Parminter, *Elizabethan Popish recusancy in the Inns of Court* (Supplement 11, *Bulletin of the Institute of Historical Research*, 1976), 8, 10, 11, 13, 22, 51–2; J. E. Neale, *Elizabeth I and her parliaments 1559–1581* (London, 1953), 118–20.

6 Harding, *A rejoinder*, 178–89; Augustine, *Epistola* clxxv, in J-P. Migne, *Patrologiae cursus completus . . . Latinae*, vol. 33 (Paris, 1841), 792ff.

7 Persons, *An epistle of the persecution*, 5–7.

8 Allen, *A true, sincere and modest defence*, chap. III.

9 Harding, *A rejoinder*, 178–89; Harpsfield, *Dialogi sex*, 638 [*vere* 739] ff; Hosius, *A most excellent treatise*, 44–6ᵛ; Rastell, *A confutation*, 166; Bristow, *Demands*, §20; Bourchier, *Historia ecclesiastica*, sig. a2ᵛ–3;

Westminster, B48/67; Southwell, *An epistle of comfort*, 212–18; cf. A. L. Rowse, 'Nicholas Roscarrock and his lives of saints', in J. H. Plumb (ed.), *Studies in social history, a tribute to G. M. Trevelyan* (London, 1955), esp. 19 note 48.

10 Stapleton, *The history*, fo. 9; *idem, A counterblast*, 60–1ᵛ; Dorman, *A proof*, 123ᵛ.

11 Allen, *A true, sincere and modest defence*, 100–17.

12 Persons, *A treatise of three conversions*, I, 299; cf. W. Haller, *Foxe's Book of Martyrs and the elect nation* (London, 1963); J. S. F. Simons, *Robert Persons, S. J., Certamen Ecclesiae Anglicanae* (Nijmegen, 1965), Intro., §vi, viii, ix; 'Certamen Ecclesiae Anglicanae' (4 vols.), Stonyhurst College, MS A II 12; Stonyhurst MS Coll. P. 288–91.

13 Persons, *A treatise of three conversions*, II and III.

14 *Ibid*, II, 153–80.

15 *Ibid*, II, 172.

16 *Ibid*, I, 538–40.

17 *Ibid*, II, 172.

18 'The copy of a letter written by Father Francis de Castro' and 'A challenge unto Foxe the martyrmonger written upon occasion of this miraculous martyrdom', P.R.O., S.P. 12/157/48.

19 Cf. below, chap. 6, p. 88.

20 J. E. Neale, *Elizabeth I and her Parliaments 1584–1601* (London, 1957), 29–30.

21 Allen, *A brief history*, sig. b4.

22 Hide, *A consolatory epistle*, sig. A2ᵛ.

23 Allen, *A brief history*, sig. c3.

24 B.L. Add. MS 34218, fo. 85ᵛ; Inner Temple, MS 538.14/no. iv.

25 Martin, *A treatise of Christian peregrination*, letter to his sisters.

26 Southwell, *An epistle of comfort*, 233; cf. Persons, *An epistle*, 45–6; Pollen, *Acts*, 322.

27 W. Harris, 'The theatre and glass of the truest and most ancient church of Great Brittany', I; Douai MS 920.1, fos. 131–3ᵛ, 110–12.

28 Bourchier, *Historia ecclesiastica*, 200–25.

29 'Canes mutos non valentes latrare, qui quidem Cerbero peiores, non solum non latraverunt verumetiam domum Dei furibus et latronibus prodiderunt', Bourchier, *op. cit.*, 213.

30 Allen, *A brief history*, sig. c6ᵛ.

31 *Idem, An apology*, 95ᵛ.

32 *Ibid*, 75ᵛ–6.

33 Alfield, *A true report*, sig. B2, G1.

34 Persons, *A brief discourse*, sig. ⧺⧺ 7ᵛ–8, cf. ⧺ 6–6ᵛ; cf. *idem, A defence of the censure*, 1—11; P. Collinson, 'John Field and Elizabethan puritanism', in S. T. Bindoff *et al.* (eds.), *Elizabethan government and society* (London, 1961), 143.

35 Persons, *An epistle of the persecution*, 3, 160–3.

36 Signed 'R. W.', Bodleian MS Rawlinson D107, fos. 134ᵛ–5ᵛ.

37 Persons, *The first book of the Christian exercise*, 239–92; cf. Southwell, *An epistle of comfort*, esp. chaps. 1–4.

38 Hide, *A consolatory epistle*, sig. F2.

39 Allen, *A defence . . . touching purgatory*, 23ᵛ.

40 *Idem, An apology* (1581), 110.

41 Hide, *op. cit.*, sig. C2–3.

42 *Ibid*, sig. D8–8ᵛ; cf. Persons, *An epistle of the persecution*, 48.

43 Alfield, *A true report*, sig. Gᵛ.

44 Allen, *A brief history*, sig. A2–2ᵛ; Alfield, *op. cit.*, sig. B3; Allen, *Apology*, 73ᵛ.

45 Alfield, *op. cit.*, sig. G; cf. E3.

46 Allen, *Apology*, 21–32.

47 *Ibid*, 6–14.

48 *Ibid*, 15–16.

49 *Ibid*, 100.

50 *Ibid*, 79ᵛ–85.

51 Persons, *A brief censure*, sigs. A2ᵛ–D7ᵛ.

52 Allen, *A true report*.

53 Persons, *A discovery*, sigs. F1ᵛ–6.

54 Persons, *An epistle of the persecution*, 62; Hide, *A consolatory epistle*, sigs. D4ᵛ–5.

55 Allen, *A brief history*, sigs. a2–3.

56 Persons, *An epistle of the persecution*, 148–50; cf. K. Thomas, *Religion and the decline of magic* (Harmondsworth, 1973), 613.

57 Campion, *Campian Englished*, 33, 183–4; *Descriptiones quaedam*, 'Admonition'; Allen, *A true, sincere and modest defence*, chaps. I–III and *passim*; Aray, *The discovery, passim*; Cresswell, *Exemplar literarum*, 35–41; Fitzherbert, *An apology, passim*; Persons, *Elizabethae Angliae*, 171–210; Stapleton, *Apologia pro rege*, 193–229; Southwell, *An humble supplication*, 11–46; Verstegan, *A declaration*, 43–5; W.R. (attrib. to Walpole), *A brief and clear confutation*, chap. xii; Worthington, *A relation of sixteen martyrs*, 34–6; 'A plea for a priest; and a plea to show that to absolve only from heresy, schism and sin; to reconcile merely to the unity of the Holy Catholic Church . . . is not treason, according to the laws' (1594–1603?), Westminster, AVII, pp. 505–51, esp. 521–32; Westminster, B48/67.

58 P. Hughes, *The Reformation in England* (London, 1954), III, 335ff; C. Read, 'William Cecil and Elizabethan public relations', in S. T. Bindoff *et al.* (eds.), *Elizabethan government and society* (London, 1961), 21–55; C. A. Newdigate (ed.), *C. R. S. Miscellanea* (1932), 389–436; Pollen, *Acts*, 75–82, 101–12, 133–4, 196, 226, 295, 303, 329–30, 335–6; *idem, Unpublished documents*, 77, 168, 177, 285–6, 325, 352–60, 372–3; J. Morris, *The troubles*, III, 20–1, 45, 94–7; Challoner, *Memoirs*, xx–xxii, 1, 48–51, 54, 56, 58–9, 62–3, 77, 78–9, 81–3, 92, 95, 99, 106, 108, 165, 166, 168, 182, 230–2; Tierney, *Dodd's Church history*, III, 135ff; M. C. Cross, 'The Third Earl of Huntingdon and trials of Catholics in the North, 1581–1595', *Recusant History* 8 (1965), 136–46; cf. O. Chadwick, *The Reformation* (Harmondsworth, 1968), 289.

59 Pollen, *Unpublished documents*, 232.

60 Pollen, *Acts*, 91–4.
61 *Ibid*, 308.
62 Pollen, *Unpublished documents*, 182–6.
63 Cf. W. K. Jordan, *The development of religious toleration in England* (London, 1932), chap. vi, and *passim*; J. Lecler, *Toleration and the Reformation* (trans. T. L. Westow, London, 1960), esp. II, 354–79; Clancy, *op. cit.*, chap. 6.
64 R. Hall, *Contra coalitionem multarum diversarum imo adversarum religionum*, in *Opuscula quaedam*.
65 Strype, *Annals*, I, i, 452–3.
66 *Ibid*, I, ii, 572–3.
67 Stapleton, *A counterblast*, 21–21^v.
68 Persons, *A brief discourse*, sig. $\neq$ 3–3^v.
69 *Idem, An epistle of the persecution*, 9, 27–41, 163–4, sig. M4^v; cf. also for requests for mercy, Allen, *An apology*, 9–10, 47–51, 104; Alfield, *A true report*, sigs. C4, D3–3^v; Allen, *A true report*, 34^v; *idem, A brief history*, sig. C8.
70 P.R.O., S.P. 12/162/14I.

5 The background to non-resistance

1 Frarin, *An oration*, sig. K6^v; cartoon reproduced in Knox, *Works*, IV, 362.
2 Osorius, *Epistle*, see esp. 7–32^v; cf. *idem, A learned and very eloquent treaty*, 51–3.
3 Hosius, *Of the express word of God*, 85, 68^v–9^v, 95ff; cf. *idem, A most excellent treatise*.
4 Staphylus, *The apology*, 141, cf. 16, 40–1, 75, 123–3^v, 139^v–42^v.
5 Albin de Valsergues, *A notable discourse*, 34–7.
6 *An edict or ordinance of the French king*, sigs. B3–4, C, C2.
7 Winzet, *Certain tractates*, I, 94–7, 121–2; Burne, *The disputation*, 134–56^v; Hamilton, *An Catholic and facile treatise*, 2^v–3; Cf. Dury, *Confutatio responsionis*, 308^v–9^v; Hay, *Certain demands*, 77.
8 Hall, *Opuscula quaedam*; *idem, Tractatus aliquot*. On Hall see F. van Ortroy, 'Vie du bienheureux martyr Jean Fisher', *Annalecta Bollandiana* x (1891), 195–7. On the Netherlands, see C. Mercier, 'Les théories politiques des Calvinistes dans les pays-bas à la fin du XVIe siècle et au début du XVIIe siècle', *Revue d'histoire ecclesiastique* XXIX (1933), 40–3; cf. Peeters, *De Christiani principis officio*; Chrysopolitanus, *De tumultuosa Belgarum rebellione sedanda*.
9 Blackwood, *De coniunctione*, esp. 67^v–107^v. On France, cf. C. Labitte, *De la démocratie chez les prédicateurs de la Ligue* (Paris, 1865), 94–102; G. Weill, *Les théories sur le pouvoir royal en France pendant les guerres de religion* (Paris, 1892), 198ff; W. F. Church, *Constitutional thought in sixteenth century France* (Cambridge, Mass., 1941), 243–71; J. W. Allen, *A history of political thought in the sixteenth century* (London, 1961), 377–80; J. N. Figgis, *The theory of the divine right of kings* (Cambridge, 1896), 128–33.

10 Blackwood, *Adversus Georgii Buchanani Dialogum*, in *Opera omnia*, 146.

11 Winzet, *Certain tractates*, I, Intro.

12 Winzet, *Flagellum sectariorum*, 155.

13 Compare *Vindiciae*, question 1 and *Flagellum*, pp. 2–3; *Vindiciae*, p. 68 and *Flagellum*, p. 6; *Vindiciae*, p. 69 and *Flagellum*, p. 31; *Vindiciae*, question 2 and *Flagellum*, p. 77; *Vindiciae*, p. 87 and *Flagellum*, p. 78.

14 Stapleton, *The history*, sig. * 3; B.L. Lansdowne MS 96/51 and 52; Strype, *Annals*, I, ii, 400, 405; Bristow, *A brief treatise*, esp. Motives 1, 2, 3, 9, 12, 14, 22, 23, 24, 27, 46; Rastell *A confutation*, 162; Persons, *A defence of the censure*, 12–18, 27ff; Crowley, *An answer to six reasons*, sigs. A4–B3ᵛ.

15 'Brief advices how to confer with ordinary heretics', Bodleian MS Jones 53, fo. 232–2ᵛ.

16 Allen, *An apology*, 3–4; Broughton, *An apologetical epistle*, 59–67, 83–4, 107–10; Strype, *Annals*, I, ii, 404; Campion, *Campian Englished*, 68–71, 182–3.

17 More, *Responsio ad Lutherum*, I, 141, 271, 691, 693 and II, 917; *The dialogue concerning Tyndale*, Book 4, chap. 18 and Book 5, chap. 14 and p. 318; *The apology*, 184; *The supplication of souls*, 55, 75–6, 92; *Epistola in qua...respondet*, A4.

18 Christopherson, *An exhortation*, sigs. TIff, Bb6ff; J. A. Muller, *Stephen Gardiner and the Tudor reaction* (London, 1926), 53, 81, 92–4, 139, 231, 274; H. F. M. Prescott, *Mary Tudor* (London, 1962), 110.

19 Acts 5.37; Josephus, *The Jewish war* (trans. G. A. Williamson, Harmondsworth, 1967), Book 2, chap. 8, 126; Hall, *De necessitate unius regis*, 4, in *Tractatus aliquot*.

20 *The New Testament*, 416 (Rom. 13.4).

21 Stapleton, *A counterblast*, 15.

22 Martial, *A reply*, sig. **; *idem*, *A treatise of the cross*, 137.

23 Bristow, *Demands*, 88; Persons, *A brief discourse*, sig. ✝ 7ᵛ; *idem*, *A brief censure*, sig. C1–1ᵛ; *The New Testament*, 659 (1 Pet. 2.16); Stapleton, *A counterblast*, 15; cf. Rainolds, *A refutation of sundry reprehensions*, 16–17.

24 Harding, *A confutation*, 173–7; Persons, *A brief censure*, sig. C4; Campion, *Campian Englished*, 143–5.

25 Persons, *A treatise of three conversions*, III, 460–5; *idem*, *An epistle of the persecution*, 24–5; cf. Dorman, *A proof*, 123.

26 Kellison, *A survey*, 600–9.

27 Luther, *Works*, vol. 45, 77–129; Frarin, *An oration*, sig. D8–8ᵛ.

28 Staphylus, *The apology*, 123, 139ᵛ–142; Persons, *A brief discourse*, sig. ✝ 7ᵛ; B. L. Woolf, *Reformation writings of Martin Luther* (London, 1970), I, 270; More, *Responsio ad Lutherum*, I, 271, and II, 917 (for reference to *Assertio septem sacramentorum*).

29 Frarin, *op. cit.*, sig. D8ᵛ; Luther, *Works*, vol. 46, 155–205.

30 Persons, *A brief discourse*, sig. ✝ 7ᵛ; Harding, *A confutation*, 173ff;

Stapleton, *A counterblast*, 15^v; Staphylus, *The apology*, 141^v. Cf. Martial, *A reply*, sig. **; Rainolds, *A refutation*, 15–16.

31 Frarin, *op. cit.*, sigs. E2^v–4^v.

32 Staphylus, *op. cit.*, 142–2^v; Harding, *loc. cit.*; Stapleton, *loc. cit.*

33 Dorman, *A proof*, 139–40; Southwell, *An epistle of comfort*, 105–6; Osorius, *An epistle*, 50^v–1; Calvin, *Institution*, IV, x (*Corpus Reformatorum*, XXXII, 762–3).

34 Persons, *A brief discourse*, sig. ╪ 7^v–8; *idem*, *A brief censure*, sig. C1^v; Calvin, *op. cit.*, III, XIX (343ff); cf. Dury, *Confutatio responsionis*, 308^v–9^v.

35 Kellison, *A survey*, 475–508.

36 Staphylus, *The apology*, 123; Allen, *An apology*, 96^v; Persons, *A Christian directory*, preface.

37 Dorman, *A proof*, 137^v–8; Frarin, *An oration*, sigs. E6^v–F2, G3–4; Harding, *A detection*, 87.

38 Harding, *A confutation*, 176; Stapleton, *A counterblast*, 16, 20^v.

39 Rainolds, *A refutation*, 16; cf. *The New Testament*, 28.

40 Persons, *A Christian directory*, preface; Allen, *Apology*, 95; Bourchier, *Historia ecclesiastica*, 70–8; Stapleton, *A counterblast*, 16^v–20^v.

41 Allen, *Apology*, 95; Stapleton, *A counterblast*, 15^v; Harding, *A detection*, 86–8.

42 Broughton, *An apologetical epistle*, 87; Foxe, *Acts and monuments*, V, 570–99; Tyndale, *Doctrinal treatises*, 127–334, footnotes to the text for these articles.

43 Rainolds, *A refutation*, 18; Persons, *A brief discourse*, sig. ╪ 8; Harding, *A detection*, 14^v; Martial, *A reply*, sig. **^{v}; Frarin, *An oration*, sigs. E6, F2–3; Rastell, *A confutation*, 166; Harding, *A confutation*, 173–3^v; Hosius, *A most excellent treatise*, sig. a4^v; Allen, *An apology*, 95^v–6.

44 Frarin, *op. cit.*, sigs. F2^v–3.

45 Stapleton, *A counterblast*, 23–6^v; Knox, *Appellation*, 77, 36 (see *Works*, IV, 497, 539–40); Goodman, *How superior powers*, 54, 96 and preface; Gilby, *An admonition*, in Knox, *Appellation*, 59^v–77; cf. Dorman, *A proof*, 119–20.

46 Strype, *Annals*, I, ii, 436–7.

47 J. Murren, 'An addition with an apology to the causes of burning of Paul's church' (1561), in Pilkington, *Works*, 484–6; Hosea 4.9.

48 Lindanus, *Certain tables*, sig. E5–5^v.

49 Dorman, *A proof*, 120.

50 Allen, *An apology*, 96.

51 T. H. Clancy, *Papist pamphleteers* (Chicago, 1964), 23, 87.

52 Persons, *A defence of the censure*, 17 (1st pagination); cf. Persons, *A brief discourse*, sigs. ╪ 8^v– ╪╪ 2.

53 Harpsfield, *Dialogi sex*, 901–2; Dorman, *A proof*, 139–40.

54 A. C. Southern (in *Elizabethan recusant prose*, 319–20) suggests that the prefatory matter to this book is by 'G. T.', who signs the epistle; I assume that this is a pseudonym for Persons.

55 Persons, *An epistle of the persecution*, 18–23; cf. Feckenham in Tomson, *An answer*, 12ᵛff.
56 Persons, *op. cit.*, 23–6.
57 Persons, *op. cit.*, 10–15.
58 Broughton, *An apologetical epistle*, 93.
59 Persons, *op. cit.*, 16–17.
60 Broughton, *op. cit.*, 90–2; Genesis 46.26; Acts 7.14; Numbers 1.
61 Persons, *A discovery*, sigs. F6–H2ᵛ; Martin, *Roma sancta*; cf. Sander, *A brief treatise of usury*.
62 Broughton, *op. cit.*, 103–4, 111; cf. J. Murren, in Pilkington, *Works*, 485–6.
63 Dorman, *A proof*, 138–8ᵛ. Cf. Broughton, *op. cit.*, 111; Wright, *A treatise*, sig. R3; H. B., *A consolatory letter*, 17–18.
64 Murren in Pilkington, *Works*, 481–6.
65 Fitzherbert, *A defence*, 45ᵛ–6.
66 Broughton, *The first part*, 129–44 (quotation at 132).

6 Recusancy

1 The name given in the seventeenth century to the doctrine that God should be obeyed before men, when it was combined with the doctrine of political non-resistance, was 'passive obedience'. As Christopher Morris points out, a better name would be passive disobedience, since it insisted on disobedience to kings in certain circumstances (*Political thought in England, Tyndale to Hooker* (London, 1953), 38). I use the term 'religious resistance': this separates it clearly from the question of political loyalty, and suggests (by 'resistance') a more determined opposition than 'disobedience' does; cf. E. Rose, *Cases of conscience* (Cambridge, 1975), 221–3, 233. The word 'resistance' was used at the time in this sense: Allen, *An apology*, 109ᵛ; Martin, 'The copy of a letter to Mr Doctor Whyte Warden of New College in Oxford', in *A treatise of Christian peregrination*; *The declaration of the fathers of the Council of Trent*, 37, in Garnet, *A treatise of Christian renunciation*; Allen, *A true, sincere and modest defence*, 100, cf. 244.
2 Acts 5.29; Matt. 22.21, etc.
3 Hide, *A consolatory epistle*, sigs. B2–3; Joshua 1.17–18.
4 J. Bossy, 'The English Catholic community 1603–1625', in A. G. R. Smith (ed.), *The reign of James VI and I* (London, 1974), 105.
5 Printed in Pilkington, *Works*, 617–39. I am grateful to Dr Norman L. Jones for bringing this tract to my attention and for telling me of the MS copy in the Archives of Corpus Christi College, Cambridge (105/39, pp. 365–71; cf. 105/38, p. 365, letter of January 1562 to the Privy Council concerning the document). On Murren, cf. C. Haigh, *Reformation and reaction in Tudor Lancashire* (Cambridge, 1975), index.
6 W. R. Trimble, *The Catholic laity in Elizabethan England* (Cambridge, Mass., 1964), 11; cf. Knox, *Letters of Allen*, 21.
7 Cf., in favour of abstention from communion, Allen, *A defence and*

declaration, sig. ** 1; and, on Aglionby's approval of attendance at church but distaste for communion, expressed in the House of Commons in 1571, J. E. Neale, *Elizabeth I and her parliaments 1559–1581* (London, 1953), 212–15.

8 The Trent declaration is printed at the end of Garnet, *A treatise of Christian renunciation.*

9 Southwell, *An epistle*, 200.

10 Vaux, *A catechism*, Intro., xxx–xxxix; cf. Haigh, *Reformation and reaction*, 249–50.

11 Sander, *A treatise*, sig. A–A6ᵛ; cf. also Lindanus, *Certain tables*, sig. A7ᵛ, where Evans told Catholics to flee from the prating of heretics in their sermons; and Allen, *A treatise made in defence*, sig. ** 1ᵛ, against taking sacraments from Protestant ministers.

12 Young, *De schismate*, republished in 1603 as *Pacis ecclesiasticae perturbator*, when old copies of the book seem to have been used with a new title-page, which suggests that the first edition did not circulate widely.

13 The booklet is entitled 'Certain considerations and causes, moving me not to be present at, nor to receive, neither use the service of the new book, otherwise called the Common Book of Prayer'. There is a MS copy at Oscott College and another in the Bodleian, Rawlinson MS D107. 4. The text is printed in Fulke, *A confutation*, see 1ᵛ–17. Cf. A. C. Southern, *Elizabethan recusant prose*, 405–6, where it is attributed to Feckenham. He, however, denied authorship (probably falsely), see *A true report of a conference betwixt Doctor Fulke and the papists* (1580), printed in R. Webster ' "Conference" at Wisbech, a glimpse of Bishop Watson and Abbot Feckenham in 1580', *Downside Review* LIV (1936), 336.

14 Cf. Haigh, *op. cit.*, 247–68.

15 Bristow, *A brief treatise*, 129ᵛff; Persons, *A brief discourse*; Richard White's Welsh verse in Pollen, *Unpublished documents*, 93–5; *The New Testament*, 27–8 (Matt. 10.32–4), 94 (Mark 3.13), 299 (Acts 4.19), 482 (2 Cor. 6.14), 590 (2 Tim. 2.17), 599 (Titus 3.10), 689–90 (2 John 10), 704 (Rev. 3.22); H. B., *A consolatory letter*; I. G., 'An answer to a comfortable advertisement', Oscott MSS; Martin, *A treatise of schism*; Southwell, *An epistle of comfort*, esp. chap. 12; Garnet, *A treatise of Christian renunciation; idem, An apology*; Hill, *A quartron of reasons*; Worthington, *A relation*; 'An exhortation by (John) Boste against going to Protestant churches (?1584)', in Pollen, *Unpublished documents*, 68–9; P.R.O., S.P. 12/136/14, 15, 16; 'The satisfaction of Mr James Bosgrave', in Allen, *A true report*, 32ᵛ–4ᵛ; Wright, *The disposition*, 'To Catholic-like Protestants'.

16 Cf. the letters at the end of Martin, *A treatise of Christian peregrination* (1583); P. Mowle's commonplace book, Oscott MSS, esp. pp. 336–9.

17 P.R.O., S.P. 12/136/15, 16 (*sub fine*); H. B., *A consolatory letter*, 55–8; Hill, *A quartron of reasons*, 178–9; Persons, *A brief discourse*, 37ᵛ–43ᵛ [*vere* 44ᵛ].

18 Persons, *op. cit.*, 58ᵛ–9.
19 1 Kings 12–13; Martin, *op. cit.*, sig. Cvii; 1 Kings 18; Worthington, *op. cit.*, 43 Daniel chaps. 1, 3 and 6; Martin, *op. cit.*, sig Diiᵛ–iii; Worthington, *op. cit.*, 43.
20 A. C. Southern, *Elizabethan recusant prose* (London, 1950), 350–3, 452–3; Martin, *op. cit.*, sig. D2; Allen, *A true, sincere and modest defence*, 69.
21 See note 15 above.
22 Garnet, *A treatise of Christian renunciation*; idem, *An apology*, 175–6.
23 *Ibid*, 164–5; Hill, *op. cit.*, 182.
24 Martin, *op. cit.*, sig. ** viiᵛ–viii.
25 Garnet, *An apology*, 69–82; Martin, *op. cit.*, sig. Ciiᵛ; Hill, *op. cit.*, 171.
26 P.R.O., S.P. 12/136/14.
27 W. Gifford, 'Theses theologicae de cultu externo contra hereticos', B.L. Lansdowne MS 96/54.
28 Persons, *op. cit.*, 8ᵛ.
29 H. B., *A consolatory letter*, 53–4; Persons, *op. cit.*, 52–8; Hill, *A quartron of reasons*, 177; Southwell, *An epistle of comfort*, 200–1.
30 Garnet, *An apology*, 131–46; Persons, *op. cit.*, 15ᵛ–18.
31 H. B., *A consolatory letter*. I would tentatively ascribe this work to Robert Southwell: the style I find very like his; he was interested in the subject of recusancy; it was the only book apart from the *Epistle of comfort* printed at Southwell's secret 'Arundel House' press (see Allison & Rogers, *op. cit.*, 184); references in the bibliographies of Southwell by C. Dodd (*Church history*, II (Brussels, 1739), 148) and G. Oliver (*Collections* (1845), 194) suggest that they confused the *Consolatory letter* and the *Epistle*. On the whole I think I prefer the *Consolatory letter* to the *Epistle* as a piece of writing.
32 H. B., *op. cit.*, 81–2.
33 *Ibid*, 105.
34 *Ibid*, 78–9.

7 *Opponents of recusancy*

1 Cf. E. Rose, *Cases of conscience* (Cambridge, 1975), esp. chap. 4; Hicks, *Letters of Persons*, 328, 338.
2 P.R.O., S.P. 12/144/69, unfoliated; Pollen, *Memoirs of Persons*, II, 27–8 and note, 179–80; Southern, *op. cit.*, 139–40; Rose, *op. cit.*, 75–7.
3 Persons, *A brief discourse*, 24ᵛ, 62–3ᵛ; Martin, *A treatise of schism*, sig. Fviᵛ; 'The satisfaction of Mr James Bosgrave', in Allen, *A true report*, 32ᵛ–4ᵛ; Garnet, *An apology*, 54–7; I. G., 'An answer to a comfortable advertisement', chap. 4, Oscott MSS.
4 Acts 5.34–42; John 3.1–21 and 19.38–9; Luke 23.50; 1 Kings 18; 2 Kings 5.
5 Martin, *op. cit.*, sigs. ** 3ᵛ, F5–7ᵛ; Persons, *op. cit.*, 24ᵛ, 62–3ᵛ; I. G., 'An answer', chaps. 3 and 4, Oscott MSS; Garnet, *Apology*, 54–5; idem, *A treatise of Christian renunciation*, 156.
6 See p. 110 and n. 6.
7 Pollen, *Memoirs of Persons*, II, 179–81, IV, 3–7.

8 B.L. Add. MS 39830, fos. 14–20.

9 Aquinas, *Summa theologica*, IIa IIae, q. 10, art. 11.

10 W. Allen to the Catholics of England, Rome, 12 December 1592, Westminster, AIV/132; P.R.O., S.P. 12/243/80, 81, 82; Knox, *Letters of Allen*, 343–6; Garnet, *A treatise of Christian renunciation*; idem, *Apology*; I. G., 'An answer to a comfortable advertisement', Oscott MSS; Southern (*op. cit.*, 139–40), following C. G. Bayne (*Anglo-Roman relations 1558–1565* (Oxford, 1913), 289) attributes this work to a layman, a certain George Cotton. The MS has no other indication of authorship than the initials with which it is signed at the end: I read these as 'I. G.', not 'G. C.', as Bayne did. The title and preface to the book say that the author is a priest, living in the southern part of England, and we are presumably to date the tract to about 1593, the date when Garnet's books were probably printed. Using G. Anstruther, *The seminary priests* (Ware, 1968), we find two men who answer this description: John Green, imprisoned at Wisbech, and the Jesuit John Gerard. Of these, Gerard seems to me the more probable author, especially when we consider the interest of his superior, Garnet, in Bell. The tract seems to be holograph, and I have compared its handwriting with that of a letter of Gerard's of 1607 (P.R.O., S.P. 14/18/35). Although the style of the writing is rather different (secretary hand in 1593 and a bastard secretary italic in 1607), there is sufficient similarity in the handwriting of the two to suggest that they were written by the same man.

11 *D.N.B.*; Bell, *Motives*; Aveling, *Northern Catholics* (London, 1966), 151–2; Haigh, *op. cit.*, 280, 289.

12 I. G., *op. cit.*, chap. 1.

13 *Ibid.*

14 *Ibid*, chap. 6.

15 *Ibid*, chaps. 2, 3, 6; Garnet, *Apology*, 156–7; Martin allowed Catholics to go to Protestant churches if they went protesting the Catholic faith and defying the heretical services of the Protestants, Martin, *op. cit.*, sig. F7–7ᵛ.

16 Garnet, *op. cit.*, 17–29; Daniel 3; 2 Kings 10.

17 I. G., *op. cit.*, chap. 1.

18 Garnet, *Apology*, 37–40; Aristotle, *Nichomachean Ethics*, Book 5, chap. 1.

19 I. G., *op. cit.*, chap. 4.

20 *Ibid*; Garnet, *op. cit.*, 143–5.

21 I. G., *op. cit.*, chap. 4.

22 *Ibid*, chap. 5.

23 *Ibid*; M. ab Azpilcueta (Navarre), *Enchiridion* (Antwerp, 1575), 696–7; Thomas de Vio (Cajetan), *Summa* (Rome, 1525), s.v. 'Excommunicatus'; Silvestro Mazzoloni da Prierio (Sylvester), *Summa summarum*, s.v. 'Excommunicatus'.

24 I. G., 'An answer', chap. 4; Bayne, *op. cit.*, 162; Hicks, *Letters of Persons*, 51; Aveling, *Northern Catholics*, 37–40; idem, *The handle and the axe*, 37–8.

25 Garnet, *A treatise of Christian renunciation*, 159–60; Bayne, *op. cit.*, 173 note; Knox, *Letters of Allen*, 100; *idem, Douai diaries*, 354–5; Bodleian MS Rawlinson D1506, fo. 106ᵛ; Persons, 'Of the life and martyrdom of Fr Edmond Campian', *Letters and Notices*, xii (Roehampton, 1878), 35–6.

26 Allen, *A true report*, 'An admonition to the reader'.

27 I. G., *op. cit.*, chap. 4; Pollen, *Memoirs of Persons*, ii, 182.

28 See pp. 198–9.

29 Pollen, *Unpublished documents*, 179–82.

30 'Quandoquidem tam Rex ipse, quam status seu respublica Anglicana persuasum sibi habere videntur, Catholicos recusantes suspectae fidei esse, seu potius proditores, eo quod ecclesias Protestantium adire recusant, nos qui neque Regem, neque rempublicam scandalizare vellemus, decrevimus eousque suae Maiestatis voluntati per leges suas explicatae hac in re nos conformare, ut praesentiam nostram dictis ecclesiis iuxta earumdem legum praescriptum exhibeamus; hocque ea sola de causa, ut Maiestati suae atque reipublicae certum faciamus, nos non ita esse reconciliatos (Ecclesiae Romanae) ut illud praeiudicio sit legitimae obedientiae, quam suae Maiestati praestare debemus. Nemo igitur hoc factum nostrum, vel male intelligat, vel sinistre interpretetur, quasi vel orandi, vel aterius cuiuslibet actus religionis praestandi causa huc venerimus.' Persons, *Quaestiones duae*, 128–9; Foley, *Records* v, 284, 371, 373–4.

31 Rose, *Cases of conscience*, 246–50; B.L. MS Sloane 1941. 12 and MS Sloane 1582; Ampleforth MS 59 ('A charitable caveat for the over confident', 1663), MSS 122 and 123 ('A final answer to an endless propounder').

8 Casuistry and recusancy

1 Cf. W. K. Jordan, *The development of religious toleration in England* (London, 1932), 382ff; C. Morris, *Political thought in England Tyndale to Hooker*, 137.

2 Hall, *De quinquapartita conscientia*, esp. 3ff; cf. Sayer, *Clavis regia sacerdotum*, 3–5; Saint-German, *Doctor and student*, Dial. i, chaps. xiii and xv.

3 Martin, *A treatise of schism*, sig. A6ᵛ; Persons, *A brief discourse*, sigs. ‡‡ 3–4; *idem, A conference*, i, 215; H. B., *A consolatory letter*, 11–12; Hill, *A quartron of reasons*, 181–2.

4 See my edition of the most important casuist documents, *Elizabethan casuistry* (Catholic Record Society, 1981).

5 Douai MS 484, pp. 408–26; Bodleian MS Rawlinson D1351, fos. 4–23ᵛ.

6 Knox, *Letters of Allen*, 66. I am grateful to Prof. John Bossy for bringing this reference to my attention.

7 Douai MS 484, pp. 422–3.

8 Douai MS 484, pp. 410, 421–2; Bodleian MS Rawlinson D1351, fos. 8, 18; Bodleian MS Jones 53, fos. 245ᵛ–6ᵛ.

9 Lambeth MS 565, fos. 16–55ᵛ.

10 *Ibid*, preface, fos. 16–17.

11 L. Vereecke, *Conscience morale et loi humaine selon Gabriel Vazquez* (Tournai, 1957), chap. ii.

12 Lambeth MS 565, fos. 16–17; Hall, *De quinquapartita conscientia,* 272–4.

13 Lambeth MS 565, fos. 30ᵛ–31ᵛ.

14 'in tali praesertim regno ubi pro dignitate ecclesiae catholicae maxime esset nobiles praesertim familias et divites in suo pristino honore dignitateque conservari ut post Reginae mortem possint sua authoritate et potentia pro fide stare et viribus atque potentia contra haereticorum audatiam eam tueri. Adde quod incredibile est quantum obsit religioni Catholicae quando aliquis nobilium detectus Catholicus punitur saepe enim eius ruina haereticus aliquis attolitur et inde status paene omnes ac tituli honorum cum magno ecclesiae detrimento ad haereticos devolvuntur'. Lambeth MS 565, fos. 24–6.

15 See pp. 110–13.

16 Lambeth MS 565, fos. 36ᵛ–7.

17 'Ad confessionem admitti potest non tum ad absolutionem', *ibid,* fo. 37–7ᵛ; Douai MS 484, p. 416.

18 'quia puto cirtissimum esse modo in Anglia non solum apud Catholicos sed etiam apud haereticos multos ex iis qui ecclesias et conciones haereticorum frequentant esse Catholicos et Catholicissimos et per ingressum illum in dictas ecclesias eos non se profiteri haereticos sed solum non detegere se Catholicos sicut nec tenentur semper se detegere sed solum in articulo necessitatis', Lambeth MS 565, fo. 37.

19 M. Creighton, 'The excommunication of Queen Elizabeth', *English Historical Review* vii (1892), 84–8; A. O. Meyer, *England and the Catholic Church under Queen Elizabeth* (trans. J. B. McKee, London, 1961), 136 note 1, 140.

20 Strype, *Annals,* ii, ii, 348–51; B.L. MS Lansdowne 96/11.

21 Bodleian MS Jones 53, fos. 193–211.

22 P.R.O., S.P. 12/279/90; E. Rose, *Cases of conscience* (Cambridge, 1975), 82–5; W. R. Trimble, *The Catholic laity in Elizabethan England* (Cambridge, Mass., 1964), 176 note.

23 P.R.O., S.P. 12/136/15, 16; Rose, *op. cit.,* 60–4; Knox, *Letters of Allen,* 359, 361; Lambeth MS 565, fo. 74ᵛ; Law, *The Archpriest controversy,* i, 152; H.M.C., *Calendar of MSS of the Marquis of Salisbury,* iv (London, 1892), 618–19; Hicks, *Letters of Persons,* 356; cf. Bossy, *The English Catholic community 1570–1850* (London, 1975), 123.

24 Knox, *op. cit.,* 344–5.

9 Casuistry and the resistance of the laity

1 Garnet, *A treatise of Christian renunciation,* 10–11, 100–1, 144–8 (quotation at 145); cf. *The New Testament,* 28 (Matt. 10.34); John Tippet's letter to his father in Pollen, *Memoirs of Persons,* ii, 80–2; cf. Morris, *Troubles,* iii, 229. Similarly in 1601 Sir Thomas Tresham argued from the fact that a wife was not subject to her husband in

spiritual matters that he was not therefore liable for any recusancy fines she might incur, see P.R.O., S.P. 12/281/fo. 90; B.L. Add MS 39829, n. 1 (and cf. Add. MS 39830, fo. 12–12ᵛ); cf. also (perhaps) J. E. Neale, *Elizabeth I and her parliaments 1559–1581* (London, 1953), 293–4.

2 H. B., *A consolatory letter*, 8–10.

3 A. C. Southern, *Elizabethan recusant prose* (London, 1950), chap. III, §3; Stapleton, *A counterblast*, 14–28; Rose, *Cases of conscience*, 58.

4 Hide, *A consolatory epistle*, sig. E7.

5 Southern, *op. cit.*, 298; Martin, *A treatise of Christian peregrination*, 'The copy of a letter to Mr Doctor Whyte, Warden of New College in Oxford'; cf. 'To my loving and best beloved sisters', in *ibid.*

6 B. Camm (ed.), *Lives of English martyrs*, II (London, 1905), chap. II; Persons, 'Of the life and martyrdom of Fr Edmond Campian', *Letters and Notices*, XI (1877), 237–9; Duke of Norfolk (ed.), *The lives of Philip Howard, Earl of Arundel and of Anne Dacres his wife* (London, 1857), 38–49; Sander, *De visibili monarchia*, 736–8; Gibbons, *Concertatio*, II, 44ᵛ.

7 Christie, *Letters of Copley*, Intro., p. 8.

8 Allen, *A brief history*, sig. C6.

9 Stonyhurst MS Anglia III, fos. 109–10ᵛ; R. B. Merriman, 'Some notes on the treatment of the English Catholics in the reign of Elizabeth', *A.H.R.* XIII (1907–8), 480–500; W. N. Sainsbury (ed.), *Calendar State Papers Colonial* IX (London, 1893), 8–23.

10 *The New Testament*, 689–90.

11 Lambeth MS 565, fos. 30ᵛ–31ᵛ.

12 R. Naz, *Dictionaire de droit canonique*, I (Paris, 1935), 250–2; J. D. Mansi, *Sacrorum conciliorum nova et amplissima collectio*, vol. 29 (Venice, 1788), 103 and vol. 32 (Paris, 1902), 958–9; Azpilcueta, *Enchiridion*, 696–7.

13 Hall, *De quinquapartita conscientia*, 537–9; Sayer, *Casuum conscientiae*, 154–5.

14 Antoninus, *Repertorium*, II, sig. NNᵛ (3a, tit. xxv).

15 Panormitanus, *Apparatus . . in Clementinas*, sigs. r3ᵛ–5ᵛ; Auximo, *Supplementum*, s.v. 'clericus', 3.

16 'hinc apparet difficultas nostrae questionis si enim sequamur relationem Antonini non tenemur vitare haereticos sive sint reconsiliati sive non cum non sint specialiter declarati excommunicati. si autem sequamur relationem Pan: eos vitare tenemur hoc ipso quod aliquando publici haeretici fuerunt sic enim sunt publici excommunicati', Lambeth MS 565, fo. 31.

17 Covarruvias y Leyva, *Opera omnia*, vol. I, 354 (*Alma mater*, 1a, §2, n. 7).

18 Lambeth MS 565, fos. 34ᵛ–35, 38–8ᵛ; Douai MS 484, pp. 408, 415; Bodleian MS Rawlinson D1351, fos. 4ᵛ–5, 6ᵛ; Bodleian MS Jones 53, fos. 210ᵛ, 239ᵛ, 240ᵛ, 250ᵛ; Strype, *Annals*, II, ii, 349, 351.

19 'melius est contrahere cum persona humilioris conditionis quam cum haeretico et ratio est propter ius naturae de evitanda malorum familiaritate, si enim aliqua familiaritas est apta ad seducendum est haec

praecipua maritalis quae ex duabus unam carnem efficit', Lambeth
MS 565, fos. 43–4, 34–5, 51ᵛ; Douai MS 484, pp. 410, 412–13; Bodleian
MS Rawlinson D1352, fos. 6ᵛ, 8, 9, 15–15ᵛ; Bodleian MS Jones 53, fos.
208ᵛ–10, 245ᵛ; cf. J. Bossy, *op. cit.*, 133ff; H. Aveling, 'The marriages
of Catholic recusants 1559–1642', *Journal of Ecclesiastical History* 14
(1963), 69–71.

20 Lambeth MS 565, fos. 41–2, 44–4ᵛ, 52–2ᵛ; Douai MS 484, pp. 410*bis*,
411, 412, 416; Bodleian MS Rawlinson D1351, fos. 8ᵛ, 9–9ᵛ; Bodleian
MS Jones 53, fo. 247–7ᵛ; Aquinas, *Summa theologica*, IIa IIae, q. 10,
art. 11; cf. Bossy, *op. cit.*, 168–81; R. Southwell, *Two letters and short
rules of a good life* (ed. N. P. Brown, Charlottesville, 1973), 49–51.

21 Lambeth MS 565, fos. 21–1ᵛ, 42–2ᵛ, 55–5ᵛ, 73ᵛ; Douai MS 484,
pp. 416–18, 421, 425; Bodleian MS Rawlinson D1351, fos. 9ᵛ, 12,
15ᵛ–16; Bodleian MS Jones 53, fos. 206–6ᵛ, 207ᵛ–8; Knox, *Letters of
Allen*, 356; *idem*, *Douai diaries*, 354–5; Hall, *De quinquapartita
conscientia*, 471–87; Azpilcueta, *Enchiridion*, chap. 21, §24 and §26;
Aquinas, *Summa theologica cum commentariis Thomas de Vio
Caietani*, in IIa IIae, q. 249, art. 4 and q. 147, art. 5; Hill, *A quartron of
reasons*, 185–7; Creighton, *art. cit.*, *E.H.R.* VII (1892), 85, 88; Meyer,
op. cit., 136 note; Rose, *op. cit.*, 85–6; Bossy, *op. cit.*, 110–21.

22 'an liceat literis, colloquiis, conviviis, aliisque amoris signis blande cum
illis agere...', 'si quis Christianus familiariter sine gravi necessitate
vellet uti Judais et Turcis, esset malum signum multo magis cum
Protestantibus, cum acerbiores sint hostes Christi et multo magis
detestandi', Lambeth MS 565, fos. 54–4ᵛ, 38ᵛ–9; Douai MS 484, p. 425;
Bodleian MS Rawlinson D1351, fo. 7.

23 'licitissimum et sanctissimum opus esse fraudare istos haereticos in
dictis solutionibus non modo ut convertant haec in subsidium Catholi-
corum quid opus est sanctissimum et omni laude dignissimum, sed
etiam si fraudant ut solum ea haereticis subtrahant ne tantum
detinentur contra catholicos immo etiam si hoc faciant ut sibi dictas
pecunias retineant ad usus suae familiae, ac postremo quocunque fine
non per se malo id faciant', Lambeth MS 565, fos. 40–1; Douai MS 484,
p. 411; Bodleian MS Rawlinson D1351, fo. 12–12ᵛ; Bodleian MS
Jones 53, fos. 205ᵛ–6, 248–9; Knox, *Letters of Allen*, 359.

24 Lambeth MS 565, fos. 42ᵛ–3, 44ᵛ–5, 48–9ᵛ, 51–1ᵛ, 73ᵛ–4; Douai MS
484, pp. 410*bis*–411*bis*, 420–1; Bodleian MS Rawlinson D1351, fos.
14–14ᵛ, 17ᵛ, 19–19ᵛ, 21–21ᵛ; Bodleian MS Jones 53, fos. 206ᵛ–7ᵛ,
251ᵛ–3ᵛ; Strype, *Annals*, II, ii, 349–50; Knox, *op. cit.*, 356, 359, 361–2;
cf. J. C. H. Aveling, *The handle and the axe*, 143–5.

25 Lambeth MS 565, fos. 52ᵛ–5; Douai MS 484, pp. 420, 423, 424;
Bodleian MS Rawlinson D1351, fo. 22; Creighton, *art. cit.*, 84, 87.

10 *Casuistry and the resistance of the clergy*

1 Lambeth MS 565, fos. 20–21ᵛ, 26ᵛ–30ᵛ, 31ᵛ–2ᵛ, 36–6ᵛ, 73; Douai MS
484, pp. 408, 409, 410, 410*bis*, 411*bis*; Bodleian MS Rawlinson D1351,
fos. 4–4ᵛ, 7ᵛ, 9ᵛ, 17–17ᵛ, 19ᵛ–20, 23–3ᵛ; Bodleian MS Jones 53, fos. 210,

239, 242ᵛ–3, 244ᵛ–5, 246ᵛ–7, 249ᵛ–50, 255; Meyer, *England and the Catholic Church*, App. xvii; Law, *Archpriest controversy*, I, 153.

2 Allen, *A true, sincere and modest defence*, 261ff; Southwell, *An humble supplication*, 8–9; Persons, *Elizabethae*, 164ff. Cf. Bodleian MS Rawlinson D107, fo. 135ᵛ; Allen to Chauncy, 10 August 1577, in Knox, *Letters of Allen*, 36; Hicks, *Letters of Persons*, 319–21; Bossy, *op. cit.*, 250–1.

3 Lambeth MS 565, fo. 17ᵛ; Luke 24.13; Galatians 2.13; Joshua 8; Adrian VI, *Quaestiones*, in 4, q. 1.

4 'valde durum est tollere aequivocationes ab humano commertio cum saepe de multis interrogemur de quibus respondere non expedit quas tum responsiones nunquam fortasse melius quam aequivocatione supterfugimus', Lambeth MS 565, fo. 18.

5 'secundum potestatem quam ego habeo, et causae cognitionem quaero ut mihi tanquam tuo superiori confitearis an tu sis Petrus', Lambeth MS 565, fo. 18ᵛ.

6 'nego me esse Petrum qui tibi tanquam iudici secundum potestatem et cognitionem quam habes teneor respondere', Lambeth MS 565, fo. 18ᵛ.

7 '1°, quia regina haeretica non est legitime regina, de qua credere est alterius negotii dubitatio est etiam de illa declaratione Pii Quinti facta in Anglia contra Reginam etc. 2°, quia saltem in hoc facto non gerit se ut reginam sed exercens tyrannidem persequendo religionem. 3°, quia clericus non tenetur respondere iudici seculari sed solum ecclesiastico. 4°, quia iudex procedit ex suspicione et coniecturis ut plurimum insufficientibus in iudicio utpote quia nullam sciant probationem et plerumque ex coniecturis quas habet tanquam privata persona non ex cognitione quam habet ut iudex', Lambeth MS 565, fos. 18ᵛ–19.

8 Lambeth MS 565, fos. 17–19ᵛ, 26ᵛ; Douai MS 484, pp. 423–4, 424–5; Bodleian MS Rawlinson D1351, fos. 22ᵛ–3, 13–14.

9 Lambeth MS 565, fos. 26ᵛ, 19ᵛ–20.

10 'dum eis ob oculos ponit viros constantes qui etiam non quaesiti offerunt se hilariter ad tormenta', Lambeth MS 565, fo. 23ᵛ.

11 Lambeth MS 565, fos. 23–4.

12 Lambeth MS 565, fos. 54ᵛ–5; Mark 6.23–7; Matt. 14.7–9; Douai MS 484, p. 423; Bodleian MS Rawlinson D1351, fo. 13.

13 Lambeth MS 565, fo. 55ᵛ; Douai MS 484, pp. 423–4, 425; Bodleian MS Rawlinson D1351, fos. 13–14; Aquinas, *Summa theologica cum commentariis Thomae de Vio Caietani*, in IIa IIae, q. 88, and q. 113.

14 C. Devlin, *Robert Southwell* (London, 1956), 311ff.

15 J. Gerard, *The autobiography of an Elizabethan* (trans. P. Caraman, London, 1956), appendix F; H.M.C., *Calendar of manuscripts of the Marquis of Salisbury*, x, 284.

16 Garnet, *A treatise of equivocation*. Authorship attributed to Garnet in J. Gerard, 'Contributions towards a life of Fr Henry Garnet S. J.', *The Month* XCI (1898), 367; cf. A. F. Allison, 'The writings of Fr Henry Garnet', *Biographical Studies* I (1951–2), 7–21. Authorship attributed to John Gerard (probably wrongly) in P.R.O., S.P. 14/17/33 and 34.

17 Garnet, *A treatise of equivocation*, 24ff; Persons, *A treatise tending to*

mitigation (1607), 358–405; *idem, A brief apology* (1601), 203; Mark 13.32.

18 Persons, *A treatise tending to mitigation*, 381–2, 285.

19 Persons, *op. cit.*, 384–6; Sepulveda, *'De ratione dicendi testimonium'* in *Opera omnia*, IV, 375–413; Morton, *A full satisfaction*, 47–103; Bagshaw, *A sparing discovery*, 11; *idem*, 'An answer', in H. Ely, *Certain brief notes*, 36–7; J. C. H. Aveling, *The handle and the axe*, 82–3; I. von Döllinger & H. Reusch, *Geschichte der Moralstreitigkeiten in der römisch-katholischen Kirche* (Nördlingen, 1889), I, 34 note.

20 Garnet, *A treatise of equivocation*, 29–31; Persons, *A treatise tending to mitigation*, 310ff; Soto, *Relectio . . . de ratione tegendi et detegendi secretum.*

21 Garnet, *A treatise of equivocation*, 45–6; Hall, *De quinquapartita*, 153ff. Cf. on probabilism, Döllinger & Reusch, *op. cit.*, esp. I, 1–5, 28–9; Rose, *op. cit.*, 72, 84.

22 Garnet, *A treatise of equivocation*, 83–4.

23 Persons, *op. cit.*, 545ff; Athanasius, *Select works* (Oxford, 1892), 255–65.

24 Persons, *op. cit.*, 547.

25 Persons, 'A discourse against taking the oath in England', dated 1606, Stonyhurst MS Coll. P, fos. 161–74^v.

26 *Ibid*, fos. 163^v, 164–4^v, 173^v–4.

27 *Ibid*, fos. 163^v, 173^v.

28 *Ibid*, fo. 164^v.

29 Douai MS 484, p. 423.

11 The development and exposition of ideas of resistance 1584–96

1 J. Bossy, 'Rome and the Elizabethan Catholics: a question of geography', *Historical Journal* VII (1964), 135–49.

2 Rainolds, *De iusta reipublicae* (Paris, 1590 and Antwerp, 1592).

3 J. Bossy, 'Elizabethan Catholicism: the link with France' (Cambridge Ph.D. thesis, 1960, 55ff, 114–30). For the use of English examples in Ligue literature, see L. d'Orleans, *Advertissement des Catholiques anglais aux français Catholiques* (1586), in M. L. Cimber & F. Danjou, *Archives curieuses* (Paris, 1836), 111–255; Bellarmine, *Responsio*, 113; Barclay, *De regno*, 340–1.

4 A. Bellsheim, *Wilhelm Cardinal Allen* (Mainz, 1885), 197, 279.

5 Cf. J. H. M. Salmon, *The French religious wars in English political thought* (Oxford, 1959), esp. chap. 2.

6 This work is now generally ascribed to Charles Arundel; see especially L. Hicks, 'The growth of a myth', *Studies. An Irish Quarterly* XLIV (1957), 91–105. For ascription to Persons, see my Cambridge Ph.D. thesis (1975), 'The political thought of the Elizabethan Catholics', 149–153.

7 Allen, *A true, sincere and modest defence*, 122–46, 56–7.

8 See pp. 29–34.

9 Allen, *op. cit.*, 198.

10 *Ibid*, 127.

11 Persons, *The copy of a letter*, 9–19.
12 *Ibid*, 218–24; cf. 17–19; Allen, *op. cit.*, 260ff.
13 Persons, *op. cit.*, 20–115.
14 *Ibid*, 115–16.
15 *Ibid*, 115–213.
16 *Ibid*, 117–36.
17 Allen, *op. cit.*, 242–3.
18 *Ibid*, chaps. v–viii.
19 G. Mattingly, 'William Allen and Catholic propaganda in England', in 'Aspects de la propagande religieuse', *Travaux d'humanisme et renaissance* 28 (Geneva, 1957), 334.
20 *The copy of a letter... concerning the yielding up of the city of Daventry* (1587), reprinted as *Cardinal Allen's defence of ... Stanley.* Cf. L. Hicks, 'Allen and Deventer (1587)', *The Month* CLXIII (1934); G. Mattingly, *The defeat of the Spanish Armada* (Harmondsworth, 1962), chap. 6; A. J. Loomie, *The Spanish Elizabethans* (London, 1963), chap. v; L. Antheunis, 'Un réfugié Catholique aux Pays-Bas: Sir Roger Ashton', *Revue d'histoire ecclésiastique* 27 (1931), 589–91.
21 *An admonition*; published also as a broadsheet, *A declaration of the sentence and deposition of Elizabeth* (1588), reprinted in Tierney, *Dodd's Church history*, III, App., pp. xliv–xlviii.
22 Persons, *Elizabethae* (several editions 1592); translated as *An advertisement* (1592). See A. J. Loomie, 'The authorship of "An advertisement..."', *Renaissance News* (1962), 201–7.
23 Persons, *News from Spain and Holland*; *idem, A relation*; I. Dodritius (*pseud.*), *Acta in comitiis Parlamentaribus.*
24 Cf. J. A. Bossy, 'The character of Elizabethan Catholicism', *Past and Present* 21 (1962), 50; T. H. Clancy, *Papist pamphleteers* (Chicago, 1964), 57ff.
25 Cresswell, *Exemplar literarum.*
26 Stapleton, *Apologia pro rege.*
27 Verstegan, *A declaration.*
28 'The copy of an answer unto a Protestant's letter to his friend beyond the seas, concerning a proclamation published in London, in November last', B.L. Add. MS 39828, fos. 154–65.
29 I. B., *The copy of a letter.*
30 Sander, *De origine ac progressu*, editions at Rheims, 1585 and Rome, 1586; see J. S. F. Simons, *Robert Persons S. J., Certamen Ecclesiae Anglicanae* (Nijmegen, 1965), 300–5.

12 The Catholic critique of Elizabethan England

1 Allen, *A true, sincere and modest defence*, chaps. I–IV; Persons, *Elizabethae*, 50–1, 164–210; *idem, An advertisement*, 46ff; Stapleton, *Apologia*, 193ff; Verstegan, *A declaration*, 43–5; Cresswell, *Exemplar literarum*, 18–33, 152ff.
2 See especially Allen, *Cardinal Allen's defence*; Sander, *De origine ac progressu*, 491–2; Persons, *Elizabethae*, 68–100; *idem, An advertisement*,

22–9; Stapleton, *Apologia*, 89–238; Cresswell, *Exemplar*, 67ff; Verstegan, *A declaration*, 13–38, 45–51.

3 Persons, *A conference*, II, 258ff and *passim*; *idem, News from Spain and Holland*, 36; *idem, Elizabethae*, 40ff; Stapleton, *Apologia*, 34; Verstegan, *A declaration*, 52; I. B., *The copy of a letter*, 32.

4 B.L. Add. MS 39828, fos. 154–65; see chap. 11, note 28 above.

5 fo. 154.

6 fo. 154^v.

7 fo. 155^v.

8 fos. 156^v, 161–2.

9 fo. 157^v.

10 fo. 163^v.

11 fo. 155–5^v.

12 fo. 155^v.

13 fo. 157.

14 fo. 157^v.

15 fo. 157^v–8.

16 fo. 160.

17 fo. 154^v.

18 fo. 157.

19 fo. 160.

20 fo. 160–160^v.

21 fo. 162.

22 fo. 162^v.

23 fos. 163, 164^v–5, 158.

24 Cf. Cresswell, *Exemplar literarum*, 34–5.

25 B.L. Add. MS 39828, fo. 164.

26 Persons, *Elizabethae*, 34; *idem, An advertisement*, 11–18; Cresswell, *op. cit.*, 61; Stapleton, *op. cit.*, 167; Verstegan, *op. cit.*, 68–75.

27 Verstegan, *op. cit.*, 53; Persons, *Elizabethae*, 14–18.

28 Verstegan, *op. cit.*, 54; Persons, *Elizabethae*, 19–20.

29 Persons, *Elizabethae*, 20–2; Stapleton, *op. cit.*, 167.

30 Persons, *Elizabethae*, 12–13; Stapleton, *loc. cit.*

31 E. A. Strathmann, 'Ralegh and the Catholic polemists', *Huntington Library Quarterly* 8 (1945), 337–58.

32 Persons, *op. cit.*, 38, 62, 104 (for example).

33 Stapleton, *Apologia*, sig. * 3, p. 126.

34 Sander, *The rise and growth*, 240, 219.

35 *Ibid*, 98–9.

36 Cf. T. H. Clancy, *Papist pamphleteers* (Chicago, 1964), chap. 11; K. Thomas, *Religion and the decline of magic* (Harmondsworth, 1973), 90–132.

37 Sander, *op. cit.*, 216–17.

38 *Ibid*, 204.

39 *Ibid*, 207.

40 *Ibid*, 221.

41 *Ibid*, 229.

42 *Ibid.*, 232–3.

43 I. B., *The copy of a letter*.

44 Rainolds, *Calvino-Turcismus*.

45 Stapleton, *Apologia*, 86–9.

46 V. J. Parry, 'The Ottoman Empire 1566–1617', in *New Cambridge Modern History*, III (Cambridge, 1968), 369; Verstegan, *A declaration*, 20–22; Rainolds, *Calvino-Turcismus*, 996–1013; B.L. Harleian MS 6265, fo. 124–4ᵛ.

47 'Ad regem Hispaniae oratio P. Personii', Stonyhurst MS Coll. PI, 248–57; W. Metcalf, 'De regem Hispaniae', oration of 1596, Stonyhurst MS Anglia II, fos. 84–5. Cf. other orations of seminarists to Spanish royal family, Stonyhurst MS Coll. PI, 256–7, 273–80; Persons, *News*, 5–13; *idem, A relation*, 26–51; Law, *Archpriest controversy*, II, 90–5.

48 Persons, *A relation*, 20.

49 'The speech that F. P. had to the English students at Rome after his arrival from Spain, 1597', Stonyhurst MS Coll. NII, fo. 126; psalm 147; cf. W. Haller, *Foxe's Book of Martyrs and the elect nations* (London, 1963).

50 M. Walzer, *The revolution of the saints* (London, 1966), chap. 8.

51 Allen, *A true, sincere and modest defence*, 160; cf. *idem, Admonition*, xli–xlii.

52 Allen, *A true, sincere and modest defence*, 161; Deut. 13.12–18; Num. 25.1–13.

53 Allen, *op. cit.*, 162; 2 Chron. 13; 2 Kings 8.20–2.

54 Allen, *Cardinal Allen's defence*, 20; cf. *idem, Admonition*, liv.

55 Allen, *Cardinal Allen's defence*, 21–7, 30.

56 Allen, *A true, sincere and modest defence*, 153–4; see pp. 111–12.

57 Allen, *Cardinal Allen's defence*, 25; *idem, A true, sincere and modest defence*, 164.

58 Allen, *A true, sincere and modest defence*, 172; Persons, *Elizabethae*, 110; *idem, Conference*, I, 213; Sander, *De visibili monarchia*, 78; Allen, *Admonition*, xxxvi.

59 Southwell, *An epistle of comfort*, 111.

60 Stapleton, *Opera omnia*, II, 524; printed separately as *Oratio academica*.

61 Stapleton, *Oratio*, 17, 13, 10–11.

62 'speciosa oratio, sed meretricia: certe mollis et faeminea nec viro digna, nedum Christiano'; 'Cum Davide dicemus, Vos haeretici venitis ad nos cum gladio et hasta et clipeo; in fastu et superbia. Nos autem Catholici venimus contra vos in nomine Domini exercituum', Stapleton, *Opera omnia*, II, 524; *idem, Oratio*, 32; Bodin, *De republica*, 731ff.

13 Resistance theory

1 Rainolds, *De iusta*, 8–18; Persons, *Elizabethae*, 107–8; *idem, Conference*, 3–13.

2 'ipsorum populorum voluntas, arbitrium, designatio, et libera . . . institutio', Rainolds, *De iusta reipublicae*, 16.

3 Persons, *Elizabethae*, 107.

4 *Idem, Conference*, I, 7.

5 Bellarmine, *Opera omnia*, II, 317; F. de Vitoria, *De indiis et de iure belli* (ed. E. Nys, Washington, 1917), 131; Aquinas, *Summa theologica*, IIa IIae, q. 10, art. 10, in A. P. d'Entrèves, *Aquinas, selected political writings* (Oxford, 1948), 152–5; Soto, *In quartum sententiarum*, I, 610; F. Suarez, *Selections from three works* (ed. G. L. Williams *et al.*, Oxford, 1944), II, 378ff (and references there); B. Hamilton, *Political thought in sixteenth century Spain* (Oxford, 1963), chap. II, §1; J. N. Figgis, 'On the political theories of the early Jesuits', *Transactions of the Royal Historical Society*, N.S. XI (1897), 102–5; M. d'Addio, *L'idea del contratto sociale* (Milan, 1954), 452 and Part III, chap. I; W. J. Bouwsma, *Venice and the defence of republican liberty* (Berkeley, 1968), 316–17.

6 Jewel, *Works*, IV, 1036 and III, 117; Harding, *A confutation*, 318ᵛ–9; cf. Sander, *The rock*, 85.

7 *The New Testament*, 657–8; Fulke, *A defence*, 241 (editor's note). For a different interpretation, cf. Kellison, *A survey*, 480.

8 Persons, *Conference*, I, 17.

9 *Ibid*, I, 8.

10 M. d'Addio, *L'idea del contratto sociale* (Milan, 1954), III, chap. I; J. W. Gough, *The social contract* (Oxford, 1957), chap. V.

11 Harding, *A confutation*, 318ᵛ–19; Allen, *A true, sincere and modest defence*, 170, 172; Persons, *Elizabethae*, 109; Rainolds, *De iusta reipublicae*, 59ff.

12 Allen, *op. cit.*, 110; *idem*, *An admonition*, xi; Sander, *Rise and growth*, chap. ii, §3.

13 Rainolds, *De iusta reipublicae*, 410–95; Persons, *Elizabethae*, 109.

14 Allen, *A true, sincere and modest defence*, 171.

15 Persons, *Conference*, I, 77.

16 *Ibid*, I, chap. V.

17 *Ibid*, I, 77.

18 *Ibid*, I, 119.

19 *Ibid*, I, 133.

20 *Ibid*, I, chap. IV.

21 *Ibid*, I, chaps. VII and VIII.

22 *Ibid*, I, 56–62.

23 *Ibid*, I, 37–8.

24 *Ibid*, I, 164.

25 *Ibid*, I, chaps. VII and VIII.

26 *Ibid*, I, 195.

27 See above, pp. 17–19 and 26–9.

28 Allen, *A true, sincere and modest defence*, chaps. V–VII; *idem*, *Admonition*, *passim*; *idem*, *Defence of Stanley*, 22ff.

29 Cresswell, *Exemplar literarum*, 98–110.

30 Persons, *Appendix ad apologiam*, 43–56; *idem*, *Manifestation*, 12ᵛ–18.

31 See bibliography in C. H. McIlwain, *The political works of James I* (Cambridge, Mass., 1918), Intro., chap. II.

32 T. Stapleton, *Relectio scholastica* III, questio v, in *Opera omnia*, I, 709; first published in 1596. See also what are apparently lecture notes

of R. Bellarmine's lectures made by R. Persons, Bodleian MSS Rawlinson C588 and e Musaeo 97; Westminster Abbey Muniments CA 33; cf. R. A. B. Mynors, *Catalogue of the MSS of Balliol College Oxford* (Oxford, 1963), 331; Pollen, *Memoirs of Persons*, II, 25 note; T. Clancy, 'English Catholics and the Papal deposing power', *Recusant History* 6 (1961–2), 120, 136.

33 Bellarmine, *Disputationum . . . de controversiis*, in *Opera omnia*, I, 524ff; J. C. Murray, 'St Robert Bellarmine on the indirect power', *Theological studies* IX (1948), 491–535; Turrecremata, *Summa de ecclesia*, 263; Cajetan, *Opuscula omnia*, 21ᵛ; Vitoria, *Relecciones teologicas* (ed. T. Urdanoz, Madrid, 1960), 290ff; Soto, *In quartum sententiarum*, I, 607–12; cf. B. Hamilton, *Political thought in sixteenth century Spain* (Oxford, 1963), chap. IV.

34 For an early English Catholic reference to Bellarmine on papal political power, see Westminster, B48/67.

35 Clancy, *Papist pamphleteers*, 54ff. He maintains that Allen's theory was the 'accidentalist' theory; see my thesis, 186–7.

36 R. M. Kingdon, Intro. to Allen, *A true, sincere and modest defence*, xxviii–xxx and text, chap. VII.

37 'De regiae successionis apud Anglos iure libri duo' (1596), Vatican Archives, Fondo Borghese IV 103; Westminster Cathedral Archives A V/122 (an abridged version). 'Sed quod boni publici causa atque inprimis religionis tuendae atque conservandae, cuius suprema Pontifici cura committitur ius ei quoque supremum competat in quaecumque reipublicae Christianae regna ac principatus, quo videat curetque ne res religionis detrimentum patiatur', fo. 124–4ᵛ.

38 'quod humana tractet', fo. 125ᵛ; John 18; 1 Cor. 6; 1 Pet. 2.13.

39 'hanc spiritualem seu ecclesiasticam tantum eminere atque praestare dignitate potestati civili, quantum anima corpori, spiritus carni, caelestia humanis, aeterna fluxis, vita futura vitae presenti et denique quantum potestas Christi potestati imperatorum', fo. 125ᵛ.

40 'qui est praecipuus ac supremus finis omnis Reipublicae et gubernationis inter fideles', fo. 126.

41 'de bono publico procurando ac inprimis de religione tuenda ac conservanda sine qua nemo aeternam vitam consequi potest', fo. 126.

42 'necessario consequi ut ubi bonum publicum atque religionis inprimis bonum illud postulat, ibi summo iure posse Pontificem summum, quemcumque magistratum civilem dirigere, moderari, reprimere, vel etiam corrigere ac castigare si a recto tramite salutis aeternae ob quam omnis magistratus institutus est cervicosus deflectat, vel alios imperio suo avertat', fo. 126–6ᵛ.

43 'cumque plurimum intersit universi orbis Christiani quis qualisve princeps ad regni Anglicani gubernacula proximus post eam quae modo sceptro fruitur reginam admittatur', fo. 128.

44 Allen, *A true, sincere and modest defence*, 168–9; *idem, Admonition*, ix–x; Leslie, *A treatise of treasons*, 86; Stapleton, *A counterblast*, 312; Persons, *A conference*, I, 56 and II, 22–3. Cf. A. O. Mayer, *England and the Catholic Church under Elizabeth* (trans. J. R. McKee, London,

1967), 319; L. von Pastor, *History of the Popes*, vol. XVIII (trans. R. F. Kerr, London, 1929), 199.

45 'sed arctiori quoque vinculo, fiduciae nimirum seu feudi particularis quo reges Angliae ab antiquissimis temporibus sedi apostolicae fiduciarii seu feudatarii aut vassalli ligei (ut iuristarum verbis utar) extiterunt', fo. 128ᵛ.

46 'Pontificiae alioquin amplitudinis non admodum studiosus', fos. 129–30; Bodin, *De republica*, 171–2 (Book 1, chap. 9); for a reference to Bodin in this context, cf. Bodleian MS ENG. th. 6. 1, p. 474.

47 'Anglos occurrentibus deinde maioribus et gravioribus difficultatibus ad sedem Romanam semper tanquam ad asylum, ac ad Pontificem tanquam ad supremum Angliae dominum recurrere solitos', fo. 130ᵛ.

48 'vel impii potius tyranni qui utrumque nepotem scelerate occiderat', 'quo Richardus diris datus, ac Henrici causa vehementer commendata fuerat', fo. 132.

49 Fo. 133–3ᵛ; M. Paris, *Historia maior* (London, 1571), 310ff.

50 'Ioannis Dei gratia rex Angliae etc. omnibus Christi fidelibus hanc cartam inspecturis salutem in Domino. Universitati vestrae per hanc cartam sigillo nostro munitam volumus esse notum quod cum Deum et matrem nostram sanctam ecclesiam in multis offenderimus, et proinde divina misericordia plurimum indigeamus, nec quid digne offere possimus pro satisfactione Deo et ecclesiae debita facienda, nisi nosmetipsos humiliemus, et regna nostra, volentes nosipsos humiliare pro illo qui se pro nobis humiliavit usque ad mortem, gratia sancti spiritus inspirante non vi interdicti nec timore coacti sed nostra bona spontaneaque voluntate ac communi consilio Baronum nostrorum conferimus et libere concedimus Deo et sanctis Apostolis eius Petro et Paulo et sanctae Romanae Ecclesiae matri nostrae ac Domino Papae Innocentio eiusque catholicis successoribus totum regnum Angliae et totum regnum Hyberniae cum omni iure ac pertinentiis suis', fos. 134ᵛ–5ᵛ.

51 R. M. Kingdon, 'William Allen's use of Protestant political argument', in C. H. Carter (ed.), *From the Renaissance to the Counter-Reformation* (London, 1966), 164–78.

52 Allen, *A true, sincere and modest defence*, 134–8.

53 *Ad persecutores Anglos*, 96. This work was further circulated as part of Gibbons, *Concertatio*.

54 Allen, *A true, sincere and modest defence*, 173–89.

55 J. Bossy, 'The character of Elizabethan Catholicism', in T. Aston (ed.), *Crisis in Europe*, 231–8.

56 J. N. Figgis, 'Political thought in the sixteenth century', *Cambridge Modern History* (Cambridge, 1907), III, 757.

14 The end of resistance: Persons' Memorial of the Reformation of England

1 *The Jesuit's Memorial*, 70–101. See T. H. Clancy, 'Notes on Persons' "Memorial" ', *Recusant History* 5 (1959–60), 17–34; J. J. Scarisbrick,

'Robert Persons' plans for the "true" reformation of England', in N. McKendrick (ed.), *Historical perspectives* (London, 1974), 19–42.

2 Persons, *The Jesuit's Memorial*, 29–45.

3 *Ibid*, 14–15.

4 *Ibid*, 117, 121–2, 130, 143–5, 149; Avila's work is 'Tratado de la reformación del estado ecclesiástico y de lo que se debe avisar a los obispos', see Q. A. Vaquero *et al.* (eds.), *Diccionario de historia ecclesiástica de España* (Madrid, 1972); cf. Juan de Avila, *Obras* (eds. L. S. Balust *et al.*, Madrid, 1970), I, intro.

5 Persons, *op. cit.*, Part I, chaps. v–vi; cf. Scarisbrick, *op. cit.*, 21–2.

6 D. Knowles, *The religious orders in England*, III (Cambridge, 1959), 444–55; J. Bossy, *The English Catholic community* (London, 1975), 29–30.

7 Douai MS 484, pp. 411*bis*, 419; Bodleian MS Rawlinson D1351, fos. 8ᵛ–9 and MS Jones 53, fos. 250–1ᵛ, 253–3ᵛ; Lambeth MS 565, fos. 38, 39–40, 46–7ᵛ, 49ᵛ–51; Meyer, *England and the Catholic church under Elizabeth*, App. xvii.

8 Pole himself had reservations about the Pope's decision, see P. Hughes, *The Reformation in England*, II (London, 1961), 230; cf. also Pastor, *op. cit.*, vol. xviii, 469 (Sander's letter of 1570).

9 Persons, *op. cit.*, 103–4.

10 *Ibid*, 205–6.

11 *Ibid*, Part III, chap. I.

12 *Ibid*, Part I, chap. x.

13 *Ibid*, 214.

14 *Ibid*, 227; J. Hurstfield, *The Queen's Wards* (London, 1958), xv, 245, 330, 348; Scarisbrick, *op. cit.*, 28–9.

15 Persons, *op. cit.*, 247–8; Allen, *A true, sincere and modest defence*, 232; cf. J. S. F. Simons, *Robert Persons S. J.*, *Certamen Ecclesiae Anglicanae* (Nijmegen, 1965), 260; Clancy, *Papist pamphleteers*, chap. v; Q. Skinner, 'History and ideology in the English Revolution', *Historical Journal* viii (1965), esp. 156–7, note 37; C. Hill, 'The Norman Yoke', in *Puritanism and Revolution* (London, 1968), 50–122. For uncomplimentary remarks about the Civil Law, cf. Sander, *A brief treatise*, 60.

16 Persons, *op. cit.*, 106.

17 *Ibid.*, 257; Part I, chap. viii; Part II, chap. v.

18 Knox, *Letters of Allen*, 394.

19 Persons, *op. cit.*, Intro. (by E. Gee).

15 Opposition to the ideas of resistance 1584–96

1 See below, p. 176.

2 See below, pp. 177–9.

3 L. Hicks, 'Allen and Deventer', *The Month* clxiii (1934), 515–17; Knox, *Letters of Allen*, 299–301; cf. C. Morris, *Political thought in England, Tyndale to Hooker* (London, 1953), 139; J. H. Pollen, *Mary Queen of Scots and the Babington plot* (Edinburgh, 1922), cciii (where Gifford's book is said to have consisted of two letters, one from a Jesuit in

Transylvania to a Dominican in Rome, the other the Dominican's reply).

4 Stonyhurst MS Coll. NII, p. 155.

5 Southwell, *An humble supplication*, 1.

6 *Ibid*, 46.

7 *Ibid*, 16.

8 *Ibid*, 35.

9 On this point see the contrasting arguments of R. C. Bald, in the Intro. to Southwell, *op. cit.*, xi and C. Devlin, in 'The patriotism of Robert Southwell', *The Month* N.S. 10 (1953), 344–54; cf. also H. C. White, *Tudor books of saints and martyrs* (Madison, 1963), 258. The latest writer in this field follows Bald, see A. Pritchard, *Catholic Loyalism in Elizabethan England* (London, 1979), 67–72.

10 Southwell, *An epistle of comfort*, 229, 240; cf. Southwell, *Two letters* (ed. N. P. Brown, Charlottesville, 1973), 84–5.

11 *Idem, An humble supplication*, App. II, 69.

12 C. Devlin, *The life of Robert Southwell* (London, 1956), 154–5.

13 'General heads of the persecution in England', Stonyhurst MS Anglia I, n. 70; Petti, *Letters of Verstegan*, 1–16.

14 Petti, *op. cit.*, 11.

15 *Ibid*, 12.

16 *Ibid*.

17 *Ibid*, 13.

18 *Ibid*, 14.

19 *Ibid*, 15–16.

20 Arber, *A transcript*, III, 97.

21 J. Bossy (Intro. to Meyer, *op. cit.*, xxi) says it was written in about 1580; he is correcting Meyer who took it to have been written at the time of its publication (*op. cit.*, 420–1); nevertheless Meyer seems to be followed by J. Hurstfield ('The succession struggle in late Elizabethan England', in S. T. Bindoff *et al.* (eds.), *Elizabethan government and society* (London, 1961), 386–7); T. Clancy says about 1574 ('English Catholics and the Papal deposing power 1570–1640', *Recusant History* 6 (1961–2), 206). The preface says the work was written some years before and refers to Bishop's own words in his damaged MS preface, 'when I saw two or three years past many seminary priests...'; I would add 'executed', or 'tried', or 'questioned' (the title of the book itself refers to the Bloody Questions), which suggests late 1581 + 2 or 3. The editor's marginal note at p. 50 suggests, perhaps pre-September 1585 (the excommunication of Henry of Navarre); p. 34 suggests post-1577–8 (Don John of Austria in the Netherlands). Above all, Bishop is surely replying to Allen's work of 1584.

22 Bishop, *A courteous conference*, 4, citing Bracton (*De legibus et consuetudinibus Angliae* (ed. G. E. Woodbine, London, 1922), II, 33).

23 Bishop, *op. cit.*, 30; cf. R. Atkinson's speech of 1563, in Strype, *Annals*, I, i, 447–8.

24 Bishop, *op. cit.*, 7, 51.

25 *Ibid*, 63–9; C. Saint-German, *Doctor and student* (ed. W. Muchall, London, 1865), Book II, chaps. 36, 39, 41, 44, 47.

26 Bishop, *op. cit.*, 69–84, 75, 84; Allen, *A true, sincere and modest defence*, 145–6; J. D. Mansi, *Sacrorum conciliorum nova et amplissima collectio*, vol. 22 (Venice, 1778), 985–90; *Corpus Iuris Canonici*, x, v. 7. 13. §3; cf. Campion's use of More as an authority on the same subject, R. Simpson, *Edmund Campion* (London, 1867), 110.

27 R. B. Manning, *Religion and society in Elizabethan Sussex* (Leicester, 1969), 157, 268; N. Tyacke, 'Popular puritan mentality', in P. Clark *et al.* (eds.), *The English Commonwealth* (Leicester, 1979), 84–5.

28 *Beautiful blossoms*, preface.

29 H.M.C., *Calendar of MSS of the Marquis of Salisbury*, Part IV, p. 274 (1592); A. Kenny, *The responsa scholarum*, I, 194.

30 T. H. Clancy, art. *cit.*, *Recusant History* 6 (1961–2), 206.

31 The same reservations apply to a book entitled *The estate of English fugitives under the King of Spain*, published from legitimate London presses in four editions in 1595 and 1596. The author, Samuel Lewknor, described his experiences as a soldier in Spanish service in the Netherlands; he attacked Spain and expressed his loyalty to the Queen. Burghley took an interest in the book and it was clearly government propaganda. See A. J. Loomie, *The Spanish Elizabethans* (London, 1963), 10–11.

16 The laity

1 J. Bossy, 'The character of Elizabethan Catholicism', *Past and Present* 21 (1962), 39–59 and in T. Aston (ed.), *Crisis in Europe*, 223–46; cf. *idem*, *The English Catholic community 1570–1850* (London, 1975), chap. 2; A. L. Rowse, *The England of Elizabeth* (London, 1953), 514ff; D. Mathew, *Catholicism in England* (London, 1948), 40ff; H. R. Trevor-Roper, *Historical Essays* (London, 1957), 91–7, 113–18; J. Hurstfield, 'The succession struggle in late Elizabethan England', in S. T. Bindoff *et al.* (eds.), *Elizabethan government and society* (London, 1961), esp. 381–2; W. R. Trimble, *The Catholic laity in Elizabethan England* (Cambridge, Mass., 1964), 116–21, 254–5, 262–3; C. Cross, *The royal supremacy in the Elizabethan Church* (London, 1969), 44–5; J. C. H. Aveling, *The handle and the axe* (London, 1976) 69–70; A. Pritchard, *Catholic loyalism in Elizabethan England* (London, 1979), esp. chap. III. For a criticism of Bossy, see, however, P. McGrath, *Papists and puritans under Elizabeth I* (London, 1967), 381, note 1; C. Haigh, 'The fall of a Church or the rise of a sect? Post-Reformation Catholicism in England', *Historical Journal* 21 (1978), 181–6. *Review article*

2 H. Aveling, *Northern Catholics* (London, 1966), 35–40; cf. A. G. Dickens, 'The first stages of Romanish recusancy in Yorkshire 1560–1590', *Yorkshire Archaeological Journal* xxxv (1953), 180–1; Bossy, *English Catholic community*, chap. 1. But according to Christopher Haigh (*Reformation and reaction in Tudor Lancashire* (Cambridge,

1975), 277) 'the Lancashire case provides little substantiating evidence' for this.

3 Trimble, *op. cit.*, 262, 119.

4 H.M.C., *Report on various collections*, III (London, 1904), 51–8; cf. 37–43, 117–23; cf. for Sir Anthony Culpepper, Bodleian MS Tanner 118, fo. 131.

5 B.L. Add MS 39828, fos. 154–65; see above, pp. 137–40.

6 H.M.C., *op. cit.*, 128–32; B.L. Add. MS 39829, fos. 119–24.

7 K. R. Wark, *Elizabethan recusancy in Cheshire* (Chetham Soc., 1971), 54; J. S. Leatherbarrow, *The Lancashire Elizabethan recusants* (Chetham Soc., 1947), 99.

8 P. McGrath & J. Rowe, 'The recusancy of Sir Thomas Cornwallis', *Proc. of the Suffolk Inst. of Arch.* 28 (1961), 257–8, 246ff.

9 Letter of 28 May 1603, signed 'J. C. (or S. ?)', Westminster Cathedral Archives AVII, pp. 437–8.

10 On the plots see J. H. Pollen, *The politics of English Catholics during the reign of Queen Elizabeth* (n.p., n.d., articles from the *Month* of 1902).

11 M. E. James, 'The concept of order and the Northern Rising of 1569', *Past and Present* 60 (1973), 49–83.

12 Sir C. Sharp, *Memorials of the rebellion of 1569* (London, 1840), 204; Trimble, *op. cit.*, 62; cf. G. R. Elton, *England under the Tudors* (London, 1969), 298.

13 Cf. A. J. Loomie, *The Spanish Elizabethans* (London, 1963), 234; Trimble, *op. cit.*, 260.

14 P.R.O., S.P. 12/154/53 and I, II. The author describes himself merely as a 'Catholic', which perhaps suggests a layman.

15 P.R.O., S.P. 12/225/35 and 35I.

16 B.L. MS Egerton 2877, fo. 183. Cf. R. Mathias, *Whitsun riot* (London, 1963); Haigh, *op. cit.*, 327–30.

17 A. J. Loomie, *The Spanish Elizabethans*.

18 Cf. A. O. Meyer, *England and the Catholic Church under Queen Elizabeth* (London, 1967), 277–301; G. Mattingly, 'William Allen and Catholic propaganda in England', in 'Aspects de la propagande religieuse', *Travaux d'humanisme et renaissance* 26 (Geneva, 1957), 325–39; R. Simpson, *Edmund Campion* (London, 1867), 336–40; T. G. Law, *Collected essays* (ed. P. Hume Brown, Edinburgh, 1904), 176–216, esp. 197. It is interesting to see the last three historians all using the same document, to the same purpose.

19 J. A. Bossy, 'English Catholics and the French marriage', *Recusant history* 5 (1959–60), 2–3.

20 E. Rose, *Cases of conscience* (Cambridge, 1975), 236ff. Some very interesting remarks on 'Church papists', and the difficulty of separating them from recusants are in Haigh, *op. cit.*, 269–78.

21 W. Richmond, 'A untrue [*sic* – 'un' presumably an addition] story of the Catholic prisoners in York Castle, their behaviour and defence of the Catholic religion when they were hailed by force to the Protestant sermons. Anno domini 1600.' B.L. Add. MS 34250, quotation at fo. 14.

Some small sections of this tract in Challoner, *Memoirs*, I, 282–95. Cf. Worthington, *A relation*, 95; Morris, *Troubles*, I, 241–2; J. C. H. Aveling, *Catholic recusancy in the city of York 1558–1791* (Catholic Record Society, 1970), 159–60.

22 Richmond, *op. cit.*, fos. 28ᵛ–9.

23 *Ibid*, fo. 23.

24 W. Wiseman, 'A treatise of three farewells taken of the world by sundry sorts departed this life', Lambeth MS 549, fo. 241.ᵛ.

25 *Ibid*, fos. 77ᵛ–8.

17 The Appellants

1 That Persons and his supporters re-adopted non-resistance (with certain qualifications) in the late 1590s is perhaps not the accepted view of historians; see, for example, C. Cross, *The royal supremacy in the Elizabethan Church* (London, 1969), 46; J. J. Scarisbrick, 'Robert Persons' plans for the "true" reformation of England', in N. Mc-Kendrick (ed.), *Historical perspectives* (London, 1974), 32–42; J. Hurst-field, 'The succession struggle in late Elizabethan England', in S. T. Bindoff *et al.* (eds.), *Elizabethan government and society* (London, 1961), 382–9; A. Pritchard, *Catholic Loyalism in Elizabethan England* (London, 1979), esp. chaps. IX and XI.

2 Although the origins of the opposition to Persons and Blackwell go back to the early 1580s, to the quarrels between on the one hand Allen and Persons and on the other Paget and Morgan (as Persons was fond of repeating), it is difficult to find any evidence of an ideological division between them at that stage. Since writing this section on the Appellants, I have seen Arnold Pritchard's excellent new book (see note 1, above), which amplifies much of what I say.

3 J. Bossy, 'Henry IV, the Appellants and the Jesuits', *Recusant History* 8 (1965–6), 80–122; *idem*, Cambridge Ph.D. thesis (see chap. 11, note 3), 144ff; W. F. Church, *Constitutional thought in sixteenth century France* (Cambridge, Mass., 1941), chap. VI; V. Martin, *Le Gallicanisme politique et le clergé de France* (Paris, 1929), chaps. III and IV; Arnauld, *Le franc discours*; Pasquier, *The Jesuit's catechism*.

4 Barclay, *De regno*; Grégoire, *De republica*; J. W. Allen, *A history of political thought in the sixteenth century*, 386–93; J. N. Figgis, *The divine right of kings* (Cambridge, 1896), 129; G. Weill, *Les théories sur le pouvoir royal en France pendant les guerres de religion*, 171–4; W. F. Church, *op. cit.*, 245–8.

5 E. Dubois, *Guillaume Barclay* (Paris, 1872), 14–17, 102–3, 113–15.

6 *D.N.B.*; Law, *Archpriest controversy*, I, 160–1, II, 196, 200–1.

7 Bagshaw, *A true relation*, 96. For expressions of loyalty to the Queen cf. Bluet, *Important considerations*, 36–43; Copley, *Another letter*, 41–2; Paget in Ely, *Certain brief notes*, 22; Mush, *A dialogue*, sig. * 4ᵛ; Law, *Archpriest controversy*, II, 195–200 and 219–21.

8 Copley, *An answer to a letter*, 66–71.

9 Bagshaw, *A sparing discovery*, 56, 59.

10 Cecil, *A discovery*, 306–7; Tertullian, 'Ad nationes libri duo', *Opera* I (Turnholti, 1951), 11ff.

11 Law, *Archpriest controversy*, II, 248; cf. Bossy, *The English Catholic community*, 38–41.

12 Clarke, *A reply*, 32ᵛ–43ᵛ; Bagshaw, *A sparing discovery*.

13 Copley, *An answer*, 69–70; Watson, *A decacordon*, 274–5; Law, *A historical sketch*, App. C. Cf. R. Parkinson in Ely, *Certain brief notes* (1601), after preface; Mush, *A dialogue*, 53ff; Charnock, *A reply*, 285ff; Law, *Archpriest controversy*, II, 62–3, 164.

14 Clarke, *A reply*, sig. A3ᵛ, 43; Law, *Archpriest controversy*, I, 20–1, 80, 201; *The copies of certain discourses*, 111; Watson, *A decacordon*, 172; 'A discourse', Lambeth MS 2007, fos. 237ᵛ–9.

15 Clarke, *A reply*, 32–2ᵛ; Watson, *A decacordon*, 45.

16 Ely, *Certain brief notes*, 18 (4th pagination).

17 Colleton, *A just defence*, 239; Law, *Archpriest controversy*, I, 93.

18 Bluet, *Important considerations*, title; Watson, *op. cit.*, 267.

19 Bagshaw, *A sparing discovery*, 10.

20 Bluet, *op. cit.*, *passim*; Bagshaw, *A true relation*, 95; *idem*, *Relatio compendiosa*, 29; Mush, *Declaratio motuum*, 25, 139.

21 Clarke, *A reply*, 31–2; Copley, *Another letter*, 19.

22 Arnauld, *Le franc discours*, sig. ¶ 3; Clarke, *A reply*, sig. A3ᵛ.

23 Ely, *Certain brief notes*, 5ᵛ; Watson, *op. cit.*, 151.

24 Bagshaw, *A sparing discovery*, 69.

25 'A discourse', Lambeth MS 2007, fo. 238ᵛ.

26 Law, *Archpriest controversy*, II, 6, 48, 112.

27 'Considerationes quaedam exhibitae Serenissime de ineunda aliqua ratione ut moderatius in Anglia cum Catholicis a persequutore agitur', Lambeth MS 2007, 259–60ᵛ (–261). Cf. Law, *op. cit.*, II, 112–13, 117–18, 185–7; Lambeth MS 2006, fo. 232.

28 Bluet, *Important considerations*, sig. ++3ᵛ; Clarke, *A reply*, 71–1ᵛ; Ely, *Certain brief notes*, 16ᵛ (2nd pagination); Mush, *A dialogue*, 91; Watson, *op. cit.*, 11; Law, *A historical sketch*, Intro.

29 Bagshaw, *A true relation*, 9; Bluet, *Important considerations*, 12; Clarke, *A reply*, 35; Watson, *A decacordon*, 284.

30 See especially Bluet, *Important considerations*, *passim*.

31 Bagshaw, *A true relation*, 55–6; Clarke, *A reply*, 73; Ely, *Certain brief notes*, 16ᵛ (2nd pagination); Mush, *A dialogue*, 91; Watson, *A decacordon*, 11, 47, 107 etc. Cf. also Law, *Archpriest controversy*, index, under 'books'.

32 J. J. Scarisbrick, *art. cit.*, 32–8. Cf. Arnauld, *Le franc discours*, sig. ¶ 3–3ᵛ; Bagshaw, *A sparing discovery*, 28–9; Bluet, *Important considerations*, sig. +++ᵛ; Clarke, *A reply*, 29ᵛ, 73ᵛ; Mush, *A dialogue*, 95–6; Law, *Archpriest controversy* index.

33 Lambeth MS 2007, fo. 238ᵛ.

34 Bagshaw, *A sparing discovery*, 6–7.

35 Arnauld, *Le franc discours*, sig. ¶ 4.

36 Bagshaw, *A sparing discovery*, 70.

37 *Ibid*, 33; Copley, *An answer*, 36–7, 91; Ely, *Certain brief notes*, 33 (4th pagination); Mush, *Declaratio motuum*, 7.

38 Clarke, *A reply*, 56; Watson, *A decacordon*, 295; Bluet, *Important considerations*, 25.

39 Clarke, *A reply*, 34ᵛ, 55ᵛ–6, 63–4; Watson, *A decacordon*, 97–8.

40 Law, *A historical sketch*, 17, note; Bennet, *The hope of peace*, 21.

41 P.R.O., S.P. 12/252/66I. Cf. Gifford to Malvasia, 17 November 1595, P.R.O. 31/9/85A (transcript of Vatican Archives, Nunz. di Fiandra 9); Knox, *Letters of Allen*, 390.

42 'Relacion del principio progresso y fin de la turbacion del collegio Ingles en Roma', B.L. Add. MS 21203, fos. 7ᵛ, 8ᵛ and Westminster Cathedral Archives, AVI/36; Agazzari to Persons, 27 August 1596, in Tierney, *Dodd's Church history*, III, App. p. lxxv.

43 Knox, *op. cit.*, 384.

44 Creighton, *An apology*, esp. 63–4.

45 Cecil, *A discovery*, esp. 306.

46 Colville, *The Palinod*, esp. sigs. A4, A5ᵛ and Intro., xxix–xxx.

47 J. Bossy, Cambridge Ph.D. thesis (see chap. 11, note 3), pp. 196–7; J. Grundy (ed.), *The poems of Henry Constable* (Liverpool, 1960), Intro., 43–4; Westminster AVI/42; *Calendar of State Papers Domestic Elizabeth 1598–1601*, 456, 460.

48 Clitheroe, *A discovery*, 49–50.

49 *Ibid*, 66, 25.

50 *Ibid*, 9.

51 Bossy, thesis (*ut supra*), 281–2; Law, *Archpriest controversy*, I, 220, 223.

52 Clarke, *A reply*, 76ᵛ–77ᵛ.

53 Bagshaw, *A sparing discovery*, 14–15, cf. 9, 56–7.

54 Copley, *Another letter*, 15. See also on the *Conference*: Bagshaw, *A true relation*, 64; Watson's dedication to Bluet, *Important considerations*, sig. + +4, cf. p. 34; Charnock, *A reply*, 82, 314; Colleton, *A just defence*, 240; Copley, *An answer*, 45–58; Ely, *Certain brief notes*, 'An answer... against... Bishop', 16; Mush, *Declaratio motuum*, 24; *idem*, *A dialogue*, 91–2, 106; Watson, *A decacordon*, 71, 107, 286, 325–6; Law, *Archpriest controversy*, index, under 'books'.

55 Mush, *Declaratio motuum*, 139; Lambeth MS 2007, fo. 261; Law, *op. cit.*, I, 98–100, 113–15, 148–9, 205–6, 206–7; II, 51, 54, 55.

56 Pasquier, *The Jesuit's catechism*, sig. A (translation of Grégoire, *De republica*, I, 935).

57 Mush, *A dialogue*, 133.

58 Watson, *A decacordon*, 221–4.

59 Bagshaw, *A sparing discovery*, 12; *idem*, 'An answer', 36–7, in Ely, *Certain brief notes*; R. Fisher in Law, *A historical sketch*, 107; Clarke, *A reply*, 22ᵛ; Watson, *A decacordon*, 32.

60 Charnock, *A reply*, 69–70; Watson, *A decacordon*, 20–33; Mush, *A dialogue*, 97–101. Cf. Vaux, *A catechism*, Intro.; Garnet, *An apology*, 150.

61 Mush, *A dialogue*, 99–101.

62 'An licitum sit Catholicis in Anglia arma sumere, et aliis modis,

reginam et regnum defendere contra Hispanos', in Strype, *Annals*, iii, ii, 583–97; T. A. Stroud, 'Fr. Thomas Wright: a test case for toleration', *Biographical Studies* i (1951), 193–5; G. R. Elton, *England under the Tudors* (London, 1974), 458.

63 Colleton, *A just defence*, 57ff; Ely, *Certain brief notes*, 116–36, 163–4; 'A discourse', Lambeth MS 2007, fo. 216ᵛ.

64 Lambeth MS 2007, fo. 217ᵛ.

65 Ely, *Certain brief notes*, 178–80.

66 'A discourse', Lambeth MS 2007, fos. 226–7; Mush, *Declaratio motuum*, 76; *The copies of certain discourses*, 181.

67 Mush, *A dialogue*, 20; cf. Charnock, *A reply*, 113–30; H.M.C., *A calendar of the MSS of the Marquis of Salisbury*, ix, 202–4.

68 Copley, *An answer*, 73; Allen, *A true, sincere and modest defence*, 210–11.

69 Copley, *Another letter*, 11–16.

70 Watson, *A decacordon*, 177; cf. his dedication to Mush, *A dialogue*, sig. ++ᵛ; Bluet, *Important considerations*, 37–8; Clarke, *A reply*, 37–42ᵛ.

71 Watson, *A decacordon*, 258–63; 1 Cor. 6.12.

72 Clarke, *A reply*, 37–41ᵛ.

73 Law, *Archpriest controversy*, ii, 52, 63–4, 68–9, 88, 182–5, 194–5.

74 C. Devlin, 'The patriotism of Robert Southwell', *The Month* n.s. 10 (1953), 348–9; Southwell, *An humble supplication*, xii–xv; J. Gerard, 'Contributions towards a life of Fr. Henry Garnet', *The Month* xci (1898), 603; H. Thurston, 'Father Southwell, the popular poet', *ibid* lxxxiii (1895), 388.

75 Southwell, *An humble supplication*, Appendix ii, 66–8 (Law, *Archpriest controversy*, ii, 95–8); 'An answer of Mr Doctor Bagshaw', 10–11, in Ely, *Certain brief notes*.

76 Clarke, *A reply*, 62 (cf. 90); Watson, *A decacordon*, 271 (cf. 11); cf. Bluet, *Important considerations*, 32; P.R.O., S.P. 12/261/99.

77 Copley, *Another letter*, 74.

18 Robert Persons and non-resistance (1596–1603)

1 On this important book, see generally, J. N. Figgis, *From Gerson to Grotius* (Cambridge, 1916), 182–9; G. Weill, *Les théories sur le pouvoir royal en France pendant les guerres de religion* (Paris, 1892), 237–8; cf. my thesis, 201ff (and references there), on the book's authorship and influence on Persons' *Conference*.

2 On 15 August 1595 a copy of the book was burned, at the command of the Archbishop of Canterbury, in the Hall of the Stationers' Company in London; see Arber, *A transcript*, ii, 40. Antwerp was the most popular place for English Catholic books to be published at that time.

3 Rainolds, *A treatise*, dedication.

4 *Idem, Calvino-Turcismus*, 707–9.

5 The story is taken apparently from Thevet, *La cosmographie universelle*, Book 1, chap. 4.

6 Persons, *A manifestation*, 55ᵛ–62ᵛ.

7 Hastings, *A watch word*; 'Ex libello quodam famoso in Anglia hoc anno 1598 edito contra Suam Sanctitatem et Regem Hispaniae ac Catholicos recusantes Reginae licentia etc.', P.R.O. 31/9/86A (transcript of Vatican Archives, Varia 264, fo. 214).

8 Persons, *A temperate ward-word*, 87–8; W. R., *A brief and clear confutation*, 206ff; Worthington, *A relation*, 36; Hill, *A quartron of reasons*, sig. A5ᵛ.

9 Broughton, *An apologetical epistle*, 53–4.

10 Fitzherbert, *An apology*, 51 (in *A defence*).

11 Chambers, *Palestina*, sig. ¶ 3–3ᵛ.

12 Persons, *A temperate ward-word*, 126–9; Worthington, *A relation of sixteen martyrs*, 38–9; Broughton, *An apologetical epistle*, 83–4.

13 *A brief censure*, 49–50.

14 Persons, *A temperate ward-word*, preface.

15 *A brief censure*, 28–31, 49–50, 87–91. (This book was possibly written by Verstegan; see Copley, *Another letter*, 28, where he attributes a 'libel upon one Digs' to Verstegan; T. Digges (or, apparently, W. Bradshaw) wrote *Humble motives for association* (1601), to which it replies. There is also a memorial attacking Digges' book in Stonyhurst Archives, Anglia III, fo. 49–9ᵛ). Cf. Broughton, *An apologetical epistle*, 85ff; Kellison, *A survey*, 475ff; Persons, *The warn-word*, 52ᵛff.

16 Persons, *A manifestation*, 102–2ᵛ.

17 Fitzherbert, *A defence*, 3ᵛ–5.

18 Persons, *A temperate ward-word*, 34–7, cf. 53–4.

19 *A brief censure*, 68–9, 74; Broughton, *An apologetical epistle*, 95–9; Persons, *Appendix ad apologiam*, 88ff; *idem, The warn-word*, 1, 81, 130.

20 Worthington, *A relation, passim*.

21 Aray, *The discovery*; Fitzherbert, *An apology* in *A defence*.

22 Aray, *op. cit.*, 1ᵛ.

23 *Ibid*, 9ᵛ.

24 *Ibid*, 14ᵛ.

25 Fitzherbert, *An apology*, 18–18ᵛ.

26 *Ibid*, 36.

27 *Ibid*, 27ᵛ.

28 *A brief censure*, 69; Persons, *A temperate ward-word*, 55–72. Cf. generally, Persons, *An Appendix to the Apology*, 14ᵛ–19; *The copy of a letter* (1601), fos. 13–14.

29 Persons, *A manifestation*, 39ᵛff.

30 W. R., *A brief and clear confutation*, 16ᵛ; Woodward, *A detection*, 84–5.

31 Fitzherbert, *A defence*, 3ᵛ.

32 Persons, *A manifestation*, 47v.

33 Persons, *A brief apology*, 170ᵛ; Inner Temple, MS 538/47, fos. 133–4ᵛ; *The copies of certain discourses*, 112–13.

34 Persons, *A temperate ward-word*, 53.

35 Persons, *A manifestation*, 98–9.

36 Pits, *Relationum historicarum*, 806; Knox, *The first and second Douai*

diaries, 409–10; A. I. Cameron (ed.), *The Warrender papers* (Edinburgh, 1932), 18–28; cf. C. Labitte, *De la démocratie chez les prédicateurs de la Ligue* (Paris, 1865), 373–7.

37 Persons, *A temperate ward-word*, 122–8; Worthington, *A relation*, 39–40; Kellison, *A survey of the new religion*, sig. A8; Broughton, *An apologetical epistle*, 50–1; Fitzherbert, *An apology*, 29–32.

38 *A brief censure*, 78–80.

39 Worthington, *A relation*, 38.

40 Persons, *A treatise of three conversions*, III, 391–6; Matthew 13.24–30; Augustine, 'Contra epistolam Parmeniani', in J-P. Migne, *Patrologiae cursus ... Latinae*, vol. 43 (Paris, 1841), 81–5.

41 A. J. Loomie, 'Spain and the English Catholic exiles, 1580–1604', London Ph.D. thesis, 1957, 462; H. Tichborne to T. Darbyshire, S.J., 2 February 1598 (P.R.O., S.P. 12/262/28) in Law, *A historical sketch*, Appendix C.

42 P.R.O., 31/9/86A (transcript of Vatican Archives, Varia 264, fo. 214).

43 A. J. Loomie, 'Philip III and the Stuart succession in England', *Revue belge de philologie et d'histoire* XLIII (1965), 498; cf. *idem*, 'A Catholic petition to the Earl of Essex', *Recusant History* 7 (1963–4), 33–42.

44 Law, *Archpriest controversy*, II, 76–86; Lambeth MS 2014, fos. 96–8ᵛ; cf. MS 2006, fos. 239–47.

45 P.R.O., S.P. 12/275/56, fos. 104–13 and 12/286/60; Inner Temple MS 538.1, fos. 18–41ᵛ; B.L. MS Lansdowne 512/2 (Petyt's copy of the previous item); two copies at Stanford Court, Worcs., the property of Sir T. Winnington, Bart (until they were destroyed by fire in 1882, see National Register of Archives), see H.M.C., *Report I* (London, 1874), App. p. 53; a copy 'penes D. Carolum Cliffordum, Baronum de Chudleigh', see MS catalogue of MSS, Stonyhurst College. This work has been discussed quite often before, see esp. J. J. Scarisbrick, *art. cit.*, 30–2.

46 *Cal. State Papers Dom. Eliz. 1601–3*, 272; cf. Law, *Archpriest controversy*, I, 243.

47 Loomie, *thesis cit.*, 388; *idem*, 'Richard Stanyhurst in Spain', *Huntington Library Quarterly* 28 (1965), 149, note 17; R. Lechat, *Les réfugiés anglais dans les pays-bas espagnols* (Louvain, 1914), App., 246–7; J. Cecil to Persons, 22 March 1601, Lambeth MS 2014, fo. 123; cf. W. Ll. Williams, 'Welsh Catholics on the continent', *Trans. of the Hon. Soc. of Cymmrodorion* (1901–2), App. B. 107–9; P.R.O., S.P. 12/271/11, 12, 13, 14, 15; Westminster B48/17; see L. Hicks, 'Father Robert Persons, S. J. and the Book of Succession', *Recusant History* 4 (1957–8), 132 and note 31.

48 P.R.O., S.P. 12/275/56 fo. 104.

49 Ortiz, *A relation of the solemnity*, 70ff; *Algunos motivos y razones, que ay para favorecer los seminarios Ingleses* (1600), Stonyhurst Archives, Anglia VI/26, 133–40; cf. *Las causas que han movido el Rey Catolico don Felipe II nuestro señor para admitir y favorecer a los seminarios de clerigos Ingleses* (Madrid, 1597), Stonyhurst MS Anglia VI, 91–6.

50 Law, *Archpriest controversy*, II, 47; J. Gillow, *A bibliographical dictionary of the English Catholics* (London, n.d.).
51 'Johannis Suiti Angli de Britaniis ab haeresi liberandis brevis admodum consultatio', Stonyhurst MS Anglia III/29, fos. 54–61.
52 Hastings, *A watch word*, 28.
53 Persons, *A temperate ward-word*, 34.
54 *Ibid*, 61–2; Rainolds, *De iusta reipublicae* (1590), 383–429^v.
55 Fitzherbert, *An apology*, 5^v–7^v, 50^v; Ortiz, *A relation*, 61, 68; Persons, *Appendix ad apologiam*, 45.
56 Persons, *A temperate ward-word*, 1–11.
57 Persons, *The warn-word*, I, chaps. x, xi, xii, xviii, esp. fo. 83–3^v.
58 Broughton, *The first part*, 132, 143; Persons, *The warn-word*, I, 129–30, 132, 141; *idem, A temperate ward-word*, 102–18.
59 Ortiz, *op. cit.*, 13.
60 Persons, *A temperate ward-word*, 118, 122; cf. Ortiz, *op. cit.*, dedication.
61 Broughton, *An apologetical epistle*, 69–82; cf. Bodleian MS ENG. th. 6. 2, pp. 422ff.
62 Law, *Archpriest controversy*, II, 148–51; Westminster Cathedral Archives, AVII, 88–114.
63 Persons, *A manifestation*, 15^v–16^v; *idem, Appendix ad apologiam*, 42–56.
64 Fitzherbert, *A defence*, 5^v, 6; Persons, *Appendix ad apologiam*, 41.
65 Worthington, *A relation*, 68–9; Persons, *A temperate ward-word*, 53; *idem, A manifestation*, 43^v.
66 Scarisbrick, *art. cit.*, 38–9.
67 Persons to Earl of Angus, 24 January 1600, P.R.O., S.P. 52/66/4 and 85/2/82; Stonyhurst MS Anglia VI/28; Westminster AVI, 101; Persons to 'N. T.', 24 May 1603, P.R.O., S.P. 14/1/84; B.L. MS Cotton Julius FVI, 146ff; Stonyhurst MS Coll. PI, 324–7. Cf. Lambeth MS 2006, fos. 206–7^v. Persons to James VI, 18 August 1602, Stonyhurst MS Anglia III, fos. 36–7^v. Persons to James I, 18 October 1603, Stonyhurst MS Anglia III, fos. 74–7^v; cf. Stonyhurst MS Anglia III, fos. 86–7^v.
68 Persons, *A brief apology*, 188^v–9; *idem, A manifestation*, 49^v–51^v; *idem, Warn-word*, 1–3.
69 Persons, *A manifestation*, 63–8.

Bibliography

Manuscript sources

Ampleforth Abbey, 59, 122, 123
Bodleian Library, Oxford
  ENG. th. 6.1
  Jones 53
  MS e Musaeo 97
  Rawlinson C588, D107, D1351, D1506
  Tanner 118–302
British Library (B.L.)
  Additional (Add.) MSS 21203, 34218, 34250, 39828, 39829, 39830
  Cotton Julius FVI
  Egerton 2877
  Harleian 6265
  Lansdowne 96, 512
  Sloane 1582, 1941
Douai Municipal Library, France, 484, 920.I
Inner Temple Library, 538. 1, 538. 14
Lambeth Library, 549, 565, 2006, 2007, 2014
Oscott College Library
  J. Feckenham, 'Certain considerations'
  I.G., 'An answer to a comfortable advertisement'
  P. Mowle, commonplace book
Public Record Office (P.R.O.)
  State Papers (S.P.) 12/136, 144, 154, 157, 162, 225, 243, 252, 261, 262,
    275, 279, 281, 286
  S.P. 14/1, 17, 18
  S.P. 52/66
  S.P. 85/2
  31/9/85A, 86A (transcripts from Roman Archives)
Stonyhurst College Archives
  A. v. 12
  Anglia I, II, III, VI
  Collectanea (Coll.) N
  Coll. P.
Vatican Archives, Fondo Borghese IV. 103
Westminster Abbey Muniments, CA 33

Westminster Cathedral Archives (W.C.A.)
AIV, AV, AVI, AVII
B48

Primary printed sources

Early printed books

The number in brackets after most entries in this list refers to A. F. Allison & D. M. Rogers, *A Catalogue of Catholic Books in English printed abroad or secretly in England 1558–1640* (London, 1968).

Adrian VI, Pope, *Quaestiones in quartum sententiarum*, Paris, 1530.

Albin de Valsergues, J., *A notable discourse, plainly and truly discussing who are the right ministers of the Catholic church*, 1575 (3).

Alfield, T., *A true report of the death and martyrdom of M. Campion*, 1582 (4).

Allen, W., *An admonition to the nobility and people of England*, 1588 (5).

Ad persecutores Anglos pro Catholicis domi forisque persecutionem sufferentibus; contra falsum, seditiosum, & contumeliosum libellum . . . responsio, trans. W. Rainolds, [Rouen], 1584.

An apology and true declaration of the institution and endeavours of the two English colleges, 1581 (6).

A brief history of the glorious martyrdom of xii reverend priests, 1582 (7).

Cardinal Allen's defence of Sir William Stanley's surrender of Deventer, ed. T. Heywood, Chetham Society, 1851 (8, 9).

The copy of a letter . . . concerning the yielding up of the city of Daventry, 1587; reprinted as *Cardinal Allen's defence of . . . Stanley* (see preceding entry).

A defence and declaration of the Catholic Church's doctrine touching purgatory, 1565 (10).

A treatise made in defence of the lawful power and authority of priesthood to remit sins, 1567 (11).

A true report of the late apprehension and imprisonment of John Nicols minister, 1583 (12).

A true, sincere, and modest defence of English Catholics, ed. R. M. Kingdon, Ithaca, 1965 (13).

Antoninus, *Repertorium totius summe*, Basle, 1511.

Aquinas, T., *Summa theologica cum commentariis Thomae de Vio Caietani*, Rome, 1888–1903.

Aray, M., *The discovery and confutation of a tragical fiction devised and played by Edward Squyer*, 1599 (35).

Aristotle, *Nichomachean ethics*, trans. R. W. Browne, London, 1901.

Arnauld, A., *Le franc discours. Discourse, presented of late to the French king*, 1602 (42).

Auximo, N. de, *Supplementum*, Venice, 1472.

Azpilcueta, M. ab, (Navarre), *Enchiridion sive manuale confessariorum et poenitentium*, Antwerp, 1575.

B., H., *A consolatory letter to all the afflicted Catholics*, 1587–8 (59).

B., I., *The copy of a letter lately written by a Spanish gentleman to his friend in England*, 1589 (60).

Bagshaw, C., *Relatio compendiosa turbarum quas Jesuitae Angli una cum D. Georgio Blackwello archipresbytero*, 1601 (63).

A sparing discovery of our English Jesuits, 1601 (64).

A true relation of the faction begun at Wisbech, in T. G. Law (ed.), *A historical sketch of the conflict between Jesuits and seculars in the reign of Queen Elizabeth*, London, 1889.

Barclay, W., *De regno et regali potestate adversus Buchananum, Brutum, Boucherium, & reliquos monarchomachos, libri sex*, Paris, 1600.

Bell, T., *Motives concerning Romish faith*, Cambridge, 1593.

Bellarmine, R., *Opera omnia*, Naples, 1856–7.

(Romulus, F., *pseud.*), *Responsio ad praecipua capita apologiae quae falso Catholica inscribitur*, Fano, 1591.

Bennet, J., *The hope of peace*, 1601 (103).

Bishop, J., *A courteous conference*, London, 1598.

(?) (Byshop, J.), *Beautiful blossoms*, London, 1577.

Blackwood, A., *De coniunctione religionis et imperii libri duo*, Paris, 1575. *Opera omnia*, Paris, 1644.

Bluet, T., *Important considerations*, 1601 (122).

Bodin, J., *De republica libri sex*, Frankfurt, 1594.

Bourchier, T., *Historia ecclesiastica de martyrio fratrum Ordinis Divi Francisci, dictorum de Observantia*, Paris, 1582.

Bracton, H., *De legibus et consuetudinibus Angliae*, ed. G. E. Woodbine, London, 1922.

Bradshaw, W., see Digges.

A brief censure upon the puritan pamphlet entitled Humble Motives, 1603 (141).

A brief form of confession, in L. Vaux, *A catechism*, 1599 (840, 143).

Bristow, R., *A brief treatise of divers plain and sure ways*, 1574 (146).

A brief treatise, 1599 (147).

Demands to be proponed of Catholics to the heretics, 1576 (148).

Broughton, R., *An apologetical epistle*, 1601 (152).

The first part of the resolution of religion, 1603 (161).

Burghley, W. Cecil, Lord, *The execution of justice in England*, ed. R. M. Kingdon, Ithaca, 1965.

Burne, N., *The disputation concerning the controversit heads of religion*, 1581 (183).

Byshop, J., see J. Bishop.

Cajetan, T. de Vio, *Opuscula omnia*, Rome, 1570. See also Aquinas.

Calvin, J., *Institution de la religion Chretienne*, in *Corpus Reformatorum*, XXXII, Brunswick, 1866.

Campion, E., *Campian Englished, or a translation of the Ten Reasons*, 1632 (193).

Canisius, P., *Certain necessary principles of religion*, 1578–9 (198).

A sum of Christian doctrine, 1592–6 (200).

Cecil, J., *A discovery of the errors committed*, 1599 (223), in J. R. Elder, *Spanish influences in Scottish history*, Glasgow, 1920.

Cecil, W., see Burghley.

Chambers, R., *Palestina*, 1600 (229).

Charnock, R., *An answer made by one of our brethren, a secular priest,* 1602 (235).

A reply to a notorious libel entitled A brief apology, 1603 (236).

Christopherson, J., *An exhortation to all men to take heed and beware of rebellion*, London, n.d.

Chrysopolitanus, C. C., *De tumultuosa Belgarum rebellione sedanda*, 1579.

Clarke, W., *A reply unto a certain libel lately set forth by Fa. Parsons,* 1603 (241).

Clitheroe, W. (?), & Constable, H. (?), *A discovery of a counterfeit conference*, 1600 (253).

Colleton, J., *A just defence of the slandered priests*, 1602 (246).

Colville, J., *Palinod*, 1600, in D. Laing (ed.), *Original letters of Mr. John Colville 1582–1603*, Bannantyne Club, Edinburgh, 1858.

The copies of certain discourses which were extorted, 1601 (254).

Copley, A., *An answer to a letter of a Jesuited gentleman by his cousin,* 1601 (257).

Another letter of Mr. A. C. to his dis-Jesuited kinsman, 1602 (258).

The copy of a letter written to a very worshipful Catholic gentleman, 1601 [by S. N.] (565).

Covarruvias y Leyva, D. de, *Opera omnia*, Frankfurt, 1592.

Creighton, W., *An apology*, 1598, in T. G. Law (ed.), *Documents illustrating Catholic policy in the reign of James VI 1596–1598*, Scottish History Society, Edinburgh, 1893.

Cresswell, J., *Exemplar literarum missarum e Germania ad D. Gulielmum Cecilium*, Rome, 1592.

Crowley, R., *An answer to six reasons*, London, 1581.

Descriptiones quaedam illius inhumanae et multiplicis persecutionis, Rome, 1584.

Digges, T., or Bradshaw, W., *Humble motives for association to maintain religion established*, London, 1601.

Dodritius, I. (*pseud.*), *Acta in comitiis parlamentaribus Londini die X. Aprilis huius anni praesentis 1593*, Antwerp, 1593.

Dorman, T., *A disproof of M. Nowell's reproof*, 1565 (274).

A proof of certain articles in religion, 1564 (275).

Dury, J., *Confutatio responsionis Gulielmi Whitakeri*, Brussels, 1582.

An edict or ordinance of the French king, 1568 (234).

Ely, H., *Certain brief notes upon A brief apology*, 1602 (291).

Evans, L., *Certain tables ... wherein is detected and made manifest*, 1565 [trans. of work of G. Lindanus] (461).

Fitzherbert, T., *A defence of the Catholic cause*, 1602 [contains *An apology*, 1602] (310).

Foxe, J., *Acts and monuments*, London, 1846.

Frarin, P., *An oration against the unlawful insurrections of the Protestants of our time under pretence to reform religion*, 1566 (344).

Fulke, W., *A confutation of a popish and slanderous libel*, London, 1571.

A defence of the sincere and true translation of the holy scripture, ed. C. H. Hartshorne, Cambridge, 1843.

Garnet, H., *An apology against the defence of schism*, 1593 (353).
　A treatise of Christian renunciation, 1593 (357).
　A treatise of equivocation, ed. D. Jardine, London, 1851.
Gibbons, J., *Concertatio ecclesiae Catholicae in Anglia*, Trier, 1588.
Gilby, A., *An admonition*, in J. Knox, *The appellation*, Geneva, 1558.
Goodman, C., *How superior powers ought to be obeyed of their subjects*, 1558.
Grégoire, P., *De republica libri sex et viginti*, Pont-à-Mousson, 1596.
Hall, R., *Opuscula quaedam his temporibus pernecessaria*, Douai, 1581.
　De quinquapartita conscientia, Douai, 1598.
　Tractatus aliquot utilissimi, pro defensione regiae et episcopalis authoritatis, Douai, 1584.
Hamilton, J., *An Catholic and facile treatise*, 1581 (370).
Harding, T., *A confutation of a book entitled An apology of the church of England*, 1565 (375).
　A detection of sundry foul errors, lies, slanders uttered and practised by M. Jewel, 1568 (376).
　A rejoinder to M. Jewel's reply against the sacrifice of the mass, 1567 (378).
Harpsfield, N., *Dialogi sex*, ed. A. Cope, Antwerp, 1566.
Hastings, Sir F., *A watch word to all religious and true hearted Englishmen*, London, 1598.
Hay, J., *Certain demands concerning the Christian religion*, 1580 (389).
Hide, T., *A consolatory epistle*, 1580 (395).
Hill, T., *A quartron of reasons of Catholic religion*, 1600 (400).
Horne, R., *An answer made*, London, 1566.
Hosius, S., *A most excellent treatise of the beginning of heresies*, trans. R. Shacklock, 1565 (403).
　Of the express word of God, trans. T. Stapleton (?), 1567 (404).
Jewel, J., *Works*, ed. J. Ayre, Cambridge, 1845–1850.
Kellison, M., *A survey of the new religion*, 1603 (429).
Knox, J., *The Appellation*, Geneva, 1558.
　Works, ed. D. Laing, Edinburgh, 1855.
Lanspergius, *An epistle or exhortation of Jesus Christ to the soul*, 1592–3 (437).
Leslie, J., *De titulo et iure serenissimae principis Mariae*, Rheims, 1580.
　Du droit et titre de la serenissime princesse Marie, Rouen, 1587.
　Pro libertate impetranda oratio, Paris, 1574.
　(?), *A treatise of treasons*, 1572 (454).
　A treatise concerning the defence of the honour of the right high, mighty and noble princess Mary of Scotland, 1571 (453).
　A treatise touching the right, title and interest of the most excellent princess Mary, 1584 (455).
Lewknor, S., *The estate of English fugitives under the King of Spain*, London, 1595.
Lindanus, G., see Evans.
Loarte, G., *The exercise of a Christian life*, 1579 (462).

Luther, M., *Works*, English trans., ed. H. T. Lehmann *et al.*, vols. 34, 45 and 46, Philadelphia, 1962.
Martial, J., *A reply to M. Calfhill's blasphemous answer*, 1566 (523).
A treatise of the cross, 1564 (524).
Martin, G., *Roma sancta*, ed. G. B. Parkes, Rome, 1969.
A treatise of schism, 1578 (535).
A treatise of Christian peregrination, 1583 (534).
More, T., *The apology*, ed. A. I. Toft, London, 1930.
The debellacion of Salem and Bizance, London, 1533.
The dialogue concerning Tyndale, ed. W. E. Campbell, London, 1927.
Epistola in qua ... respondet libri Ioannis Pomerani, Louvain, 1568.
Responsio ad Lutherum, ed. J. M. Headley, New Haven, 1969.
The supplication of souls, ed. E. Morris, n.p., n.d.
Mush, J., *Declaratio motuum ac turbationum quae ex controversiis inter Jesuitas ... et sacerdotes seminariorum in Anglia*, 1601 (552).
A dialogue betwixt a secular priest and a lay gentleman, 1601 (553).
N., S., see *The copy of a letter*.
The new testament of Jesus Christ, translated faithfully into English, Rheims, 1582 (567).
Ortiz, A., *A relation of the solemnity wherewith the Catholic princes K. Phillip III and Queen Margaret were received in the English College of Valladolid*, 1601 (584).
Osorius, H., *An epistle of the reverend father ... to the most excellent princess Elizabeth*, trans. R. Shacklock, 1565 (585).
A learned and very eloquent treaty, trans. J. Fen, 1568 (587).
Panormitanus, N. de Tudeschis, *Apparatus ... in Clementinas*, Paris, 1515.
Paris, M., *Historia maior*, London, 1571.
Pasquier, E., *The Jesuit's catechism*, 1602 (596).
Peeters, C., *De Christiani principis officio*, Cologne, 1580.
Persons, R., *An advertisement written to a secretary of my L. Treasurer's of England*, trans. R. Verstegan, 1592 (264).
An appendix to the Apology, 1602 (612).
Appendix ad Apologiam, Rome, 1602.
A brief apology or defence of the Catholic ecclesiastical hierarchy, 1601 (614).
A brief censure upon two books, 1581 (615).
A brief discourse containing certain reasons why Catholics refuse to go to church, 1580 (616).
A Christian directory, 1585 (621).
A conference about the next succession to the crown of England, 1594 (271).
The copy of a letter written by a Master of Art of Cambridge, 1584, ed. J. Burgoyne as *History of Queen Elizabeth, Amy Robsart, and the Earl of Leicester, being a reprint of 'Leicester's Commonwealth'*, London, 1904 (261).
A defence of the censure, 1582 (626).
De persecutione Anglicana, Rome, 1582. First published 1581.
A discovery of J. Nicols minister, 1581 (627).

Elizabethae Angliae reginae haeresim Calvinianam propugnantis, saevissimum in Catholicos sui regni edictum, Augusta (Augsburg ?), 1592.

An epistle of the persecution of Catholics in England, 1582 (629).

The first book of the Christian exercise appertaining to resolution, 1582 (619).

The Jesuit's memorial for the intended reformation of England, ed. E. Gee, London, 1690.

A manifestation of the great folly and bad spirit of certain in England, 1602 (633).

News from Spain and Holland, 1593 (634).

'Of the life and martyrdom of Fr Edmond Campian', *Letters and Notices*, XI and XII, Roehampton, 1877–8.

Quaestiones duae, Rome, 1607.

A relation of the King of Spain's receiving in Valladolid, 1592 (636).

A temperate ward-word, 1599 (639).

A treatise tending to mitigation, 1607 (641).

A treatise of three conversions, 1603 (640).

The warn-word to Sir Francis Hastings' Waste-word, 1602 (642).

Pilkington, J., *Works*, ed. J. Scholefield, Cambridge, 1842.

Pits, J., *Relationum historicarum de rebus Anglicis*, Paris, 1619.

R., W., *A brief and clear confutation* (attrib. to R. Walpole), 1603 (874).

Rainolds, W., *Calvino-Turcismus id est Calvanisticae perfidiae cum Mahumetana collatio*, Antwerp, 1597.

De iusta reipublicae Christianae in reges impios et haereticos authoritate, Antwerp, 1592.

A refutation of sundry reprehensions, cavils and false sleights, 1583 (702).

A treatise containing the true Catholic and Apostolic faith of the holy sacrifice and sacrament ordained by Christ, 1593 (703).

A treatise entitled beware of M. Iewel, 1566 (709).

Rastell, J., *A confutation of a sermon pronounced by M. Jewel*, 1564 (705).

Romulus, F., see Bellarmine.

Saint-German, C., *Doctor and student*, ed. W. Muchall, London, 1815.

Sander, N., *A brief treatise of usury*, 1568 (749).

De clave David, Rome, 1588.

De origine ac progressu schismatis Anglicani libri tres, Rome, 1586.

De visibili monarchia ecclesiae, libri octo, Rome, 1571.

The rise and growth of the Anglican schism, ed. D. Lewis, London, 1887.

The rock of the church, 1624 (751).

A treatise of the images of Christ, 1567 (754).

Sayer, G., *Casuum conscientiae sive theologiae moralis thesaurus*, Douai, 1620.

Clavis regia sacerdotum, casuum conscientiae, Münster, 1628.

Sepulveda, J. G., *De ratione dicendi testimonium*, in *Opera omnia*, Madrid, 1780.

Silvestro Mazzoloni da Prierio (Sylvester), *Summa summarum*, Bologna, 1515.

Soto, D., *In quartum sententiarum commentarii*, Douai, 1613.

Relectio . . . de ratione tegendi et detegendi secretum, Salamanca, 1566.

Southwell, R., *An epistle of comfort*, ed. M. Waugh, London, 1966.

An humble supplication to Her Majesty, ed. R. C. Bald, Cambridge, 1953.

Two letters and short rules of a good life, ed. N. P. Brown, Charlottesville, 1973.

Staphylus, F., *The apology*, trans. T. Stapleton, 1565 (794).

Stapleton, T., *Apologia pro rege Catholico Philipo II*, 1592.

A counterblast to M. Horne's vain blast against M. Feckenham, 1567 (796).

A fortress of the faith, 1565 (797).

(trans.), *The history of the Church of England compiled by the Venerable Bede*, 1565 (82).

Opera quae extant omnia, Paris, 1620.

Oratio academica an politici horum temporum in numero Christianorum sint habendi, Munich, 1608.

Thevet, A., *La cosmographie universelle*, Paris, 1575.

Tomson, L., *An answer to certain assertions of M. Feckenham*, London, 1570.

A treatise of treasons, see Leslie.

Turrecremata, I. de, *Summa de ecclesia*, Venice, 1561.

Tyndale, W., *Doctrinal treatises*, ed. H. Walker, Cambridge, 1848.

Vaux, L., *A catechism*, ed. T. G. Law, Chetham Society, 1885.

Verstegan, R., *A declaration of the true causes of the great troubles*, 1592 (844).

Theatrum crudelitatum haereticorum, Antwerp, 1592.

Vindiciae contra tyrannos, ed. H. J. Laskie, as *A defence of liberty against tyrants*, London, 1924.

Vitoria, F. de, *Relecciones teologicas*, ed. T. Urdanoz, Madrid, 1960.

Walpole, R., see W. R.

Watson, W., *A decacordon of ten quodlibetical questions*, 1602 (883).

Winzet, N., *Certain tractates together with the book of fourscore three questions*, ed. J. K. Hewison, Scottish Text Society, Edinburgh, 1888–90.

Flagellum sectariorum, Ingolstadt, 1582.

Woodward, P., *A detection of divers notable untruths, contradictions, corruptions and falsifications*, 1602 (906).

Worthington, T., *A relation of sixteen martyrs*, 1601 (917).

Wright, T., *The disposition or garnishment of the soul*, 1596 (923).

A treatise showing the possibility and convenience of the real presence, 1596 (925).

Young, J., *De schismate, sive de ecclesiae unitatis divisione liber unus*, Louvain, 1573.

Pacis ecclesiasticae perturbator, sive de schismate, Douai, 1603.

Collections of letters etc.

Arber, E., *A transcript of the registers of the Company of Stationers*, vol. 2, London, 1875, vol. 3, London, 1876.

Challoner, R., *Memoirs of the missionary priests*, ed. T. G. Law, Edinburgh, 1878.

Christie, R. C., *Letters of Sir Thomas Copley*, Roxburghe Club, London, 1897.

Foley, H., *Records of the English province of the Society of Jesus*, vol. 5, London, 1879.

Hicks, L., *Letters and memorials of Father Robert Persons, S.J.*, Catholic Record Society 39, London, 1942.

Kenny, A., *The responsa scholarum of the English College, Rome*, vol. 1, Catholic Record Society 54, London, 1962.

Knox, T. F., *The first and second diaries of the English College, Douai*, London, 1878.

The letters and memorials of William Cardinal Allen, London, 1882.

Law, T. G., *The Archpriest controversy*, 2 vols., Camden Society, London, 1896, 1898.

A historical sketch of the conflict between Jesuits and seculars in the reign of Queen Elizabeth, London, 1889.

Lettenhove, K. de, *Relations politiques des Pays-Bas et de l'Angleterre*, vol. 7, Brussels, 1888.

Morris, J., *The troubles of our Catholic forefathers*, ser. 1, London, 1872, ser. 2, 1875, ser. 3, 1877.

Petti, A. G., *The letters and despatches of Richard Verstegan*, Catholic Record Society 52, London, 1959.

Pollen, J. H., *Acts of the English martyrs*, London, 1891.

Memoirs of Father Robert Persons, Catholic Record Society 2 & 4, London, 1906, 1908.

Unpublished documents relating to the English martyrs, Catholic Record Society 5, London, 1908.

Strype, J., *Annals of the Reformation*, Oxford, 1824.

Ecclesiastical memorials, Oxford, 1822.

Tierney, M. A., *Dodd's Church history*, vol. 3, London, 1840.

Index